GLOBAL TALENT MANAGEMENT

Sara Miller McCune founded SAGE Publishing in 1965 to support the dissemination of usable knowledge and educate a global community. SAGE publishes more than 1000 journals and over 800 new books each year, spanning a wide range of subject areas. Our growing selection of library products includes archives, data, case studies and video. SAGE remains majority owned by our founder and after her lifetime will become owned by a charitable trust that secures the company's continued independence.

Los Angeles | London | New Delhi | Singapore | Washington DC | Melbourne

Sonal Minocha & Dean Hristov

GLOBAL TALENT MANAGEMENT

AN INTEGRATED APPROACH

Los Angeles | London | New Delhi
Singapore | Washington DC | Melbourne

Los Angeles | London | New Delhi
Singapore | Washington DC | Melbourne

SAGE Publications Ltd
1 Oliver's Yard
55 City Road
London EC1Y 1SP

SAGE Publications Inc.
2455 Teller Road
Thousand Oaks, California 91320

SAGE Publications India Pvt Ltd
B 1/I 1 Mohan Cooperative Industrial Area
Mathura Road
New Delhi 110 044

SAGE Publications Asia-Pacific Pte Ltd
3 Church Street
#10-04 Samsung Hub
Singapore 049483

Editor: Matthew Waters
Editorial assistant: Jasleen Kaur
Production editor: Sarah Cooke
Copyeditor: Sharon Cawood
Proofreader: Audrey Sciven
Indexer: Silvia Benvenuto
Marketing manager: Alison Borg
Cover design: Francis Kenney
Typeset by: C&M Digitals (P) Ltd, Chennai, India
Printed in the UK

Library of Congress Control Number: 2018960401

British Library Cataloguing in Publication data

A catalogue record for this book is available from
the British Library

ISBN 978-1-5264-2422-8
ISBN 978-1-5264-2423-5 (pbk)

At SAGE we take sustainability seriously. Most of our products are printed in the UK using responsibly sourced papers and
boards. When we print overseas we ensure sustainable papers are used as measured by the PREPS grading system. We
undertake an annual audit to monitor our sustainability.

CONTENTS

PREFACE

THE RATIONALE BEHIND THIS TEXTBOOK

The vision for this text is to provide a holistic account of strategic Global Talent Management (GTM) perspectives – current and future – which shape and are shaping the global workplace and workforce landscape through academic, policy and practitioner lenses. As such, the text will give its readership – students, academics, practitioners and policymakers – a holistic overview of key GTM perspectives, which determine the inter-linked nature of individuals as global talent, organisations as hubs for global talent, and policy across sectors and industries. Characterising the text is its international, cross-disciplinary and cross-industry approach through the use of original, contemporary cases as illustrative examples.

This collation of policy, practice and academic lenses in GTM enables you to develop a holistic picture of this domain, emergent as it is in modern-day management practice. Hence, the textbook intends to broaden the foundations for the future study of Global Talent Management as a strategic management practice distinct from its current consumption largely as a subset of the Human Resource Management (HRM) subject. This text positions GTM as a holistic and integrative practice and discusses the notion of individuals as global talent, organisations as hubs for global talent, and the role of systemic policy in global talent development.

The study of management often bifurcates itself into a study of the composite functions, for instance HRM, Marketing and so forth. This text steers away from doing so or from specialising in any one of the three main component parts of this book – Global, Talent and Management. Instead, we invite the reader to experience a fusion of these three domains of modern-day practice – individual, organisational and policy – in providing an integrative perspective into how we view and subsequently manage talent in a global context (Figure 0.1).

Talent being the central core for the text, it is important to discuss up front our perspective on this and what we mean by it. Several texts before us discuss 'individuals' as talent (see Boucher, 2016; Kuptsch and Pang, 2006; Scullion and Collings, 2010), albeit from a narrow perspective, where the dominant focus on internationally mobile talent

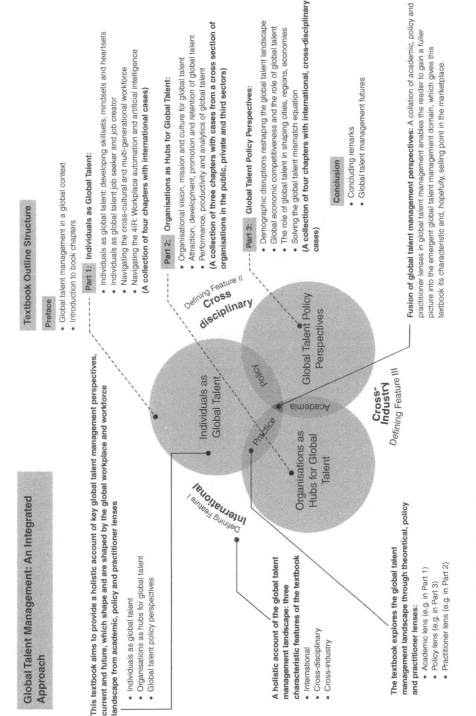

Global Talent Management: An Integrated Approach

This textbook aims to provide a holistic account of key global talent management perspectives, current and future, which shape and are shaped by the global workplace and workforce landscape from academic, policy and practitioner lenses

- Individuals as global talent
- Organisations as hubs for global talent
- Global talent policy perspectives

A holistic account of the global talent management landscape: three characteristic features of the textbook:

- International
- Cross-disciplinary
- Cross-industry

The textbook explores the global talent management landscape through theoretical, policy and practitioner lenses:

- Academic lens (e.g. in Part 1)
- Policy lens (e.g. in Part 3)
- Practitioner lens (e.g. in Part 2)

Textbook Outline Structure

Preface
- Global talent management in a global context
- Introduction to book chapters

Part 1: Individuals as Global Talent:
- Individuals as global talent: developing skillsets, mindsets and heartsets
- Individuals as global talent job seeker and job creator
- Navigating the cross-cultural and multi-generational workforce
- Navigating the 4IR: Workplace automation and artificial intelligence
(A collection of four chapters with international cases)

Part 2: Organisations as Hubs for Global Talent:
- Organisational vision, mission and culture for global talent
- Attraction, development, promotion and retention of global talent
- Performance, productivity and analytics of global talent
(A collection of three chapters with cases from a cross section of organisations in the public, private and third sectors)

Part 3: Global Talent Policy Perspectives:
- Demographic disruptions reshaping the global talent landscape
- Global economic competitiveness and the role of global talent
- The role of global talent in shaping cities, regions, economies
- Solving the global talent mismatch equation
(A collection of four chapters with international, cross-disciplinary cases)

Conclusion
- Concluding remarks
- Global talent management futures

Fusion of global talent management perspectives: A collation of academic, policy and practitioner lenses in global talent management enables the reader to gain a fuller picture into the emergent global talent management domain, which gives this textbook its characteristic and, hopefully, selling point in the marketplace.

Defining Feature II
Cross disciplinary

Individuals as Global Talent

Global Talent Policy Perspectives

Policy

Academia

Practice

Organisations as Hubs for Global Talent

Cross-Industry Defining Feature III

Defining Feature I **International**

Figure 0.1   A visual structure for the text

and its management is the focus. In this book, we widen our perspective and discuss how people from any origin and any background can still stage themselves globally as talent – this is the space where this book is positioned. Hence, through this book, we assist our readership – whether students, staff, practitioners or policymakers – view and develop themselves as global talent.

WHAT WOULD OUR READERSHIP GAIN FROM THIS TEXT?

The somewhat fragmented nature of key texts to date, which suggests a focus on specific GTM themes, provides an opportunity for this textbook to deliver an authoritative and holistic account of the timely GTM field. This field, despite being in its infancy, has the potential to shape individuals as global talent, organisations as hubs for global talent, and global talent policy across organisations, sectors of the economy, cities, regions and countries.

Unlike key GTM contributions, this textbook goes beyond organisations and their relationship with the emergent discipline to provide insights into 'self' as global talent, i.e. you as global talent and the need to develop global skills, competencies and attributes to succeed as future-ready talent in a fast-paced and highly competitive global labour market. Our student readership will also gain an insight into how to confidently navigate through a range of cultural, generational and technological disruptions.

Characterising this text is its international, cross-disciplinary and cross-industry approach through the use of original cases of diverse organisations and individuals as illustrative examples throughout. As such, this textbook can appeal to a broad readership and be adopted as a core university text by students on a number of undergraduate, postgraduate and executive management courses and PPD/CPD modules.

As this text targets global talent management in its broadest sense, in addition to individuals as global talent and organisations as hubs for global talent, you will also have the opportunity to gain critical insight into the relationship of global talent with policy, society and economy across cities, regions and countries. This insight also considers the inclusion of current agendas, such as the global talent mismatch, demographic disruptions, and the role of global talent in shaping cities, regions, economies and societies, among others. These themes highlight the influence and role of global talent beyond the subject field and into its relationship with a number of interrelated global trends and developments.

This text, one might argue, is perhaps ahead of its time because organisation studies and business and management studies often tend to focus on people-management approaches rather than development. This is by no means a comprehensive text on strategic workforce management and planning, nor is it solely about the management of individual talent. Its perspective is a lot broader regarding what it is revealing to the reader, including practical insights from international people and organisations and cases concerning what it takes to build the right environment to attract, retain and sustain talent.

PART 1: INTRODUCTION

Through Part 1 of this text, we provide in-depth insights into 'individuals as global talent' through both concept building and future self-reflection and a development perspective. The building blocks of the concept of global talent – global mindsets, heartsets and skillsets are introduced in depth. At the heart of our global talent definition is how an individual, i.e. you, as global talent, can navigate through the ever-changing world of work, including the ability to thrive in a cross-cultural workforce and work efficiently across different generations in the workforce.

This part will help you understand why and how you could develop yourself not only as a confident job seeker but also as a job creator in an environment where the gig economy and enterprise are set to dominate the future world of work. You will develop an appreciation for the notion of hybrid global talent amid developments and innovations in the 4th Industrial Revolution, including artificial intelligence, automation, and robotics, and their implications for the workforce and workplace.

Our focus in **Chapter 1** is for our readers to gain a clear understanding of our definition of global talent. In unpacking the concept, we discuss it as being a unique combination of mindsets, skillsets and heartsets that allows an individual to place themselves confidently in a dynamic, global marketplace. We provide a critical perspective on these including the importance of developing global competence, emotional intelligence and learnability as expressions of the global talent attributes. We conclude that these attributes work uniquely and in different combinations and cannot be homogenised or formulised as the basis of development as future global talent.

Talent development, however, is not an individual process – it is relative to the employment marketplace and the economy. This marketplace is increasingly global and continuously disrupted by developments in the technology and service space. This means that there is the need to prepare for greater flexibility in careers as job seekers and creators, not only to avoid future displacements but also to maximise the opportunities available in a gig economy of the future. **Chapter 2** deals with these contemporary challenges in self-development as future global talent. You will also have the opportunity to gain insight from practice through the perspective of a job-seeker-turned-job-creator at Alibaba India.

The employment and enterprise marketplace is, by its very nature, cross-cultural and multi-generational, further enabled by the forces of globalisation. We acknowledged at the very start that the primary readers of this text might well be students but, of course, those in their 30s, 40s and 50s and beyond are also in that workforce. Hence, the ability of highly effective and adaptive global talent to navigate through generations and cultures in the workforce is essential. **Chapter 3** delves into navigation as global talent in such a diverse workforce environment, illustrated through current case study examples.

Chapter 4 sets the scene for global talent against an increasingly automated and AI-oriented world of work, the impact that these disruptions might have on the workforce and workplace, and how you as global talent need to adapt to the future world of work. In this chapter, we provide a discussion of the impact of workplace automation and advancements in robotics on the workforce through a look at contemporary illustrative examples of this phenomenon.

PART 2: INTRODUCTION

Part 2 of this text shifts its focus from the individual to the organisation as hubs for global talent development. It delves into the vision and mission shaping in organisation that place people management at its core, such that the attraction, development and retention of global talent become central to their purpose. As advances in AI invade organisations, humans will be the single most powerful differentiator for every organisation – this is our central argument in this part of the text. We posit that good organisations focus on human resource management while great organisations concentrate their efforts on talent development and management.

In pushing the boundaries of organisations, as we know them, this part will look at newer/different forms of organisations – for example, football clubs and innovation-driven enterprises where people are the heart of organisational existence and purpose. Increasingly, established and corporate forms of the organisation would have to think of ways to scale up such a talent focus to sustain their competitive positioning in the attraction and retention of global talent.

In **Chapter 5**, we scene-set the organisational perspective and discuss how global talent builds on the more established concept of strategic Human Resource Management. We provide a considered insight into the importance of developing a global talent-orientated vision and mission in organisations. This chapter then goes on to explore current organisational approaches in the corporate and public sectors to the development and promotion of an enabling, inclusive and open culture for global talent management in organisations. We conclude the chapter by positioning global talent as a source of competitive advantage, with implications for organisational strategy and management.

The attraction, development and retention of global talent in organisations is the focus for **Chapter 6**. In this chapter, you will gain an insight into the importance of establishing an organisational strategy for the attraction of global talent, and explore current developments in organisational practice in this area. The chapter proceeds to a discussion of strategies to develop and retain global talent, including challenges faced by management in sustaining good practice in this area. Through international case study insights, you will have the opportunity to reflect on a diverse set of organisational strategies to attract, develop and retain global talent.

In **Chapter 7** we provide a rich perspective on the role, place and influence exerted by performance, productivity and data analytics in shaping effective global talent management in organisations. You will be given the opportunity to critically reflect on approaches to identifying, measuring and improving performance and productivity and gain practical insights into innovative organisational practice in these areas. This will help you understand the role that performance and productivity play in global talent management. The chapter then explores the role of global talent analytics in improving performance and productivity, and provides a range of examples from organisational practice including the hybrid people analytics approach that LinkedIn (2018) has taken to strengthen its organisational productivity.

PART 3: INTRODUCTION

As this text targets global talent management in its widest sense, in addition to individuals as global talent (Part 1) and organisations as hubs for global talent (Part 2), we examine and appraise the relationship of global talent management within policy, society and the economy at large in this Part. Critical contemporary policy challenges, including the global talent mismatch and demographic disruptions, are discussed alongside the role that global talent plays in shaping cities, regions, economies and society at large. These themes of global relevance highlight the integrative and interdependent nature of global talent development as a concept, beyond the management domain.

In **Chapter 8,** we provide a discussion into current demographic disruptions that have the potential to reshape the talent landscape of the future. These include demographic trends and developments, such as the ageing workforce in developed economies alongside the demographic dividend, which is seen as a game-changer in developing countries. We appraise the challenges and opportunities resulting from these trends and give you insights into possible policy responses and approaches. This is relevant to both students and workforce professionals and policymakers with an interest in the broader implications of demographics in the global workforce and workplace. The in-depth comparative case study will introduce you to contrasting demographic perspectives from China and India.

Chapter 9 presents the interplay between global talent and economic competitiveness. It discusses the inclusion of global talent in socio-economic plans and the development of targeted strategies and interventions that utilise global talent in driving their competitiveness. National approaches to talent are discussed against the context of the Global Talent Competitiveness Index and the role it plays in measuring global talent competitiveness at a national level. A discussion of Singapore's talent-driven policy approach to support national competitiveness concludes this chapter.

The role of global talent in shaping cities, regions and economies is the focus of **Chapter 10**. Throughout this chapter, we provide in-depth insights into the economic, socio-cultural, demographic contributions and impact of global talent across a range of cities, regions and countries. This will help you to identify critical components of the economic, socio-cultural and demographic contribution of global talent. Through examples and cases, we provide ideas to harness global talent in a variety of contexts. We look at how policy interventions aimed at talent serve as both enablers and barriers to realising the multidimensional contribution of global talent to the economy.

Chapter 11 provides an introduction to the global talent mismatch as a key global challenge and its implications for countries, sectors of the economy and individual organisations. The role of education in addressing this challenge through a focus on skills development is discussed alongside other policy responses. You will also gain insight into the role of university–academia collaboration and large-scale multilateral partnerships between government and other bodies in addressing the global talent mismatch. The Hays Global Skills Index is introduced as a measurement of the talent mismatch at a country level.

Part 3 concludes the text by bringing in a cross-disciplinary, cross-industry perspective from a city/economy-shaping perspective and diversifies the study of global talent management away from the narrow perspectives of an individual or organisation. These perspectives operate in a context provided by policy and practice in a city, along with the socio-economic levels of an economy. This impact determines how individuals and organisations shape their global talent management strategies. In concluding this text, we hope to have provided a comprehensive study into contemporary and future perspectives of an emergent field in management practice.

REFERENCES

Boucher, A. (2016). *Gender, Migration and the Global Race for Talent*. Manchester: Manchester University Press.

Kuptsch, C. and Pang, E. F. (2006). *Competing for Global Talent*. Geneva: International Labour Organisation.

Scullion, H. and Collings, D. (2010). *Global Talent Management*. London: Routledge.

PART I

Individuals as Global Talent

1

DEVELOPING MINDSETS, HEARTSETS AND SKILLSETS

Chapter contents

Demystifying the concept of global talent

- An introduction
- Global talent and globalisation
- Global talent and the wider management literature
- Defining global talent in a world of work context

Developing global mindset attributes

- Bennett's concept of 'mindsets' and its global dimension
- Global competence as a core global mindset attribute

Developing global heartset attributes

- Bennett's concept of 'heartsets' and its global dimension
- Emotional intelligence as a core global heartset attribute

Developing global skillset attributes

- Bennett's concept of 'skillsets' and its global dimension
- Learnability as a core global skillset attribute

Global talent activity

Learning objectives

After reading this chapter, you will be able to:

- articulate the concept of global talent and how it relates to human resource management
- appreciate the different definitions of global talent, including the one adopted in this text
- understand the concept of global mindsets, heartsets, skillsets and related attributes
- evaluate yourself as global talent.

DEMYSTIFYING THE CONCEPT OF GLOBAL TALENT
An introduction

Global talent and the concept of talent can be found in common parlance, sometimes as a buzzword, but mostly for its significance to organisations and economies at large. According to Ilian Mihov, Dean at INSEAD Business School, one of the world's leading and largest graduate business schools, talent is now increasingly seen as a currency (Adecco Group, 2015) and as a competitive advantage that is sought after by organisations, cities, regions and nations:

> We live in a world where talent has become the core currency of competitiveness – for businesses and national economies alike. Businesses and governments need new kinds of leaders and entrepreneurs, equipped with the skills that will help their firms and countries to thrive in the global knowledge economy.

Undoubtedly, a lot has been written and is still being written about talent, considering how important talent is to organisations, businesses and national economies. We look at the concept and its definitions in greater detail next in order to frame the foundations of this text.

Talent and globalisation

One of the big five global management-consulting firms, McKinsey and Co., provides the most cited and widely accepted definition of talent through a seminal study compiled by consultants Ed Michaels, Helen Handfield-Jones and Beth Axelrod – *The War for Talent* (Michaels et al., 2001).

Talent is 'the sum of a person's abilities … his or her intrinsic gifts, skills, knowledge, experience, intelligence, judgment, attitude, character and drive. It also includes his or her ability to learn and grow', Michaels et al. argue (2001: xii). Twenty one years on, the study is still relevant in defining and contextualising the notion of talent in the world of work.

However, within a world of unprecedented challenges, industry demands new kinds of talent, which can 'learn and grow' (Michaels et al., 2001) and quickly adapt to a range of macro-level political, environmental and societal trends and developments which are occurring on a global scale. These macro-level trends include globalisation, constant technological innovations and demographic developments, emphasising the need to prepare future-ready and globally-aware talent.

Professor Ian Goldin, of Oxford University, argued in his book that 'globalisation is an increase in the impact on human activities of forces that span national boundaries' (Goldin and Reinert, 2013: 2). The forces of globalisation, together with rapid techno-logical advancements, require a forward-thinking workforce – global talent with the dexterity and expertise to think and work globally.

Global talent and the wider management literature

Since *The War for Talent*, a plethora of texts have discussed the concept of global talent. This extant literature has covered important interrelated concepts and developments that go hand in hand with global talent, including:

- the management of global talent (Schuler et al., 2011; Stahl et al., 2012)
- the competition for global talent (Beechler and Woodward, 2009)
- global perspectives of talent management (Scullion and Collings, 2011)
- global talent mobility (Welch and Zhen, 2008)
- the conceptualisation of talent (Adamsen, 2016)
- global talent policy (Allan, 2006)
- the global talent supply pipeline (Gordon, 2009).

Directly relevant to our work is Gordon's (2009) critical account of the challenge in developing a well-rounded future workforce, which draws particular focus to the education to employment link in his book, *Winning the Global Talent Showdown: How Businesses and Communities Can Partner to Rebuild the Jobs Pipeline*. He contends that the education system is outdated and broken, and fails to prepare students with the skills they need to thrive in the rapidly changing workforce and workplace of the future. Similarly, Adamsen's (2016) *Demystifying Talent Management: A Critical Approach to the Realities of Talent* is pertinent in its conceptualisation of talent, albeit without a global dimension to it. In *Global Talent Management*, Scullion and Collings (2011) provide a discussion on recent theoretical contributions in the area of global talent management, key challenges and opportunities facing the field and emerging developments around global talent management in key economies such as China, India, the Middle East and Eastern Europe.

Specifically, HR management students and professionals may be interested in exploring further texts that specifically discuss talent management (see, for example, Brewster et al., 2011 and Scullion and Collings, 2011). Also pertinent is Johnson's work (2014) which advances our understanding of how organisations can prepare for and capitalise on major global talent trends. In their 'Global Talent Management' chapter in *The Routledge Companion to International Human Resource Management*, Vaiman and Collings (2014) put the spotlight on organisational approaches to global talent management and provide a critical discussion on the global context of global talent management. Scullion and Collings (2011) discuss emerging trends in global talent management in emerging economies such as China, India, the Middle East and Eastern Europe.

This textbook builds on these works by providing a comprehensive and more integrative perspective on global talent management and does not focus merely on the HR aspects of talent management.

International perspectives on talent tend to focus on the issues and challenges related to mobility and migration specifically. For example, Cerna (2016) provides a comprehensive account of the interplay between the highly skilled migration of global talent and immigration policy in her book *Immigration Policies and the Global Competition for Talent*. Through the adoption of a global talent policy perspective, the author provides a critical account of high-skilled immigration policies of countries seen as hubs for global talent. *Gender, Migration and the Global Race for Talent* by Boucher (2016) reflects on international country-level policy and practice in skilled migration with a particular focus on gender. The author provides an in-depth discussion of the rationale behind governments' decision making to adopt gender-aware skilled immigration policies for global talent. Similarly, Duncan (2012) provides a comparative account of the legal and political efforts and challenges in managing the recruitment of high-skilled global talent in the text *Immigration Policymaking in the Global Era: In Pursuit of Global Talent*.

Our text is positioned as a contemporary text that presents to its readers an integrated perspective that is relevant for current and future managers and leaders across sectors and disciplines.

Most of these texts play on the interrelatedness of concepts such as mobility, competition, policy and supply of talent. Some other perspectives focus on the management and development perspective. For example, Salomaa (2014) explored perspectives in global talent development through the coaching of talent in multinational companies. Similarly, Garavan et al. (2012) have mapped global talent development through its definition, scope and challenges related to formulating global talent development strategies in organisations.

Talent in a global context, or rather the notion of global talent, has been discussed by some others. In her 'Going Global' article for *Coaching Today*, Wendy Wilson, an executive coach and mentor, defines the concept of global talent as 'a workforce already known variously as local plus, global nomads, frequent business travellers and virtual commuters' (Coaching Today, 2012). By drawing on earlier work, Professor Brenda Yeoh and Dr Lai Eng, of the National University of Singapore, see global talent as 'comprising highly mobile skilled workers such as business creators, technical experts, technology innovators, health professionals, and those in scientific, educational and cultural sectors' (Yeoh and Ah Eng, 2008: 235).

Global talent has been viewed through a range of prisms, but mostly either individual or organisational understandings and definitions result. We attempt to provide a more integrative and holistic positioning for the concept in the section that follows.

Defining global talent in a world of work context

In attempting to amplify the concept of global talent, there is a need to define global talent more practically and in the context of the world of work. This includes attributes, skills and competencies that individuals seen as global talent should be able to demonstrate.

We use a three-pillared approach to unpacking our definition of global talent. For us, global talent carries with it a unique combination of mindset, skillset and heartset attributes (Figure 1.1).

Global talent cannot however be reduced to an equation or a formula. Each human talent is unique and even more so as it adapts and evolves in a global context. However, in unravelling the concept we provide illustrative areas of knowledge, skills

Figure 1.1   Global talent as the sum of global mindsets, heartsets and skillsets

and values that allow individuals to position themselves confidently on the global stage. As such, these individuals:

> don't just demonstrate a combination of global mindset, heartset and skillset attributes that are in demand by the future workforce and workplace but are also able to make a meaningful contribution to their organisations and communities.

Our definition therefore assumes that a global talent is a global practitioner who is ready to embrace, lead and inspire change in the world of work around them. Equipped with global, yet diverse knowledge, skills and training, such individuals are capable of taking a visionary approach to their personal professional practice and the organisations they contribute to and lead. Global talent is also boundaryless and inclusive of its local, regional and national contexts. Such individuals recognise diversity as an enabler of prosperity across communities and organisations and understand the benefits of fostering intercultural engagement as part of their professional practice and beyond. They are also naturally driven by a curiosity about the world they live in. They act as catalysts of innovation for their communities and organisations. Global talent is best placed to respond to the rising challenges of sustainability across the economy, environment and society.

The conceptualisation of global talent in this text premises that global talent is not just a reference to the international or expat workforce. Nor is it, as we said earlier, formulaic; it is unique in the combinations of attributes it possesses and utilises. As such, our aim in conceptualising of global talent is to widen its definition, usage and application in the management of human development – as individuals in organisations or by society.

In the section that follows, we explore the triple attributes of a global mindset, heartset and skillset in further detail.

DEVELOPING GLOBAL MINDSET ATTRIBUTES

Bennett's concept of 'mindsets' and its global dimension

A mindset, according to Bennett (2008: 18), is informed by a set of cognitive competencies, which 'include cultural-general knowledge, culture-specific knowledge, identity development patterns, cultural adaptation processes, and the first priority: cultural self-awareness' (2008: 18). If you add a global dimension to this set of cognitive competencies, the sum is – a global mindset.

However, a global mindset is a complex set of cognitive competencies and perhaps is not as simplistic as this. Let us examine some other perspectives here.

Mansour Javidan, a Garvin distinguished professor and director at the Najafi Global Mindset Institute, views a global mindset through the perspective of leadership. He highlights that 'leaders with a strong stock of Global Mindset know about cultures and political and economic systems in other countries and understand how their global industry works. They are passionate about diversity and are willing to push themselves' (*Harvard Business Review*, 2010). He positions adaptability in a global context as a key differentiator for individuals with a global mindset who, according to him, 'are comfortable with being uncomfortable in uncomfortable environments'.

The World Bank provides a different perspective on how global mindsets are defined and seen in the professional world, this time through the perspective of global health and social care. Jules Duval, senior medical officer at the World Bank, emphasised the implications of having a global mindset for global healthcare: 'as the next generation works, travels, and lives with a global mindset unlike any generation before them, they will start to see health and well-being as common values shared by all people' (Dorn, 2016). Mi Ja Kim, professor and Dean Emeritus at the College of Nursing, University of Illinois, has also written about the need to develop a global mindset for the nursing and health industry. Professor Kim emphasised the 'urgent need to develop nurse leaders who have a global mindset and who can advance nursing scholarship and health policies worldwide' (Kim, 2005: 6).

So far, we have explored the concept of a global mindset from the perspective of global business, healthcare and leadership. The working definition of a global mindset that this text proposes builds on these definitions and places emphasis on a wider understanding of the world that talent with a global mindset should be able to demonstrate:

> An individual with a global mindset is open-minded, aware of cross-cultural differences and is creative in thought and gesture. They can demonstrate a broad understanding of key global economic, societal, environmental and political themes and the potential impact these can and are having.

The definition of this textbook implies that you, as someone with a global mindset, should understand current global developments and challenges in the world around you and the impact they have on the global economy, society, environment and politics. Having the ability to grasp and navigate through an ever-changing, complex global context and its implications for individuals, communities and organisations will inevitably put you in a better standing among your peers. If you want to develop a global mindset, you will need to be able to broaden and expand your thinking.

By now, you will have noted that in our discussion of definitions of a global mindset, we have highlighted some 'attributes' of talent with a global mindset – an understanding of global themes, cross-cultural awareness and working within an international context. Understanding what constitutes the key attributes of talent with a global mindset is important.

In your conversations with people and, indeed, when scrolling through the learning materials, you may note that some of them refer to global citizenship as a key attribute when they define a global mindset. However, the premise of this text is that in order to be considered a talent with a global mindset, a much wider set of attributes needs to be demonstrated.

We structure global mindset attributes alongside six distinctive themes – awareness, openness, ethics, intelligence, creativity and opportunism – as shown in Table 1.1. These themes provide a more holistic view of one's global mindset. Three categories of global mindset attributes are provided – based on prior level and experience. We see these categories or, indeed, sets of global mindset attributes as progression levels through which you acquire new attributes as you progress in your studies or career.

If you were an undergraduate student, you would be required to develop and demonstrate attributes such as global awareness, curiosity and social ethics. If, however, you were a postgraduate student, you would be expected to build on attributes shown in the entry-level attributes by also developing and demonstrating attributes such as cultural awareness, creativity and social intelligence. The advanced set of global mindset attributes shown in Table 1.1, targeted at postgraduate research students and established professionals, provides attributes such as understanding cross-disciplinarity, recognising interconnectedness and having a growth mindset.

Table 1.1 Global mindset attributes

Global mindset attributes	Entry level attributes for youth	Professional attributes for graduates	Advanced attributes for experienced managers/ levels
Awareness	Global awareness	Global awareness Global competence Cultural awareness	Advance (practice) awareness (+ prior levels)
Openness	Curiosity	Curiosity Open-mindness	Cognitive flexibilty Understanding cross-disciplinarity (+ prior levels)
Ethics	Social ethics	Social ethics Cultural ethics Environmental ethics	Social ethics Cultural ethics Environmental ethics Business ethics
Intelligence	Emotional intelligence Social intelligence	Cultural intelligence Social intelligence	Practice intelligence (+ prior levels)
Creativity	–	Creativity	System 2 thinking Leveraging cross-disciplinarity
Opportunism	–	–	Growth mindset Recognition of inter-connectedness and resourcefulness

Global competence as a core global mindset attribute

An important milestone in the wider recognition of the importance of developing a global mindset has been the OECD's work on the PISA Global Competence Framework. The OECD's Directorate of Education and Skills, together with the Harvard Graduate School of Education, developed and launched the framework with the purpose of explaining, fostering and assessing global competence (OECD, 2017). The framework is seen as a potential intervention tool for policymakers, education and industry leaders, alongside teachers interested in nurturing global competence as a core attribute among young people across the world.

The framework defines global competence as follows:

> Global competence is the capacity to examine local, global and intercultural issues, to understand and appreciate the perspectives and world views of others, to engage in open, appropriate and effective interactions with people from different cultures, and to act for collective well-being and sustainable development.

But why do we need global competence? The OECD highlighted the importance of global competence for the workforce and workplace alongside its wider societal benefits. The organisation concluded that talent needs to be globally competent in order to live harmoniously in multicultural communities; to thrive in a changing labour market; to use media platforms effectively and responsibly; and to support the Sustainable Development Goals (OECD, 2017).

Being globally competent, you would understand the importance of the interrelated nature of the world we all live in, the challenges we are faced with and the developments we care about in our own pursuit and collectively as a community (Figure 1.2).

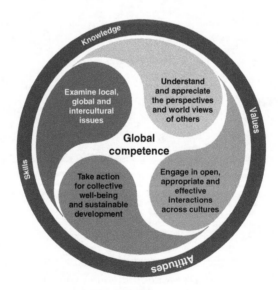

Figure 1.2   OECD's Global Competence Framework

(Source: OECD, 2017)

This work raises some important questions for talent with a global mindset, particularly how talent as citizens of the world understand, make sense of and respond to these challenges and opportunities.

The OECD's definition is aligned, to a degree, with this text's definition of a global mindset as it touches on the importance of themes and developments of global relevance and being open-minded and engaged across cultures and borders.

DEVELOPING GLOBAL HEARTSET ATTRIBUTES
Bennett's concept of 'heartsets' and its global dimension

In this section, we explore the concept of a global heartset, what it means for you and how you know you have developed a global heartset. You may question whether 'heartsets' is an official word. This is a common question we get asked when we deliver our global talent programmes and modules, both in the UK and internationally.

Whilst *The Oxford English Dictionary*, does not recognise it as a word officially, it has been defined by Bennett.

Bennett (2008: 19), who describes a heartset as being informed by a set of affective competencies, which include 'curiosity, initiative, risk taking, suspension of judgment, cognitive flexibility, tolerance of ambiguity, cultural humility, and resourcefulness'. Bennett also concludes that a heartset takes into account one's 'maintenance of attitudes such as curiosity and tolerance of ambiguity that act as motivators for seeking out cultural differences'. If we attach a global dimension to this set of affective competencies, the sum of which forms one's heartset, we come up with a new concept – a global heartset. Simply put, one then might conclude that having a global heartset is about being able to understand your inner world and how it interacts with the inner worlds of other people around you.

By seeing global heartset through the perspective of leadership as a discipline and one's quality, Joann Ross and Willa Zakin Hallowell, associates at Grovewell Global Leadership Solutions, argue that successful global leaders are those who can demonstrate that they have a good awareness of their own and others' emotions. Through their work in organisational leadership, the authors conclude that 'global leaders use more than their minds. A global "heartset" allows them to be aware of their own and others' emotions, enabling them to make meaningful connections across differences' (Ross and Hallowell, 2016). The authors conclude that while the dominant discourse has been focused on the importance of developing a global mindset, the latter is only half of the equation and the other half is exactly the importance of nurturing a global heartset.

The working definition of a global heartset that this text puts forward places an emphasis on the need for a thorough understanding of oneself and the relationship between oneself and others that talent with a global heartset should be able to demonstrate:

> An individual with a global heartset is empathetic, respectful and conscientious. They can demonstrate a well-developed set of intra- and inter-personal traits and qualities and understand how different cultures operate.

This means that you, as someone with a global heartset, should have a good understanding of your personal traits and qualities as well as how they enable you to understand others and their personalities beyond your immediate network, across cultures and across borders. In other words, if you want to develop a global heartset, you need to be able to broaden your understanding of yourself, along with how your inner traits and qualities enable you to understand others' traits and qualities.

Though being relatively complex and unexplored, the concept of a global heartset can act as a key differentiator in the job market and some influential voices have spoken about how one's unique personality can make a difference in the workplace. Alastair Cox, CEO of Hays global recruiting firm, highlighted the importance of taking advantage of your unique personality through authenticity and passion (Cox, 2016). In his 'If You Fake It, You Won't Make It' article, Cox argues that personality is what makes us different at work and in our personal lives. Cox concluded that 'your purpose here is to identify the real you, not your perfect persona. And whatever you conclude is you is fine, and it's unique' (Cox, 2016).

Global heartset attributes can be structured along two distinctive themes – intra-heartset and inter-heartset – shown in Table 1.2. These themes provide a more inclusive and holistic view of one's global heartset. Though the intra- and inter-heartset themes of attributes might sound similar, they are very different. If intra-heartset attributes are concerned with the understanding of oneself, the inter-heartset ones are focused on one's understanding of others.

This text provides three categories of global heartset attributes – youth and undergraduate student, graduate and postgraduate taught student, postgraduate research student and professional. These categories, which are also sets of global heartset attributes, are again seen as progression levels that enable you to acquire newattributes.

Early career professionals, for example, should develop and demonstrate global heartset attributes that include sensitivity, openness, honesty and respect, as evident in the entry-level attributes shown in Table 1.2. Graduates and postgraduate taught students progress on to the next stage by having to develop attributes such as emotional intelligence, empathy, an understanding of oneself and others, alongside passion and respect. At the advanced level, we have postgraduate research students and professionals who, by building on the previous sets of global heartset attributes, are also expected to demonstrate that they possess conscientiousness, inclusivity, compassion and integrity among other attributes (Table 1.2).

Table 1.2   Global heartset attributes

Global heartset attributes	Entry level attributes for youth	Professional attributes for graduates	Advanced attributes for experienced managers/ leaders
Intra-heartset	Sensitivity	Sensitivity	Conscientiousness
	Morality	Morality	Inclusivity
		Passion	Integrity
		Personality	Sensibility
		Emotional intelligence	Ambiguity
		Honesty (self)	(+ prior levels)
		Awareness (self)	
		Understanding (self)	
		Respect (self)	
Inter-heartset	Tolerance	Global citizenship	Compassion
	Openness	Diversity	Empathy
	Respect (others)	Tolerance	Otherness
	Honesty (others)	Openness	(+ prior levels)
		Empathy	
		Respect (others)	
		Honesty (others)	
		Understanding (others)	
		Awareness (others)	

Emotional intelligence as a core global heartset attribute

The concept of a global heartset and its importance, as in the case of the global mindset, has been recognised by the world of work and is receiving growing attention from global recruiters and talent evangelists alike. One example of this is emotional intelligence, which this text sees as a core attribute for talent with a global heartset (see Table 1.2). Emotional intelligence has recently made headlines in influential business and management outlets such as the *Harvard Business Review* and the World Economic Forum's *Agenda*. Emotional intelligence is a core attribute and something that should be developed should you see yourself as a talent with a global heartset.

Dr Travis Bradberry, co-author of *Emotional Intelligence 2.0*, and the co-founder of Talent Smart, the world's leading provider of emotional intelligence tests and training, has argued that emotional intelligence is 'the "something" in each of us that is a bit intangible. It affects how we manage behaviour, navigate social complexities, and make personal decisions that achieve positive results' (Bradberry, 2017). Bradberry defines emotional intelligence in the following way: 'Emotional intelligence is your ability to recognize and understand emotions in yourself and others, and your ability to use this awareness to manage your behaviour and relationships.'

According to Bradberry, emotional intelligence is made up of four skills falling under two overarching competencies – personal and relational (social), which are shown in Figure 1.3. *Self-awareness* is defined as one's ability to accurately perceive one's own emotions and stay aware of them as they happen, while *self-management* influences one's ability to use awareness of one's emotions to stay flexible and demonstrate positive behaviour. Both skills contribute to the personal competence of Bradberry's concept of emotional intelligence.

Social or relational competence may comprise *social awareness* and *relationship management*. One's ability to accurately pick up on emotions in other people and understand them is at the core of social awareness, while *relationship management* forms one's ability to use an awareness of one's own and others' emotions to navigate through interactions with success and confidence (Figure 1.3).

An interesting fact from Bradberry's research into professionals is that 90% of top performers in the sample are also thought to be high in emotional intelligence. The research, on the other hand, found that just 20% of bottom performers are high in emotional intelligence.

Bradberry's definition of emotional intelligence is aligned with this text's definition of a global heartset and global heartset attributes. Earlier in this chapter, we defined a global heartset as the sum of intra- and inter-personal traits and qualities (Table 1.2). The intra- and inter-personal attributes this text puts forward express some similarities with Bradberry's self and social elements of emotional intelligence as they both take on board attributes in relation to self and in relation to others.

Thus one can safely conclude that understanding others is just as important as understanding yourself and the traits and qualities that make up your global heartset.

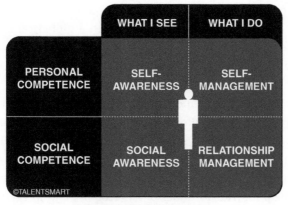

Emotional intelligence is
made up of four core skills.

Figure 1.3   Emotional intelligence defined

(Source: Bradberry, 2017)

DEVELOPING GLOBAL SKILLSET ATTRIBUTES

Bennett's concept of 'skillsets' and its global dimension

Our discussion of the global mindset and heartset concepts and attributes demonstrated the diverse aspects one has to appreciate and focus on in the journey to becoming a global talent. The final component of our global talent equation, as shown in Figure 1.1, is the concept of global skillsets.

A skillset is defined by Bennett (2008: 20) as a set of behavioural competencies which include 'such characteristics and skills as the ability to empathise, gather appropriate information, listen, perceive accurately, and manage social interactions and anxiety'. Equally, Chuck Ridley, Professor of Counselling Psychology at Texas A and M University, sees a skillset as 'a behavioural repertoire. It consists of a range of proficiencies. It is needed to accomplish a particular task or perform a given function' (Ridley, 2012). A global dimension added to this set of behavioural competencies would make this a global skillset.

If having a global mindset is about demonstrating a broad awareness of the wider world around you and your global heartset indicates your understanding of your inner world and that of others, for someone with a global skillset it is important to be able to put this awareness and understanding of self, others and the world into practice, where one example is to deliver or accomplish a task or assignment. In simple terms, one might argue that talent with a global skillset are those who understand and leverage their acquired skills and abilities to make the most of the world around them, to make a meaningful contribution to their community, or to deliver impact in their organisations.

We now go on to explore how individuals and organisations define the concept of global skillsets in practice. Linda Brimm, Emeritus Professor of Organisational Behaviour at INSEAD Business School and author of *Global Cosmopolitans*, highlights that the key components for the development of a global skillset include adaptive capacity, relational awareness and different ways of knowing and navigating through multiple lenses and perspectives that help individuals understand, recognise and integrate complex global dynamics (Brimm, 2015).

This may sound complex. What are the specific attributes employers might be looking for in you so that they can see you have a global skillset? This is a standard question that students often ask us when we define the concept of global skillsets. Ananthram and Nankervis (2013) provide one answer to this question as they explore the global skillset concept through the perspective of management. They conclude that 'the particular skillsets required by global managers include the capacities for self-awareness, intuition, and contextual flexibility along with an overarching global mindset' (Ananthram and Nankervis, 2013: 303).

They go on to identify five components of global managerial skillsets, which they consider key to success in international business: global mindset; cross-cultural sensitivity; adaptability; communication; and knowledge of global markets.

Douglas Bourn provides a Science, Technology, Engineering and Mathematics (STEM) perspective on talent, and concludes that 'a wide range of employers are looking for people who are well-rounded, can take on complex global challenges, be socially aware, have excellent communication and intercultural skills and be compassionate' (Bourn, 2008: 10).

The conceptualisation that this text puts forward emphasises the importance of developing soft skills and attributes that are valued by employers:

> An individual with a global skillset is capable of complex problem solving, possesses great people and leadership skills and is highly adaptable. They can demonstrate having the key skills required by employers.

This definition implies that you, as someone with a global skillset, would have developed resilience and adaptability as core attributes, alongside the ability to communicate and lead, both on your own and in collaboration with other individuals. Having an understanding of the core competencies, skills and attributes required by employers in your field is of equal importance. If you are keen on developing your global skillset, you will need to be adaptive and prepared for continuous learning.

Through our discussion of the concept of a global skillset so far, we have come across a range of attributes – adaptability, leadership, communication – all of which hold importance in today's world of work. This text puts forward some key global skillset attributes that you, as a global talent, develop and demonstrate to succeed in the workplace. We structure global skillset attributes alongside five distinctive themes – communication, technology, people, leadership and business – which are provided in Table 1.3. These themes provide a more holistic view of one's global skillset.

Three categories, shown in Table 1.3, which are also sets of global skillset attributes – aimed at entry level, professional and advanced experienced – are provided by

Table 1.3   Global skillset attributes

Global skillset attributes	Entry level attributes for youth	Professional attributes for graduates	Advanced attributes for experienced managers/ leaders
Communication	Cross-cultural communication	Borderless networking Cross-cultural communication	Borderless networking Cross-cultural communication Cross-generational communication
Technology	Digital engagement and identity New media literacy	Digital engagement and identity Ability to comprehend and process new data New media literacy Learnability	Ability to comprehend and process big data Computational thinking (+ prior levels)
People	Active listening People skills	Active listening People skills Adaptability	Influence and persuasion (+ prior levels)
Leadership	Digital leadership	Digital leadership Empowerment of others	Change leadership Agile leadership Visionary leadership (+ all youth & graduates)
Business	N/A	Entrepreneurship Critical thinking	Complex problem solving Resilience (c) (+ all youth & graduates)

this text. They are again seen as progression levels that enable you to acquire new attributes as you progress with your studies or move on to a professional role. Recent graduates and postgraduate taught students would be required to develop further global skillset attributes, such as adaptability, critical thinking and the ability to comprehend and process new data.

Cross-cultural communication, digital engagement and identity and people skills are global skillset attributes that students at undergraduate level would be required to develop and demonstrate alongside other attributes, as evident in the first set of attributes shown in Table 1.3. The last set of global skillset attributes shown in Table 1.3 is targeted at postgraduate research students. Building on the previous two sets of global skillset attributes, talent in this category would also be expected to demonstrate that they have developed the ability to influence and persuade, resilience, complex problem solving and agile leadership, among other attributes.

Learnability as a core global skillset attribute

Processing global skillset attributes has gained a lot of recognition among recruiters, and recent work by ManpowerGroup, one of the largest global recruiters, provides evidence of this through the introduction of 'learnability' as a core attribute for talent with a global skillset.

ManpowerGroup's (2018) rationale behind improving the ability to pick up new skills and knowledge and, indeed, learnability is simple:

> In a dynamic market environment, it's important for individuals to seek out continuous skills development in order to remain attractive to employers, and for companies to enable their workforce to learn new skills and to adapt to new processes and technologies.

Learnability is defined as 'the desire and ability to quickly grow and adapt one's skillset to remain employable throughout their working life' (ManpowerGroup, 2018). It is, therefore, clear that one's ability to adapt to change in the workforce and workplace is something that very much underpins learnability as a core global skillset attribute. In an ever-changing world of work, you will be required to constantly learn and adapt. Hence, there may be a requirement for you to improve or refresh and develop your learnability.

With the importance of learnability in mind, ManpowerGroup has developed and launched the Learnability Quotient (LQ) (LQ, 2018) with the purpose of measuring one's level of learnability. The LQ represents a new way for talent to assess their learning styles and receive recommendations that help them better engage with learning that will help them improve the pace with which they pick up new knowledge and skills.

LQ, as highlighted by Mara Swan, Executive Vice President, Global Strategy and Talent, ManpowerGroup, is and has been important in defining one's success in the competitive job market, particularly in the era of super computers, robots and artificial intelligence – concepts we will discuss in Chapter 4 of this text.

So, why is it important to understand your LQ and take actions to improve it? What does your LQ say about you and your learning style? We would encourage you to take Manpower's LQ test yourself to evaluate your LQ and improve your learning style. The web link to the test is available in the further reading section of the chapter.

GLOBAL TALENT ACTIVITY – INDIVIDUAL AND COLLABORATIVE ACTIVITY OPTIONS

In this first chapter of the text, you have had the opportunity to consider diverse perspectives on global talent as well as how we define the concept as the sum of global mindset, heartset and skillset attributes. You now have the opportunity to consider how you see yourself as global talent. What follows are 10 questions which allow you to test your global mindset, heartset and skillset attributes.

Here are the parameters for this activity: You have two options – a self-reflection exercise and/or global talent activity. If you find yourself studying independently at home or in the university library, then take up the self-reflection exercise and write in no more than 50 words your answer to each of the 10 questions below. You also have the opportunity to discuss your reflections by organising an impromptu global talent activity with your peers in class, or perhaps you could ask your tutor to organise one. From our own experience of running self-reflection exercises and global talent activities with students, the latter option works brilliantly if you are in a social setting and you are keen to share your reflections and ideas and explore what your fellow students think about global talent.

Global mindsets: Chapter 1 of this text introduced you to the concept of a global mindset and, with it, a number of key global themes related to the global economy, environment, politics and the social agenda that you, as global talent, should have an awareness of. You were also given the opportunity to learn about the key global mindset attributes that are sought after by employers, leading voices in the world of education and the authors of this text.

Question	Response
1: From your perspective, which key global economic, environmental, political and social themes should a person with a global mindset be aware of and why?	
2: Which key global mindset attributes should a person with a global mindset be able to develop and demonstrate?	
3: Which global mindset attributes do you feel you have already developed and which ones do you feel you need to do more work on? For example, would you need to work harder on your global competence?	

Global heartsets: The concept of a global heartset that characterises global talent is something that we also covered in this first chapter; we discussed a number of attributes that you, as global talent, should be able to develop and demonstrate to be successful in the global workplace and workforce. You were also introduced to a range of perspectives on global heartsets from different disciplines and organisational contexts.

Question	Response
4: From your perspective, what kind of values do you think the world needs and how will you make a difference by being global talent with a global heartset?	
5: Which key global heartset attributes should a person with a global heartset be able to develop and demonstrate?	

6: Which global heartset attributes do you feel you have already developed and which ones do you feel you need to do more work on? For example, would you need to work harder on your emotional intelligence?	

Global skillsets: Chapter 1 introduced you to the concept of global skillsets and discussed a number of attributes that you, as global talent, should be able to develop and demonstrate to employers. We explored various discipline perspectives and sectoral voices on what constitutes a global skillset and the imperative for developing one.

Question	Response
7: From your perspective, which attributes, skills and competencies are sought after by employers in your subject discipline and why?	
8: Which key global skillset attributes do you think that someone who regards themselves as global talent should be able to demonstrate and why?	
9: Which global skillset attributes do you feel you have already developed and which ones do you feel you need to do more work on? For example, would you need to work harder on your learnability?	

We have developed an extra question for postgraduate taught and research students but we would also welcome undergraduate students to take up the challenge, test their creativity and further develop their global mindset, heartset and skillset attributes.

Being a global talent requires that you have a good understanding of a range of themes of global relevance, such as poverty, sustainability and economic development, and have the ability to provide responses and actionable solutions to these challenges.

10: Which key global challenge should be addressed by governments and why? Please provide your top three ideas on how this global challenge may be addressed.	

We hope you enjoyed playing the global talent activity.

Further reading and resources

Bradberry, T. (2017). *Why you need emotional intelligence.* Available at: www.weforum.org/agenda/2017/02/why-you-need-emotional-intelligence [Accessed 22 January 2018].
British Council (2017). *How to succeed in the global workplace MOOC.* Available at: www.futurelearn.com/courses/global-workplace [Accessed 19 February 2018].
LQ (2018). *Learnability quotient assessment.* Available at: www.learnabilityquotient.com/en/assessment [Accessed 22 January 2018].

REFERENCES

Adamsen, B. (2016). *Demystifying talent management: A critical approach to the realities of talent.* London: Palgrave Macmillan.

Adecco Group (2015). *Growing talent for today and tomorrow: Report highlights importance of 'employable skills' and vocational education amid changing labour markets and rising unemployment.* Available at: https://press.adeccogroup.com/news/second-edition-of-global-talent-competitiveness-index-released-switzerland-singapore-and-luxembourg-lead-rankings-2b2b-2cb12.html (Accessed 24 January 2018).

Allan, M. (2006). *Brain strain and other social challenges arising from the UK's policy on attracting global talent.* Geneva: International Labour Organization.

Ananthram, S. and Nankervis, A. (2013). Global managerial skill sets, management development, and the role of HR: An exploratory qualitative study of North American and Indian managers. *Contemporary Management Research,* 9(3), 299–322.

Beechler, S. and Woodward, I. C. (2009). The global 'war for talent'. *Journal of International Management,* 15(3), 273–85.

Bennett, J. M. (2008). On becoming a global soul: A path to engagement during study abroad. In V. Savicki (ed.), *Developing intercultural competence and transformation: Theory, research, and application in international education* (pp. 13–31). Sterling, VA: Stylus.

Boucher, A. (2016). *Gender, migration and the global race for talent.* Oxford: Oxford University Press.

Bourn, D. (2008). *The global engineer incorporating global skills within UK higher education of engineers.* London: UCL Institute of Education.

Bradberry, T. (2017). *Why you need emotional intelligence.* Available at: www.weforum.org/agenda/2017/02/why-you-need-emotional-intelligence [Accessed 22 January 2018].

Brewster, C., Mayrhofer, W. and Reichel, A. (2011). Riding the tiger? Going along with Cranet for two decades: A relational perspective. *Human Resource Management Review*, 21(1), 5–15.

Brimm, L. (2015). *How to learn from a global life*. Available at: https://knowledge.insead.edu/blog/insead-blog/how-to-learn-from-a-global-life-4134 [Accessed 27 July 2017].

Cerna, L. (2016). *Immigration policies and the global competition for talent*. Basingstoke: Palgrave Macmillan.

Coaching Today (2012). *Going global: Coaching with a global mindset*. Available at: www.wendywilsonconsulting.com/wp-content/uploads/Going-global-CTJuly-2013.pdf [Accessed 24 January 2018].

Cox, A. (2016). *If you fake it, you won't make it*. Available at: https://social.hays.com/2017/04/25/if-you-fake-it-you-wont-make-it [Accessed 21 January 2018].

Dorn, D. (2016). *International corporate health leadership council launches global culture of health whitepaper*. Available at: https://dorncompanies.com/culture-health-whitepaper [Accessed 22 January 2018].

Duncan, N. (2012). *Immigration policymaking in the global era: In pursuit of global talent*. New York: Springer.

Garavan, T. N., Carbery, R. and Rock, A. (2012). Mapping talent development: Definition, scope and architecture. *European Journal of Training and Development*, 36(1), 5–24.

Goldin, I. and Reinert, K. A. (2013). *Globalisation for development*. Oxford: Oxford University Press.

Gordon, E. E. (2009). *Winning the global talent showdown: How businesses and communities can partner to rebuild the jobs pipeline*. San Francisco, CA: Berrett-Koehler.

Harvard Business Review (2010). *Bringing the global mindset to leadership*. Available at: https://hbr.org/2010/05/bringing-the-global-mindset-to.html [Accessed 21 January 2018].

Johnson, M. (2014). *The worldwide workplace: Solving the global talent equation*. Berlin: Springer.

Kim, M. J. (2005). Editorial: Developing a global mindset for nursing scholarship and health policy. *Australian Journal of Advanced Nursing*, 22(3), 6–7.

LinkedIn (2018). *About us*. Available at: https://press.linkedin.com/about-linkedin [Accessed 22 January 2018].

LQ (2018). *Learnability quotient assessment*. Available at: www.learnabilityquotient.com/en/assessment [Accessed 22 January 2018].

ManpowerGroup (2018). *What is learnability*? Available at: www.manpowergroup.com/workforce-insights/expertise/learnability-quotient [Accessed 22 January 2018].

Michaels, E., Handfield-Jones, H. and Axelrod, B. (2001). *The war for talent*. Boston, MA: Harvard Business Review Press.

OECD (2017). *PISA 2018 global competence*. Available at: www.oecd.org/pisa/pisa-2018-global-competence.htm [Accessed 22 January 2018].

Ridley, C. (2012). *Mindset, heart set and skill set: Ties that bind doctoral students, Gideon's warriors, and church planters*. Available at: www.churchplanting.com/mindset-heart-set-and-skill-set-ties-that-bind-doctoral-students-gideons-warriors-and-church-planters/#.WmS2B62cZTZ [Accessed 21 January 2018].

Ross, J. A. and Hallowell, W. Z. (2016). *Getting to the heart of global leadership*. Available at: www.fletcherforum.org/home/2016/9/22/getting-to-the-heart-of-global-leadership [Accessed 27 July 2017].

Salomaa, R. (2014). Coaching of key talents in multinational companies. In *Global talent management* (pp. 43–63). Berlin: Springer International Publishing.

Schuler, R. S., Jackson, S. E. and Tarique, I. (2011). Global talent management and global talent challenges: Strategic opportunities for IHRM. *Journal of World Business*, 46(4), 506–16.

Scullion, H. and Collings, D. (2011). *Global talent management*. London: Routledge.

Sorrell, M. (2016). *To move upward, move outward*. Available at: www.linkedin.com/pulse/move-upward-outward-sir-martin-sorrell [Accessed 23 January 2017].

Stahl, G., Björkman, I., Farndale, E., Morris, S. S., Paauwe, J., Stiles, P., et al. (2012). Six principles of effective global talent management. *Sloan Management Review*, 53(2), 25–42.

Vaiman, V. and Collings, D. G. (2014). *Global talent management: The Routledge companion to international human resource management*. London: Routledge.

Welch, A. R. and Zhen, Z. (2008). Higher education and global talent flows: Brain drain, overseas Chinese intellectuals, and diasporic knowledge networks. *Higher Education Policy*, 21(4), 519–37.

Yeoh, B. S. and Ah Eng, L. (2008). Guest editors' introduction: 'Talent' migration in and out of Asia – Challenges for policies and places. *Asian Population Studies*, 4(3), 235–45.

2

JOB SEEKERS AND JOB CREATORS

Chapter contents

Routes to employment

- Traditional routes to employment
- The need to nurture both job seekers and job creators

Global talent as job seekers

- Deconstructing global talent as job seekers
- Global talent and the growth of the gig economy
- Innovative company models embracing the gig economy model

Global talent as job creators

- The rise in global talent entrepreneurs and start-up creators
- Africa's emerging social entrepreneurship models

Hybrid global talent: job seekers and job creators

- The challenges of navigating through uncertainty in the job market
- Learnability as a core attribute of hybrid global talent

Interview with global talent job seeker turned job creator Sandeep Deshpande

Reflective exercise: Global entrepreneurship quiz

> ## Learning objectives
>
> After reading this chapter, you will be able to:
>
> - identify and draw upon different routes to employment
> - understand the concept of global talent as job seekers and creators
> - explore the importance of being prepared for hybrid careers
> - gain insights from practice on hybrid global talent.

ROUTES TO EMPLOYMENT

Traditional routes to employment

As global talent, there are many different routes to employment that you have the opportunity to take. A graduate in the UK might be looking at employment in one way and a rural youth in India from a completely different perspective. Talent in Australia, China or other countries may look at routes to employment perhaps from a contextual or economy-specific way.

In addition to routes to employment varying across geographies, there are, in addition, different entry points to employment. You may well start your professional career in a graduate-level job. However, you may enter the workforce as an intern, an apprentice or even a freelancer working on multiple projects and for more than one employer instead! For those of you with an entrepreneurial mindset, you may be passionate about establishing a business focused on the development of a product or delivery of a unique service. Alternatively, you may take up the opportunity to be both an employee global talent as well as a job creator!

The purpose of this text is not to homogenise, nor generalise different routes to employment. Instead, what it aims to do is to include all those different perspectives on employment and discuss them through examples from international practice in organisations and communities. By doing this, we would like to encourage you to reflect on employment more broadly and have a deeper understanding of the changing nature of employment.

It is important for someone, say a fresh graduate, who might be going into their first employment placement for a large multinational organisation, a third-sector body or a small business, to understand that this is not the only labour market step you'd take.

You will be reinventing yourself throughout your career! We will explore this further in the chapter when we discuss the option to develop yourself as both a global talent job seeker and a job creator.

Different people in different parts of the world have diverse perspectives and varied opportunities to engage in employment. One needs to be mindful of this and embrace the importance of developing a global mindset. We will explore more of that in Chapter 3 where we will discuss the importance of being able to navigate through and communicate across cultures, boundaries and generations as global talent.

What one needs to note in the context of our discussion of routes to employment is that the world of work has evolved profoundly over the centuries, with advancements in agriculture, manufacturing, engineering and three industrial revolutions – developments which we will discuss in detail in Chapter 4. We are now in the midst of the 4th Industrial Revolution, or 4IR, which is fundamentally reshaping the workforce and the workplace.

What does this mean for employment? Global talent needs to be more agile and flexible in the way it engages with employment opportunities. Often, this engagement will include more than one employment opportunity at a time. Traditional routes to entering the workforce and well-established forms of employment may no longer be relevant. While there are many routes to employment, there are two established forms of employment that we will discuss in the following chapter.

The need to nurture both job seekers and job creators

The world is changing and there is a need to nurture both job seekers and job creators, the two established forms of 'employment' across the world today. As we live in a world of rapid technological, demographic, economic, political and environmental disruptions, talent that is truly global will need to demonstrate great flexibility in the way they engage with employment opportunities.

This may well mean that if you have been an entrepreneur and a job creator for a period of time, say 5–10 years, you may well need to join the workforce as an employee or a job seeker at some stage of your working life. Take, for example, Barnaby Voss, co-founder of BlikBook, a virtual platform for students and academics in higher education, who moved to a corporate role at Google after being an entrepreneur for five years (Jacobs, 2015). After his company was acquired by Civitas Learning, Voss opted for greater job security (than that afforded to him as an entrepreneur) as Head of Marketing at Google.

Chloe Macintosh, co-founder of the online furniture retailer Made.com, has now become a creative adviser at Soho House due to the complexities surrounding entrepreneurship and sustaining your start-up ideas over time. After five years of experience in building a company from scratch, Chloe Macintosh seized the market opportunity to apply her entrepreneurial skills and progress to the corporate world (Jacobs, 2015).

Alternatively, if you have been an employee of a large international organisation for many years and you have acquired considerable experience and knowledge in order to develop your own ideas, you may want to become a CEO or an entrepreneur who starts their own business, employs people and is ultimately considered a job creator. A good example is Elizabeth Zeigler, CEO of Graham-Pelton Consulting, who became the first woman to lead a global fundraising and non-profit management firm after 16 years of part-time employment (Fast Company, 2017). Another example is Mike Kappel, who worked as a systems programmer for a big, multinational company before establishing his own business and becoming CEO of Patriot Software. Mike started his business in the basement of a factory and grew it into a multi-million-dollar company that employs well over 300 people and serves small businesses in the USA (Forbes, 2017).

There are many such stories from the world of work: how entrepreneurs have joined the 'gig economy' and become employees, and vice versa. We now go on to discuss in more detail established forms of employment and to define global talent as job seekers and job creators.

GLOBAL TALENT AS JOB SEEKERS
Deconstructing global talent as job seekers

In moving towards a discussion of the concept of global talent as job seekers and what it means to you, we would like to point out that this text is not limited to graduates entering the job marketplace, and this is not what we mean by job seekers. Yes, the primary focus of this text (as it is a textbook) is concerned with you being a graduate and being a talent entering the graduate job market, but there are different entry points into this market.

There are different levels of entry, such as apprenticeships, internships, traineeships and short assignments. Later, this text will discuss the gig economy, which serves as one such example. Equally, the employment landscape is far more complex across the spectrum of vocational, technical, trainee middle-management, senior management, executive level, and so forth.

So, it is not just the point of entry we reflect on in terms of job seeking and creating, nor is it the level – we are concerned with the entire spectrum.

Global talent as job seekers is not a new idea. In fact, around 80% of the world's 3 billion workforce fall into this category, whereby they are employed by a company and their status is as an employee for that company or organisation, be it a business, a public sector body or a non-profit entity.

For the purpose of this text, job seekers are talent who are in employment or seeking new employment.

The International Labour Organisation (ILO), a United Nations agency dealing with labour problems, international labour standards, social protection and work opportunities for all, defines an employee as a 'worker holding an explicit or implicit employment contract which gives him or her a basic remuneration which is not directly dependent upon the revenue of the unit for which he or she works' (ILO, 2018a).

The UK government defines an 'employee' as 'someone who works under an employment contract'. It goes on to suggest that all employees have an employment contract with their employer, which sets out an employee's employment conditions, rights, responsibilities and duties, all included in the 'terms' of the contract (UK Government Portal, 2018a). Global talent who are employed then have certain rights and responsibilities that they are expected to fulfil as part of their employment contract with the organisation that employs them. This is what differentiates 'employees' from individuals in the workforce with fewer rights and responsibilities, who in the UK are considered as 'workers' – workers who are in employment through an agency. We will discuss this new development in more detail when we cover the growth of freelance work and the gig economy.

Talented job seekers in employment or simply employees have an important role as they are often seen as an important asset to organisations, which helps achieve their organisational mission and objectives. Wright et al. (2006), for example, see employees as an integral part of an organisation and go on to suggest that 'a firm's human resources are an important potential source of sustained competitive advantage'. Equally, 'Valuing Your Most Valuable Assets', a *Harvard Business Review* article by Teresa Amabile, a professor at Harvard Business School, and Steven Kramer, a psychologist and independent researcher, highlighted that 'corporate leaders often proclaim that their employees are their most valuable asset' (*Harvard Business Review*, 2011).

Now that we have explored different perspectives and concepts of job seekers as talent in employment and their value to organisations, the definition of global talent as job seekers and employees that this text puts forward is the following:

> Global talent as job seekers are current or future temporary and permanent employ-
> ees of small- to large-scale organisations in public, private and non-profit sectors, who
> use their global mindset, heartset and skillset attributes to create value and develop a
> product or deliver a service that is aligned with their employer's organisational vision,
> mission and objectives.

We now provide an in-depth account of the forms of employment that global talent considered as job seekers take up throughout the course of their career. As the
definition of this text implies, global talent who are job seekers can be employed on
a part-time or full-time basis. They may also be self-employed talent, who work for a
company on a short-term contract or project, or as a freelancer. This latter mode of
employment, which some experts in the field argue provides flexibility to employees,
is gaining considerable attention from employers, governments and society more
generally. Global talent job seekers, employed on both a full-time and part-time
basis, have been dominating the labour market and thus have been recognised by
employment law. Talent who fall within the self-employment mode of employment
alongside talent on short-term assignments nevertheless reflect a more recent trend,
which is growing in importance – the gig economy and the rise of flexible modes of
employment.

Global talent and the growth of the gig economy

The term 'gig economy' was first coined at the peak of the global financial crisis
'when the unemployed made a living by gigging, or working several part-time jobs,
wherever they could', says Leslie Hook, a *Financial Times* San Francisco correspondent (Hook, 2015). The *Cambridge Dictionary* defines the term 'gig economy' as 'a way
of working that is based on people having temporary jobs or doing separate pieces
of work, each paid separately, rather than working for an employer' (*Cambridge
Dictionary*, 2018).

Building on these, the House of Commons Work and Pensions Committee in the UK
provides a fuller and more comprehensive conceptualisation of the gig economy, emphasising the main catalyst of its growth and the wide-reaching implications for this mode
of employment (House of Commons, 2017):

> The term 'gig economy' is used to refer to a wide range of different types and models of
> work. A common feature of many of these is a reliance on intermediary digital platforms
> or apps to connect self-employed workers with work. Gig economy companies often

operate in industries that have historically relied on self-employed workforces. New technology, however, enables them to operate on a scale which has substantial implications for the nature of work, the sectors in which they operate and the welfare state.

In the aftermath of the global financial crisis, the gig economy has become synonymous with a new wave of work, technology-enabled talent, the flexible nature of employment, short-term assignments and the associated insecurity of employment that it offers, which we will also discuss a bit later in this section.

The scale of the gig economy is impressive, indicating its possible upward trajectory and growing significance in the global labour market. According to a study in the USA, more than one in three workers is freelance – a figure expected to grow to 40% by 2020 (Deloitte, 2016); 34% of the Asia-Pacific workforce consists of freelancers and gig economy workers, according to Kelly Services, global recruiters (Kelly Services, 2015); in the UK, over 1.1 million people work in the gig economy – approximately the same number as in the National Health Service, the country's largest employer (*Financial Times*, 2017); equally, in the EU, between 20% and 30% of the workforce is estimated to be taking part in the gig economy (Moncada, 2017).

The growth in this freelance or casual employment has been recognised by UK employment law. The House of Commons Work and Pensions Committee in the UK published in 2017 its 'Self-employment and the gig economy' report, suggesting that 5 million people or 15% of the UK workforce is now self-employed (House of Commons, 2017). This serves as recognition of the growing scale and scope of the gig economy. Equally, new employment status definitions have emerged in UK employment law that build on the more traditional definition of an 'employee'. These include terms and definitions such as 'workers', 'agency workers' and 'self-employed contractors' who generally have fewer rights than employees but greater flexibility in terms of choosing their employment and the amount of work they are willing to commit to.

Agency workers in the context of the UK, for example, are a growing segment of the gig economy. Agency workers in the UK are set to reach 1 million by 2020 (*Financial Times*, 2016). According to the UK government's definition of an agency worker, 'you're an agency worker if you have a contract with an agency but you work temporarily for a hirer. Agencies can include recruitment agencies, for example "temp agencies"' (UK Government Portal, 2018b).

In other countries, such as Singapore, the USA and Germany, talent who are engaged in employment that is considered to be part of the gig economy have been recognised as job seekers in employment under different terms. In Germany, for example, they are considered as temporary agency workers who now form well over 5% of the country's workforce (Sandra and Birgit, 2016).

In Singapore, talent engaged in the gig economy are considered as 'contingent workers' or simply freelancers, and recent figures suggest that contract workers make up approximately 11% of the country's workforce (CIPD Asia, 2017). In the USA, on the other hand, the Bureau of Labour Statistics often adopts the term 'contingent worker' to define workers employed in alternative work, who are now believed to represent over 15% of the country's total workforce (Fallon, 2017).

Despite the high degree of autonomy that it offers, what is common among all gig economy workers across different countries are the somewhat limited rights and responsibilities that freelancers have in contrast to employees. We now go on to provide an insight into businesses that have embraced the gig economy and positioned 'flexiwork' at the core of their organisational models.

Innovative company models embracing the gig economy model

There have been a number of innovative and arguably successful companies, such as Deliveroo and Uber that have embraced the new flexible mode of employment as the new norm. The rise of these technology-enabled companies has challenged the very definition of a worker or an employee.

Uber, a San Francisco-based global taxi company, has been disrupting the transportation sector in large cities across the world since 2008. In less than a decade, Uber's global network of taxis has reached over 600 cities worldwide. The company's business model is simple – its app pulls together gig economy talent in the transportation industry to offer customers a reliable taxi service, which they can book through their smartphone and pay for online. The success of Uber very much depends on its network of over 2 million gig economy drivers worldwide who either own or lease a car, which can be turned into an Uber taxi. Uber orchestrates this global network of talent drivers and prospective customers by offering value for money and a driver ratings system, and charging drivers between 20% and 25% for each customer journey made through the Uber app.

Nevertheless, it is not only developed countries that benefit from the transportation industry disruptors riding the gig economy wave. India, for example, has developed its own Uber-like service. Ola Cabs is India's response to Uber – an innovative start-up founded in Mumbai in 2011 shortly after its San Francisco-based competitor, which provides employment opportunities to over one million gig economy drivers.

INDUSTRY INSIGHT

Ola versus Uber

Which app holds the largest market share and gig economy talent in India?

Ola Cabs has grown exponentially over the past five years due to the ongoing penetration of technology in India and the introduction of smartphones at an affordable price. Uber's disruptor now claims to have over 125 million users of its app in India, which connects with around one million gig economy drivers in over 110 cities across the country. Uber entered the Indian market in 2013 and the two companies now hold a 90% share of the market. Uber nevertheless currently operates in only 29 Indian cities. According to KalaGato's research report, in mid-2017, Uber had a market share of 50%, while Ola had 44.2% (BBC, 2018).

Ola Cabs also rivals Uber with an incredible fleet of 12 types of cars, ranging from tuk tuks, sedans and SUVs to luxury cars, kaali peeli and airport shuttles. Ola Cabs has recently announced that it is entering the Australian market in what is believed to be its first international venture. This will be an opportunity to tap into a large network of gig economy workers, many of whom are Indian-born drivers from the country's diaspora in Australia.

Deliveroo, a British-based upmarket food delivery service launched in London in 2013 is another illustration of the gig economy. Deliveroo's business model is similar to the one developed by Uber and Ola Cabs as it connects a fleet of cyclists and bikers with upmarket food customers of restaurants that do not usually deliver. Deliveroo's presence stretches across 35 UK cities and 40 cities internationally. This global market reach is enabled through its network of over 5000 gig economy workers (StartUps, 2017).

Amazon, the largest online retail platform, also taps into the gig economy as it employs a large number of employees on a short-term and an ad-hoc basis to cover busy periods of the year, such as Christmas and Easter where shoppers usually make more online purchases. Not needing to employ a permanent headcount enables Amazon to reduce operational costs and offer competitive prices for its products and services. Gig economy talent at Amazon are often taking up employment under the terms of agency workers, which we briefly discussed earlier in this chapter.

But it is not just technology-enabled and internet businesses that are rethinking their dominant model of talent recruitment – we see it in other sectors, such as banking, healthcare, education and hospitality where job seekers or employees are also part of the gig economy, as they are often employed on a fixed-term or 'zero hours contract' basis. Talent on 'zero hours contracts', currently over 3% of the UK's workforce, are also considered gig economy workers.

Sarah O'Connor, a *Financial Times* employment correspondent on the world of work, highlights the primary drive for employees to engage with the gig economy – the considerable degree of flexibility they are given to work whenever and wherever they want to (*Financial Times*, 2017):

> Ask someone who works in the 'gig economy' what attracted them and they almost always say 'the flexibility'. The promise of being able to choose when to work is a powerful one, particularly for lower-paid workers whose other job options can be inflexible and disempowering.

While the gig economy provides a number of opportunities for employees to take up flexible employment, the downside of it is that talent in this category are not in permanent employment and, as such, they don't often enjoy the stability of a minimum number of guaranteed hours at work per week, nor company benefits and perks, in the same way as permanent employees.

There has been some controversy recently, particularly around Uber and Deliveroo, both of which have been questioned over organisational practices related to basic worker and employee benefits, such as paid holiday time and pensions.

While employers of gig economy workers have largely been the main beneficiaries of tech disruption in the workplace, governments across the world are taking steps to secure certain rights and benefits for the growing talent pipeline involved in the gig economy.

In the UK, *Good Work: The Taylor Review of Modern Working Practices*, a government-commissioned report, has introduced a series of proposed changes that could significantly alter the way gig economy companies operate in Britain. If implemented, recommendations from this review might force companies such as Uber and Deliveroo to pay tax, holiday and sick pay (Taylor, 2017). In the European Union, Brussels is looking into opportunities to introduce social protection for gig economy workers, such as healthcare insurance and unemployment benefits (Brunsden, 2017).

Asian countries that have been disrupted by gig economy employment, such as India, have also stepped up to offer employees certain benefits and protection in line with those provided for regular employees. The *Economic Times*, an influential news outlet in India, invites the country's government to step in and 'build worker and workplace protection into the system' (*Economic Times*, 2017).

Whist the gig economy faces its own challenges and will evolve rapidly in the coming years, job seekers need to be prepared for the disruptions and opportunities that consequently impact their working lives.

GLOBAL TALENT AS JOB CREATORS

While job seekers who are engaged in employment are considered as employees, job creators could be regarded as employers. The ILO defines employers as talent 'who hold self-employment jobs, i.e. whose remuneration depends directly on the profits derived from the goods and services produced and engage one or more persons to work for them as "employees", on a continuous basis' (ILO, 2018b).

The 1996 Employment Rights Act in the UK defines an employer as 'the person by whom the employee or worker is (or, where the employment has ceased, was) employed'. In the context of the UK, we may also have job creators serving as company directors, who are employed by their company, usually one with limited responsibility. This makes them not only job creators but also employees of their company, mainly for tax and national insurance purposes (UK Government Portal, 2018c).

We understand that employment law and international definitions of employers may be a bit confusing and vary greatly from country to country. The aim of this text is not to delve into the definitions of employers but to focus on job creators and key expressions of this term instead. So who really are the job creators? Could companies, in addition to individuals, also fall within this category?

Global talent as job creators is a form of employment, which has a range of definitions and contextual applications in addition to the Employment Rights Act and the ILO's classification of 'employers'. Job creators can be owners of a small start-up company, employing a handful of people, or large-scale entrepreneurs and owners of ventures providing employment opportunities to hundreds and thousands of people, often internationally.

The term 'job creator' is also used to define organisations and businesses themselves as the primary sources of growth in employment opportunities. A study carried out by Magnus Henrekson, Professor at the Research Institute for Industrial Economics in Sweden, suggests that small and young firms, such as SMEs and start-ups established by entrepreneurs, are often the main creators of employment opportunities (Henrekson and Johansson, 2010). Henrekson, who calls these organisations 'gazelles', concludes that they are found to be outstanding job creators.

This view is consistent with the findings of an international large-scale study carried out by Ernst & Young, a global consultancy firm. The *EY Global Job Creation Survey* highlights that 'entrepreneurship has long been the driving force behind economic growth and job creation' (Ernst & Young, 2016). Studies in the UK have also found that small enterprises and entrepreneurs are responsible for recent growth in the provision of employment opportunities.

Sir Richard Branson, serial entrepreneur, founder of Virgin Group and an influential voice in business, also views job creators as small companies run by passionate entrepreneurs that seek to disrupt the status quo in the business world. He highlights the large-scale contribution of successful entrepreneurs as job creators as they provide employment opportunities both in the UK and internationally. 'The entrepreneurs of today will be the job creators of tomorrow' is what Branson often says.

Another view into job creation is provided by Martin Fridson, Chief Investment Officer of Lehmann, Livian, Fridson Advisors LLC and editor of Forbes, who highlights that 'the term "job creation" really should be reserved for activities that increase the number of jobs the economy can support when it is achieving its full potential' (Forbes, 2013). According to him, not only do job creators then open up new employment opportunities, they do so in a way that builds on the strength of the employment market, which does not simply fill a gap or respond to demand. Hence, Martin Fridson's definition implies an increase in the number of jobs in the economy in real terms.

Now that we have explored some perspectives and definitions of organisations and individuals that create employment opportunities, the working definition of global talent as job creators and employers that this text puts forward is as follows:

> Global talent who are job creators are CEOs, entrepreneurs and owners of small- to large-scale organisations in public, private and non-profit sectors, who use their global mindset, heartset and skillset attributes to create employment opportunities at every level of the organisation. Not only do job creators work towards their future but also the futures of other people, by creating self-employment and part-time and full-time employment opportunities – their contribution to and scale of impact on the global job market is immense.

Among the large group of job creators, there is one notable segment and this is the start-up creators, who have created millions of jobs in key sectors of the global economy such as technology, healthcare, agriculture, transportation, financial and professional services, to name a few.

The rise in global talent entrepreneurs and start-up creators

Global talent entrepreneurs or start-up creators are the backbone of modern employment due to the scale and impact of the businesses they establish in the world of work. Entrepreneurs also support the creation of job opportunities and, importantly, the development of other entrepreneurs who are likely to create further employment opportunities should their business idea be successful. We cover this group too and discuss in depth how global talent entrepreneurs and start-up creators drive the new employment wave. In addition, we go through some of the building blocks or enablers of entrepreneurship.

Definitions of entrepreneurs and start-up creators as global talent are varied and we have handpicked some influential ones. The *Financial Times Lexicon* (*Financial Times*, 2018) defines entrepreneurs as individuals who are often owners or co-owners of their company and who pursue opportunities for financial or social gain, often at great financial risk. An important characteristic of entrepreneurs as job creators is their focus on creating 'social and economic wealth through the creation of companies and jobs, as well as frequently innovating through the development of new products and services' (*Financial Times*, 2018). A new company that has been initiated and founded recently by entrepreneurs is considered a start-up.

Returning to our Virgin Group example and Richard Branson, we provide further insight into the organisation as an example of how entrepreneurs and start-up creators both generate large-scale employment opportunities and develop future entrepreneurs to start up their own business and create further jobs. They do so through what is known as a multiplier effect.

INDUSTRY INSIGHT

A global job creator footprint

The Virgin Group and Sir Richard Branson

Richard Branson and Nik Powell established Virgin Group back in 1970 when the very first business of the company was also launched. Fast forward to 2018 and Virgin Group is a successful capital investor, with a globally recognised and respected brand boasting

(Continued)

(Continued)

over 60 businesses under its umbrella that serve 53 million customers across the world (Virgin, 2018). Virgin Group businesses occupy some strategic sectors of the economy such as transportation, financial and professional services, entertainment, insurance and healthcare, mobile networks and technology, among others.

Virgin has a strong job creator footprint on a global scale. The Virgin Group of businesses employs over 69,000 talent from 35 countries (Virgin, 2018). Over the years, Virgin Group has created immense value and impact in the world of business and services and this is often attributed to Branson's entrepreneurial mindset and passion for doing business. Not only is Virgin Media a large-scale global job creator, but it is also committed to nurturing entrepreneurs who ultimately create further employment opportunities beyond the company's network of businesses.

Branson's initiative to support entrepreneurship and job creation, Virgin Start Up, has founded over 400 businesses and ventures that have created new products and jobs. Virgin Start Up provides financial resources for novice entrepreneurs to establish or grow their business, supported by a network of over 500 mentors who provide tailored mentoring and support for new ventures (Virgin Start Up, 2018).

Behind the success of Virgin and other large-scale job creators, is a range of enablers for entrepreneurship to thrive and these include tools such as crowdfunding platforms and start-up finance, entrepreneur and start-up co-working spaces, alongside tailored mentoring and support. The case of Virgin Start Up illustrates that business mentoring and support are integral to nurturing entrepreneurs. Mentors, who often provide advice, constructive critique and new ideas, are instrumental to improving one's business idea or strategy.

Co-working spaces have only recently emerged as a trend but provide opportunities for like-minded entrepreneurs and job creators to work together while cutting the operational costs of their start-up or company. Equally, the rise of crowdfunding as a crucial enabler to entrepreneurs and the creation of jobs also deserves our attention – crowdfunding enables wannabe entrepreneurs to realise their business ideas through the funding support of many, sometimes thousands of, backers who 'invest' in a business idea or a company to enable it to grow in scale and scope. Establishing an enabling infrastructure in place and its many expressions, including start-up resources, is thus crucial to nurturing global talent job creators, businesses and ultimately the creation of new jobs.

However, entrepreneurs can be job creators without making a profit or directly benefitting from the realisation of their business or organisation. Evidence of this form of entrepreneurship is provided through the rise of social entrepreneurship models across the world.

J. Gregory Dees, a Duke University professor highlights that the essence of entrepreneurship is the opportunity to provide entrepreneurial approaches to social problems. He argues that social entrepreneurship 'combines the passion of a social mission with an image of a business-like discipline, innovation and determination commonly associated with, for instance, the high-tech pioneers of Silicon Valley' (2001).

As such, social entrepreneurs address larger, often non-corporate and non-organisational goals and objectives that deliver impact on or improve the state of communities, societies, economies and environments. The Schwab Foundation for Social Entrepreneurship, founded by Claus Schwab, the father of the World Economic Forum (Davos, Switzerland), provides a good insight into global talent as social entrepreneurs (Schwab Foundation for Social Entrepreneurship, 2018):

> Social entrepreneurs drive social innovation and transformation in various fields including education, health, environment and enterprise development. They pursue poverty alleviation goals with entrepreneurial zeal, business methods and the courage to innovate and overcome traditional practices. A social entrepreneur, similar to a business entrepreneur, builds strong and sustainable organizations, which are either set up as not-for-profits or companies.

Emerging global social entrepreneurship models

Now that we have explored some definitions, we discuss a range of social entrepreneurship business models that are disrupting the traditional space. Africa has become a hotbed for social entrepreneurship in recent years. Not only do social entrepreneurs create new businesses and products, but they also help people get skilled, employed and create employment opportunities themselves.

Luvuyo Rani, co-founder and managing director of Silulo Technologies operates IT training centres in towns and rural areas of South Africa, providing re-skilling and up-skilling initiatives alongside job opportunities for unemployed youth (WEF, 2016).

Building on this, Manav Subodh, co-founder of 1M1B (1 Million for 1 Billion), provides another example of how social entrepreneurship initiatives, driven by Indian global talent who aspire to be job creators, provide employment opportunities for people, after spending 10 years in the corporate world working for Intel (Entrepreneur India, 2018). Behind 1M1B sits Subodh's aspiration to create a million entrepreneurs and leaders who will drive a billion people out of poverty by providing employment and entrepreneurship development opportunities to youth aged 18–25 in rural India.

What do these examples from practice tell us? In a world of constant change, you need to be able to learn, adapt and be prepared to take up employment and become both an employee and an employer at various stages of your professional life – something that we will discuss in the next section of this chapter.

Jack Ma, founder and executive chairman of Alibaba Group, said at the 2018 World Economic Forum that talent in their 20s should join the workforce, follow a good employer and develop new skills and abilities. Armed with new skills and knowledge, talent in their 30s can then become entrepreneurs and set up their own ventures and businesses (WEF, 2018).

HYBRID GLOBAL TALENT: JOB SEEKERS AND JOB CREATORS

The challenges of navigating through uncertainty in the job market

So far in this chapter, we have covered traditional routes to employment and discussed global talent as job seekers and job creators. The chapter has also provided an international insight into a range of individual and organisational perspectives on these forms of employment.

But what if we tell you that there is a third employment mode on the horizon, which is also poised to become an established one? Yes! There is a third one and it is called 'hybrid global talent' – which, in simple terms, is defined as global talent that is prepared to be both job seekers and job creators at various stages and over the course of their professional life.

Continuous uncertainty in the labour markets globally, the changing profile of the global workforce and the emergence of new technologies are disrupting the landscape of work as we know it. These disruptions on a global scale are likely to bring new forms of employment and require different kinds of flexible future-ready, globally minded and technology-savvy talent, as we will discuss in Chapters 3 and 4. Hence, we need to stay alert to new developments in the world around us and constantly adapt to them.

We now go on to discuss hybrid global talent in further detail. Is there even such a thing as hybrid global talent? Hybrid talent in the corporate world has often been narrowly defined as organisations having both a permanent and flexible workforce engaging in the gig economy. Jennifer Singleton, Senior Vice President of Marketing at Skillsoft, sees hybrid talent as companies that employ freelancers alongside full-time employees. Intel's Freelance Nation programme has adopted a hybrid talent approach where both permanent employees and freelancers co-exist and contribute to the organisation's vision and objectives (People Matters, 2017). Many technology-enabled and internet-based companies have embraced this approach to hybrid talent according to Upwork, a popular freelancing marketplace connecting talent with employment opportunities worldwide (Upwork, 2018).

We want you, however, to reflect on hybrid global talent in its broadest sense, whereby hybrid characteristics are available in a single individual, not the many – hence our focus is on individuals who are hybrid global talent as opposed to organisations employing global talent teams and which end up with hybrid workforces models.

The working definition of hybrid global talent that this text puts forward therefore is based on individuals as hybrid global talent – a definition that is influenced by the global dimension of the world of work, characterised by not only opportunity but also uncertainty. It positions hybrid global talent as those who are capable of transcending disciplines and industries:

> Hybrid global talent are individuals who have the ability to continuously evolve their global mindset, heartset and skillset attributes and adapt to established and new forms of employment and employment opportunities. They have an adaptive mindset that enables them to take up multiple job seeker and job creator roles throughout their professional life, both in their country of residence and internationally. Hybrid global talent take up employment and creates employment opportunities beyond their discipline, industry or field of specialisation.

Our definition suggests that a key property or attribute of hybrid global talent is the ability to learn and adapt with a view to seamlessly transition from one mode of employment to another – for example, from an employee in a large blue-chip organisation to an entrepreneur or a founder of a small technology-enabled company. In Chapter 1, we briefly discussed learnability as a core attribute that needs to be nurtured in global talent. Learnability is at the essence of creating hybrid global talent.

Learnability as a core attribute of hybrid global talent

Having a global mindset, heartset and skillset together with the ability to constantly learn new skills and knowledge is not, however, enough to prepare you for a hybrid career. The ability to stay relevant and gain meaningful employment and/or create employment opportunities for yourself and others is very much the focus of learnability. Mara Swan, Executive Vice President, Global Strategy and Talent at ManpowerGroup, has made the case for the importance of one's pace of learning and adaptation to a changing employment marketplace (Swan, 2016):

When new skills become in demand as fast as others become extinct, employability is less about what you already know and more about your capacity to learn. It requires a new mindset for both employers trying to develop a workforce with the right skillsets and for individuals seeking to advance their careers.

We seek to take the learnability concept and build on it, as we also believe that hybrid global talent means having an understanding of sometimes different or contrasting fields of specialisation to your own. So learnability should not only be narrowly defined as the ability to develop new skills and knowledge in order to stay relevant, employable and employed – a definition that has been coined by ManpowerGroup and discussed in Chapter 1 – but also as the ability to do so in subject disciplines and professional areas that are different from your own. This approach implies true flexibility and adaptability. Having the ability to cross disciplines and industries in learning new knowledge and skills is therefore crucial if you want to call yourself a hybrid global talent. Being a hybrid global talent is being comfortable with this cross-disciplinary and cross-industry environment and thriving on it.

In order to do so, you may wish to read books and resources in disciplines that are different from the discipline you are studying at college or university, or follow developments in industries that are different from the one you aspire to work in. You will be surprised at how quickly traditional industries evolve and often merge to create new ones. Examples include autonomous transportation, Fintech and blockchain, biomedical technologies, smart cities and urbanisation, and sustainable food production, to name a few. Then you need to be prepared to navigate through this fast-evolving employment landscape, and developing yourself as a hybrid global talent.

Interview: with global talent job seeker turned job creator Sandeep Deshpande, former CEO at Alibaba India

Q: Tell us more about your early career journey and early employment years, in particular when you joined the world of work as a job seeker.

So that was in a very different era, almost about three decades ago. There were very few opportunities back then and the economy in India was more closed – what we call 'license raj' – meaning in order to set up a business you needed a government license and very many categories of very many industries were reserved for public sector companies and the government. As a result, the Indian economy was highly protected and foreign investors had a limited role to play because the government wanted to build Indian companies and their capabilities to function in this market.

So there were very few opportunities to do business and join a private sector company back then. There were very few good companies in the private sector. So most people those days would dream of getting a government job or joining a public sector bank, for example, because that offered them job security. India's private sector which is thriving today was a very small portion, if you like, of the employment opportunities offered to talent.

I was lucky to get a sales job initially as part of a campus placement during my time at university. We were about 60 people in a batch of Master of Business Administration (MBAs) at the University of Pune and we had only a handful of companies that came on campus to recruit. Probably less than half of the MBA batch was placed in companies. University of Pune's business school was a tier two business school and it was therefore hard to attract companies to come on campus. So that's why only 40–50% of the batch secured a placement with those companies.

Back in the day we had to create a student committee for placements whose task was to reach out to HR people and companies and lobby for fresh graduates to be recruited and offered placements. I was also part of that committee. So by and large it was hard to get a job in those days.

Receiving a placement opportunity during my MBA is how I started my career journey as an employee or a job seeker talent – I became an employee in an air-conditioning company which was a collaboration with Hitachi Japan and that's how I started my career in sales. Again, as I said, there were very few private sector employment opportunities back then.

But I always wanted to work in product management and sales was not my primary area of passion and interest. So it took me almost two years to transition from sales to an assistant product manager role. But those days there were very few opportunities and if you were doing something which was not your primary passion, then it wasn't very easy to change that – especially if you were not from a top Higher Education (HE) institution like Indian Institutes of Technology (IITs) and Indian Institutes of Management (IIMs). So if a graduate was not from those top institutions it was very hard to get hold of employment opportunities in good companies.

And then things started to change around 1995 when new sectors of the economy emerged in India. Government policies around foreign investment also changed in the late 1990s and then things changed rapidly and more opportunities for employment and

(Continued)

(Continued)

business emerged. There were a lot of joint ventures of multinational companies that were created during that time.

Q: What do you think will be the role of the gig economy in redefining traditional employment going forward? We see companies such as Uber and Deliveroo that disrupt the traditional model of employment.

So Uber and Delivero and Amazon, also Ola Cabs, Flipcart and Swiggy in India, are thriving gig economy businesses. Companies like these are not necessarily creating entrepreneurs but there is a huge number of jobs that have been created in the past seven or eight years in the gig economy and the e-commerce sector in India. They play a big job creation role – my guestimate is that at least 500,000 to a million jobs would have been created in India thanks to Uber, Ola and other gig economy businesses.

So these companies have created a lot of jobs but it remains to be seen how this mode of employment will fare in the long term. For example, food delivery talent at Uber Eats are probably not building any other skills rather than driving and delivering and acquiring some customer-facing experience. The challenge however is – what happens to a person who is in their late 30s or 40s and they are not able to work say 10 hours at the same pace and under the same pressure. What happens to that gig economy talent if they don't build any skills other than the skills they acquire through Uber Eats? So you really don't develop any additional skills other than the ability to use the app, navigate the map and find locations to deliver products and services. So whilst the benefit of these gig economy businesses is that they have created some jobs, the challenges are related to the narrow skillset that talent involved in the gig economy have the opportunity to acquire.

I am sure that some of the gig economy talent that is a bit more entrepreneurial start from say driving a Uber car and then they figure out how to buy a car or two and hire another driver to utilise the capacity of a car whereby Uber services are provided 24 hours a day. So this way these people have created one more job, they learn how to excel in customer experience and increase their driver rating. This is one example of how even drivers can maximise their employment opportunities by becoming small entrepreneurs themselves.

Global talent individuals as job creators

Q: Tell us more about your recent career journey and employment years, in particular when you turned into a job creator and led on the establishment of Alibaba's base in India which resulted in the creation of many jobs in the country.

So Alibaba were very interested in the Indian market as India is the second largest manufacturing and supply-based economy after China with a large number of businesses exporting products, goods and services to the rest of the world.

The growth for Business 2 Business (B2B) at Alibaba was stagnating in China and the trade was declining and the company found it difficult to grow the business in China itself, that's when they started to look at India. The company had very ambitious goals in India and they wanted to have as many Indian suppliers on the online platform in India as possible – over 100,000 suppliers across different sectors and industries. So the aim for Alibaba India was to really become as big as the China-based business.

My contribution was to essentially help Alibaba build their team in India and hire a large sales team of over 100 people – this was effectively a distributed team across six or seven Indian cities which are large export hubs such as Mumbai, Delhi, Chennai and Bangalore.

We recruited a centralised customer service team that was assisting Indian suppliers on Alibaba with practical matters such as using the online platform to grow their businesses. We also built a lot of supplier education and training programmes.

So essentially the key goal during my journey with Alibaba was to build Alibaba as a premium world number one online platform for Indian businesses and suppliers across a range of sectors of the economy to grow their business internationally. We developed a very large network of free members or companies, mainly SMEs, who created their product listings on Alibaba.

In the two years I worked at Alibaba, we were able to grow the Alibaba India revenue to a substantial extent – we have grown the company's revenue from operations in India by three to four times. I have met suppliers and exporters from India listed on Alibaba's platform. Some of those companies have grown from less than 10 employees with having predominantly family members as employees to expanding its workforce to several hundred employees. One company I remember is a supplier which started from a small workshop in their house to having multiple factories in Mumbai because of the number of enquiries and business they generated through their membership at Alibaba India.

So one can imagine the amount of jobs being created through these fast-growing entrepreneurs and start-ups. So we had several thousand membership fee-paying gold members in addition to about 500,000 free suppliers on Alibaba's online platform. So there were thousands of additional jobs – or indirect jobs if you like – that were created through these over half a million suppliers on Alibaba India. So there is a significant contribution to job creation through my involvement with Alibaba India.

(Continued)

(Continued)

Q: What would be the role of entrepreneurs and start-ups in creating job opportunities going forward? Do you think that entrepreneurs and start-ups might overtake traditional employers such as large corporations as the main source of employment opportunities in the future?

Uber and Ola Cabs is probably one example where companies create a lot of jobs at the lower end of the career ladder. But there are obviously other impacts generated by such businesses. Ola Cabs, for example, has also created thousands of mid-level and senior-level jobs in specialisms such as engineering, marketing and sales, partnerships development and other areas.

So all these start-ups in India have a very thriving start-up community and every time a start-up is successful, those companies are looking for talent with higher-level skills and more specialist jobs are created. Internet-enabled and tech-related start-ups are the major player in this start-up community as they don't just create lower-skilled jobs – there are also significant numbers of jobs being created in engineering, analytics, distribution and product development, for example.

Particularly when it comes to engineering, I don't think India is producing engineers that are able to join the workforce and have the right skills to be recruited. So there is a skills gap – a gap between what the industry or start-ups are looking for and the quality of engineers graduating from Indian HE institutions to meet these requirements. So despite the fact that India produces a lot of engineers from colleges and universities, the number of those engineers who meet the requirements of businesses is generally low. So probably around 1% of engineers graduating from universities meet employer criteria as they are ill equipped.

I think that entrepreneurs and start-ups might overtake traditional employers such as large corporations as the main source of employment opportunities in the future. This will certainly happen but how soon this happens in India is a million-dollar question and I doubt anyone would be able to tell us this. But definitely if you add all Internet-enabled and tech-related companies together with manufacturing and a whole lot of other booming sectors with a lot of start-ups and entrepreneurs, they are probably creating more jobs and more employment opportunities than traditional employers.

Q: What would be your single most important advice for global talent individuals, who are job creators – these are entrepreneurs and start-ups – advice that will help them thrive in the highly competitive global marketplace for services and products?

Because there are very few people who are job-ready, who will meet the exact criteria of the skills businesses require? My advice for these entrepreneurs and start-up companies would be to create a good structure, internship programmes and offer comprehensive internships to both undergraduate and postgraduate students, and have some of their best managers oversee these graduate talent development programmes so that these companies actually help universities and also give those individuals opportunities to understand what different industries, entrepreneurs and start-ups require from them and this way they are more job-ready when they graduate. This is something that is missing completely and because there is a skills gap, it creates a lot of disruption at both ends – for talent and employers.

The problem is that smaller entrepreneurs and start-ups don't always have the time or resources to focus on placements and graduate talent development and larger companies don't do that very well either.

Q: What would be your advice for those individuals who may not have had the opportunity to go to college or university but still want to create their start-up or become entrepreneurs? You have seen and worked with a lot of entrepreneurs so what do you think are the key ingredients for success in entrepreneurship?

I have had the opportunity to meet a lot of people, great entrepreneurial talent who have done a reasonable job in setting up a small business, but who have not had the chance to go to university or college. I don't think that education or going to college or university is a prerequisite for one to become an entrepreneur or to create a start-up. If one has the burning desire to do something on their own such as building a business, then these people will find ways to do that.

The most important ingredient for success is persistence. Beneath that is your ability to think big and to even dream. Another feature of successful entrepreneurs is their determination as they don't give up. Those are the two key qualities I have seen among successful entrepreneurs I have had the opportunity to interact with in the past.

Chapter 2 discussed individuals as job seekers and job creators and the rise of the gig economy on a global scale and its implications for the global workforce. We also discussed the concept of 'hybrid global talent' – a label for individuals who are prepared to be both job seekers and job creators – and the importance of being able to navigate through uncertainty in the job market and a longer working life and develop 'learnability' as a skill amid these challenges and opportunities. You also had the opportunity to find out more about Sandeep Deshpande, consultant and former CEO of Alibaba India – a global talent job seeker who turned into a successful job creator.

REFLECTIVE EXERCISE

Global entrepreneurship quiz – what is your global entrepreneurship IQ?

Reflective exercise: Having read Chapter 2 and the interview with Sandeep Deshpande in the last part of this chapter, take the following global entrepreneurship quiz, which will help you understand the level of your global entrepreneurship IQ.

Question	Response
1: Global entrepreneurs are individuals who use their global understanding and networks to identify international and cross-cultural opportunities that can create value.	True/False
2: The key to successful global entrepreneurship is to develop an idea that has a market with a need for the product or service idea conceived on a global level or in a specific country.	True/False
3: In their ability to navigate through uncertainty in global labour markets, global entrepreneurs who are hybrid global talent need to consider several factors. Which of the following is not a factor for consideration? (A) Lifelong learning and developing learnability as a core skill (B) High level of specialisation in a given economic sector, market or field (C) Understanding global trends affecting job seekers and job creators (D) Ability to shift the business focus to adapt to a changing environment	A B C D
4: Global talent can take more than one route to employment at the same time – they can be both employed and employ others.	True/False
5: Global talent, who are job seekers, need to develop a high degree of self-flexibility that will enable them to update their skillsets.	True/False

6: Global talent who are job creators need to develop a high degree of business flexibility that will enable them to adapt to a changing business environment.	True/False
7: The gig economy provides high flexibility to adapt to individual work patterns but limited job security and regularity of income.	True/False
8: The gig economy as a concept has several characteristics. Which of the following statements is not a characteristic of the gig economy? (A) The gig economy often operates without any formal employment agreements (B) The proportion of Australians and Americans employed in the gig economy is set to rise to over 30% by 2025 (C) Technology enables the gig economy to connect talent with opportunities (D) The majority of gig economy talent comes from emerging and developing countries	A B C D
9: Global entrepreneurs should have a good level of understanding of global economic, environmental, political and social themes and development that are likely to influence their business.	True/False
10: Global entrepreneurs should also have a good level of understanding of key elements of the global social entrepreneurship agenda. Which of the following statements is not an element of the social entrepreneurship agenda? (A) Social entrepreneurship promotes sustainable business models and frameworks (B) Social entrepreneurship has its primary focus on maximising profits from emerging economies (C) Social entrepreneurship provides a platform for entrepreneurs to address global challenges (D) Social entrepreneurship delivers social change through harnessing the power of market forces and business principles	A B C D

Responses to questions

Q1:   True

Q2:   True

Q3:   Option B

Q4:   True

Q5:   True

Q6:   True

Q7:   True

Q8:   Option D

Q9:   True

Q10: Option B

Further reading and resources

Financial Times (2015). *What is the gig economy?* Video. Available at: www.ft.com/video/c70a617f-3ecc-37aa-af51-0d3d9e57c212 [Accessed 30 January 2018].

World Economic Forum (2015). 10 lessons from leaders: Social entrepreneurs tell all. Available at: www.weforum.org/agenda/2015/12/10-lessons-from-leaders-social-entrepreneurs-tell-all (Accessed 28 March 2018).

World Economic Forum (2018). Meet the leader with Jack Ma. Video. Available at: www.youtube.com/watch?v=4zzVjonyHcQ [Accessed 31 January 2018].

REFERENCES

BBC (2018). *India ride-sharing firm Ola to enter Australia*. Available at: www.bbc.co.uk/news/business-42868296 [Accessed 30 January 2018].

Brunsden, J. (2017). *Brussels in push on social protection for gig economy workers*. Available at: www.ft.com/content/bff01a7a-29cb-11e7-bc4b-5528796fe35c [Accessed 30 January 2018].

Cambridge Dictionary (2018). *Gig economy*. Available at: https://dictionary.cambridge.org/dictionary/english/gig-economy [Accessed 30 January 2018].

CIPD Asia (2017). *Asia's rising 'gig' economy is creating a challenge for HR*. Available at: www.cipd.asia/news/hr-news/asia-gig-economy-challenge-hr [Accessed 30 January 2018].

Dees, J. G. (2001). *The meaning of social entrepreneurship*. Available at: https://entrepreneurship.duke.edu/news-item/the-meaning-of-social-entrepreneurship [Accessed 31 January 2018].

Deloitte (2016). *The gig economy: Distraction or disruption?* Available at: www2.deloitte.com/insights/us/en/focus/human-capital-trends/2016/gig-economy-freelance-workforce.html#endnote-sup-3 [Accessed 30 January 2018].

Economic Times (2017). *Prepare regulation for the gig economy*. Available at: https://blogs.economictimes.indiatimes.com/et-editorials/prepare-regulation-for-the-gig-economy [Accessed 8 August 2018].

Employment Rights Act (1996). *Section 230*. Available at: www.legislation.gov.uk/ukpga/1996/18/section/230 [Accessed 30 January 2018].

Entrepreneur India (2018). *This social entrepreneur is creating employment in undeserved areas*. Available at: www.entrepreneur.com/article/307190 [Accessed 31 January 2018].

Ernst & Young (2016). *Does disruption drive job creation? EY Global Job Creation Survey 2016*. Available at: www.ey.com/Publication/vwLUAssets/ey-job-creation-survey-2016/$FILE/ey-job-creation-survey-2016.pdf [Accessed 31 January 2018].

Fallon, N. (2017). *The growth of the gig economy: A look at American freelancers*. Available at: www.businessnewsdaily.com/10359-gig-economy-trends.html [Accessed 30 January 2018].

Fast Company (2017). *How I became a CEO after starting as a flextime employee*. Available at: www.fastcompany.com/40408150/how-i-became-ceo-after-starting-as-a-flextime-employee [Accessed 29 January 2018].

Financial Times (2016). *UK to have 1m agency workers by 2020*. Available at: www.ft.com/content/ff371b92-ba32-11e6-8b45-b8b81dd5d080 [Accessed 30 January 2018].

Financial Times (2017). *Driven to despair: The hidden costs of the gig economy*. Available at: www.ft.com/content/749cb87e-6ca8-11e7-b9c7-15af748b60d0 [Accessed 30 January 2018].

Financial Times (2018). *Definition of entrepreneur*. Available at: http://lexicon.ft.com/Term?term=entrepreneur [Accessed 31 January 2018].

Forbes (2013). *Who are the real job creators?* Available at: www.forbes.com/sites/investor/2013/06/17/who-are-the-real-job-creators/#3ef9843a79e4 [Accessed 31 January 2018].

Forbes (2017). *Making the transition from employee to entrepreneur*. Available at: www.forbes.com/sites/mikekappel/2017/06/28/making-the-transition-from-employee-to-entrepreneur/#569448261fc8 [Accessed 29 January 2018].

Harvard Business Review (2011). *Valuing your most valuable assets*. Available at: https://hbr.org/2011/10/valuing-your-most-valuable [Accessed 30 January 2018].

Henrekson, M. and Johansson, D. (2010). Gazelles as job creators: A survey and interpretation of the evidence. *Small Business Economics*, 35(2), 227–44.

Hook, L. (2015). *Year in a word: Gig economy*. Available at: www.ft.com/content/b5a2b122-a41b-11e5-8218-6b8ff73aae15 (Accessed 30 January 2018).

House of Commons (2017). *Work and Pensions Committee: Self-employment and the gig economy*. Available at: https://publications.parliament.uk/pa/cm201617/cmselect/cmworpen/847/847.pdf [Accessed 30 January 2018].

International Labour Organisation (ILO) (2018a). *ILO thesaurus: Employee*. Available at: http://ilo.multites.net/default.asp [Accessed 29 January 2018].

International Labour Organisation (ILO) (2018b). *Current guidelines*. Available at: www.ilo.org/global/statistics-and-databases/statistics-overview-and-topics/status-in-employment/current-guidelines/lang—en/index.htm [Accessed 29 January 2018].

Jacobs, E. (2015). *A pivot back to corporate life*. Available at: www.ft.com/content/a1bb4992-8eab-11e5-8be4-3506bf20cc2b?ftcamp=published_links%2Frss%2Fmanagement_entrepreneurship%2Ffeed%2F%2Fproduct [Accessed 19 February 2018].

Kelly Services (2015). *Agents of change: Independent workers are reshaping the workforce*. Available at: www.kellyservices.com/global/siteassets/3-kelly-global-services/uploadedfiles/3-kelly_global_services/content/sectionless_pages/kocg1047720free agent20whitepaper20210x21020final2.pdf [Accessed 30 January 2018].

Moncada, R. (2017). *The coming of the 'gig economy': A threat to European workers?* Available at: https://europe-liberte-securite-justice.org/2017/11/22/the-coming-of-the-gig-economy-a-threat-to-european-workers [Accessed 30 January 2018].

People Matters (2017). *Companies need to stay nimble and responsive to stay relevant*. Available at: www.peoplematters.in/article/talent-management/how-to-drive-talent-agility-to-increase-productivity-and-efficiency-16233 [Accessed 31 January 2018].

Sandra, V. and Birgit, K. (2016). *Germany: Compromise struck on new temporary agency work legislation*. Available at: www.eurofound.europa.eu/observatories/eurwork/articles/working-conditions-industrial-relations-law-and-regulation/germany-compromise-struck-on-new-temporary-agency-work-legislation [Accessed 30 January 2018].

Schwab Fundation for Social Entrepreneurship (2018). *What is a social entrepreneur?* Available at: www.schwabfound.org/content/what-social-entrepreneur [Accessed 8 August 2018].

StartUps (2017). *Will Shu: How I went from investment banker to founder of $857m-backed tech start-up Deliveroo*. Available at: https://startups.co.uk/will-shu-how-i-went-from-investment-banker-to-founder-of-200m-backed-tech-start-up-deliveroo [Accessed 30 January 2018].

Swan, M. (2016). *This skill could save your job – and your company*. Available at: www. weforum.org/agenda/2016/08/this-little-known-skill-will-save-your-job-and-your-company [Accessed 31 January 2018].

Taylor, M. (2017). *Good work: The Taylor review of modern working practices*. Available at: www.gov.uk/government/uploads/system/uploads/attachment_data/file/627671/good-work-taylor-review-modern-working-practices-rg.pdf [Accessed 30 January 2018].

UK Government Portal (2018a). *Employment status: Employee*. Available at: www.gov.uk/employment-status/employee [Accessed 30 January 2018].

UK Government Portal (2018b). *Employment status: Your rights as an agency worker*. Available at: www.gov.uk/agency-workers-your-rights [Accessed 30 January 2018].

UK Government Portal (2018c). *Employment status: Director*. Available at: www.gov.uk/employment-status/director [Accessed 30 January 2018].

Upwork (2018). *How these 4 major companies are using hybrid teams*. Available at: www. upwork.com/hiring/enterprise/how-these-4-major-companies-are-using-hybrid-teams [Accessed 31 January 2018].

Virgin (2018). *About us*. Available at: www.virgin.com/virgingroup/content/about-us [Accessed 31 January 2018].

Virgin Start Up (2018). *Virgin StartUp infographic: Journey so far*. Available at: www.virgin startup.org/news/virgin-startup-infographic-journey-so-far [Accessed 31 January 2018].

World Economic Forum (WEF) (2016). *A quarter of South Africans are unemployed – but this social entrepreneur has a plan*. Available at: www.weforum.org/agenda/2016/03/interview-luvuyo-rani-of-silulo-technologies [Accessed 31 January 2018].

World Economic Forum (WEF) (2018). *Meet the leader with Jack Ma*. Available at: www. youtube.com/watch?v=4zzVjonyHcQ [Accessed 31 January 2018].

Wright, P. M., McMahan, G. C. and McWilliams, A. (2006). Human resources and sustained competitive advantage: A resource-based perspective. *International Journal of Human Resource Management*, 5(2), 301–26.

3

UNDERSTANDING THE CROSS-CULTURAL AND MULTI-GENERATIONAL WORKFORCE

Chapter contents

Global workforce dynamics

- Globalisation and its contribution to the rapid growth in the mobility of talent
- Greater workforce mobility contributes to a growth in the cross-cultural workforce
- Longevity contributes to a growth in the cross-generational workforce

Navigating a cross-cultural workforce

- Understanding the cross-cultural workforce
- Implications for global talent amid growth in the cross-cultural workforce
- Legal frameworks and organisational good practice in promoting values of equality and diversity
- The link between diversity and innovation

Navigating a multi-generational workforce

- The multi-generational workforce and implications for global talent

- Five generations in the workforce and the place of millennials
- Opportunities and challenges related to having five generations in the workforce
- Generation U on the horizon
- Generation One in the workforce

The importance of cross-cultural and cross-generational communication

- Developing your communication skills and effectively communicating across cultures and generations
- The complexity of the cross-cultural and cross-generational developments

Case study 3.1: Global business approach to the changing workforce composition

The World's Workforce in 2025 and 2050 Quiz

Learning objectives

After reading this chapter, you will be able to:

- understand key global workforce dynamics
- identify key characteristics of the cross-cultural workforce and its implications for talent
- understand developments in the multi-generational workforce and its impact on talent
- appreciate the importance of developing cross-cultural and cross-generational communication.

GLOBAL WORKFORCE DYNAMICS

Globalisation and its contribution to rapid growth in the mobility of talent

In the first chapter of this text, we provided a discussion on how globalisation, alongside other disruptive global trends, is reshaping the very definition and purpose of talent from individual, organisational and policy perspectives. However, global talent should also be aware of key workforce dynamics such as the cross-cultural and multi-generational workforce that reshape the world of work, as we know it today.

The rise of the cross-cultural workforce as the new normal and a growing multi-generational workforce are perhaps the two most notable global workforce dynamics. If the former is influenced by globalisation trends, the growth in the latter can be attributed to an increase in quality of life and longevity. We critically examine both dynamics before we proceed to discuss how you, as global talent, may develop the ability to navigate through the cross-cultural workplace and multi-generational workforce.

As discussed in Chapter 1, global talent with a global mindset needs to be aware of globalisation and its influence on the global workforce and workplace. The dynamism in which the world is becoming more interconnected and interdependent influences the world of work, particularly the mobility of talent internationally. Globalisation has undoubtedly accelerated the growth of this mobility.

Greater workforce mobility contributes to growth in the cross-cultural workforce

This greater workforce mobility across borders contributes to a highly diverse, cross-cultural workforce where global talent will be required to work and contribute to organisations, often working in teams of diverse talent that come from different parts of the world and bring in different world views and perspectives to the office.

A recent PricewaterhouseCoopers (PwC) report, *Recent Talent Trends Forcing Strategic Approaches* (2016), highlighted that global talent of the future would need to develop cross-cultural skills and an inclusive mindset in order to be successful in the workforce. The report concluded that 'global acumen and the ability to work effectively across cultures' are critical attributes that talent should be able to develop and demonstrate to employers (PwC, 2016).

Longevity contributes to growth in the cross-generational workforce

Alongside greater workforce mobility of talent internationally, another trend influencing the world of work is longevity whereby people born in the latter part of the 20th century live longer than those born in the first part of the 20th century. Longevity and increased life expectancy are the result of improvements in global health, working conditions and an improved quality of life of the working classes more generally. Longevity and higher life expectancy mean that people remain active in the workforce for longer.

We now reflect on some official statistics to see how longevity as a trend has impacted on the lives of people over time. The World Health Organisation (WHO), an international organisation operating in over 150 countries across the world, highlights that the average life expectancy of those born in 1955 was just 48 years, while in 1995 it was 65 years (WHO, 2018). This means that people in 1995 lived 17 years longer on average when compared to data from 40 years ago. Over 5 billion people in 120 countries today have a life expectancy of more than 60 years.

In an even shorter time period, overall life expectancy has risen from 65 years for men and 69 years for women in 2000–05 to 69 years for men and 73 years for women in 2010–15, despite large disparities across countries, which are still prevalent and which we cannot ignore. This longevity among the global population leads to profound changes in the profile of the global workforce, whereby the result is likely to be at least four generations of talent co-existing in the workplace, if not five, but we will discuss this later in the chapter.

Within a cross-cultural workforce context, talent that is global in nature would also need to adapt to working with people of different ages. Talent should be able to comfortably navigate through this generational diversity – a challenge that is seen as such by both organisations and individuals themselves. Sharon Aut, Global Inclusion and Diversity Lead at Slalom, a $1 billion global consultancy firm, highlights that one's ability to understand generational differences and embrace new ways of working contributes to a more open, flexible and culturally agile workforce and organisation (Slalom, 2017).

In the following two sections of this chapter, we will discuss in detail how you as global talent can understand and interpret the cross-cultural and multi-generational workforce and workplace. We will then provide insights from industry, policy and academia into the implications and impacts of these two global workforce dynamics and what they mean for you.

NAVIGATING A CROSS-CULTURAL WORKFORCE
Understanding the cross-cultural workforce

Cross-cultural workforce is a term that has only recently started to attract attention in the world of work, particularly as a result of globalisation factors such as the increased mobility of talent internationally. Despite its popularity, only a handful of organisations and individuals have defined the term and its understanding is thus still limited. Cross-cultural workforce, multi-cultural workforce and diverse workforce are terms that have been used interchangeably. It is in the latter – diverse workforce – that we find most evidence of theorising and definitions that bring together a multitude of cultures.

A large part of the academic body defines a multi-cultural and diverse workforce as one that comprises of people from different cultural and racial backgrounds, but we argue that this definition has a broader remit. A cross-cultural workforce or having diversity in the workforce, according to the *Business Dictionary* (2018), is a workforce that is characterised by 'similarities and differences among employees in terms of age, cultural background, physical abilities and disabilities, race, religion, sex, and sexual orientation'.

The working definition of a cross-cultural workforce that this text puts forward brings together the above key characteristics of the concept and positions global talent at the heart of it:

> Cross-cultural workforce is a term that reflects a talent pool of globally-minded individuals engaging with work on a team, corporate, city or even national level. This workforce brings together a multitude of cultural backgrounds, world views, identities and personal and professional perspectives for the benefit of delivering individual and organisational value, product, service or impact.

This would mean that global talent are firmly embedded in the cross-cultural workforce, naturally promote values such as inclusiveness and integrity, and have the ability to understand, embrace and make the most of a diverse workforce through proactive engagement.

Implications for global talent amid growth in the cross-cultural workforce

From these definitions, it becomes clear that global talent needs to navigate a workforce that is diverse in nature. In an influential *Harvard Business Review* piece – 'How to Successfully Work Across Countries, Languages, and Cultures' – Tsedal Neeley, an associate professor at the Harvard Business School and the founder of the consulting firm Global Matters, proposed five key actions to support the integration of global talent in the cross-cultural workforce and promote a culture of diversity and inclusiveness: embracing positive indifference; seeking commonality between cultures; identifying with the global organisation rather than your local office; seeking interactions with others, geographically distant partners, colleagues and clients; and, importantly, aspiring to a global career (*Harvard Business Review*, 2017).

Cross-cultural understanding, abilities and competencies should nevertheless be nurtured from early on, ideally ahead of the start of one's professional career. Exposure to diversity at college or university is important in nurturing skills and attributes that can help graduate global talent to embrace, succeed and thrive in cross-cultural teams and organisations. Uma Jayakumar, an associate professor at Michigan University, argues that it is essential for students to develop cross-cultural workforce competencies – that is, understanding diversity and having the ability to communicate effectively across cultures, which collectively contribute to the development of graduate talent who 'can lead and compete in a diverse and global marketplace' (Jayakumar, 2008).

In terms of one's place in a cross-cultural workforce, very often the focus is solely on cross-cultural competencies and attributes, such as the understanding of different languages. And yes, all of these skills and abilities are important but they are primarily referred to and attributed to one's skillset. Hence, we would urge you as global talent to unlock your global mindset and reflect on the importance of inculcating diversity into this mindset. This is about how one's mindset stretches its boundaries of ethics, stereotypes and differences.

The case of the Middle East and its inclusion (or not) of women in the workforce provides an insight into the importance of shifting these boundaries. The participation of Middle Eastern women in the world of work is yet to be recognised as an opportunity due to societal perceptions and ethical considerations of the role of women in the family. Saudi Arabia has taken steps to increase the number of women in its workforce from 22% to 30% by 2030, thus rethinking its workforce ethics code as the country has not historically been engaged in, nor supported, women joining the workforce.

So, what might be considered ethical in one cultural context is not necessarily considered as such in another context. Global talent capable of functioning in cross-cultural teams and understanding the value of diversity in the world of work need to critically reflect on and comprehend these cultural and geographic differences in the understanding and notion of diversity in the workplace, and contribute to the promotion of good practice and the raising of awareness.

As we discussed at the outset of this chapter, talent mobility is intensifying on a global scale, which is driven by a combination of factors, including increased globalisation, the opening up of economies, the rise of citizens of the world, one's desire to explore new countries, multinational companies tapping into country talent pools, and so on.

In its 'World of Work' report, the International Labour Organisation (ILO, 2014) estimates that there are 232 million global talent that are mobile globally – a figure which has increased by 57 million since 2000. Another study, conducted by the Organisation for Economic Co-operation and Development (OECD, 2015), estimated that there were over 115 million mobile talent in OECD countries alone – a figure that comes to 10% of the population of these countries. This mobility of talent internationally is, therefore, a major global workforce dynamic.

Talent mobility has been traditionally and narrowly associated with the mobility of highly skilled talent from one country to another, but this is now on course to change. Contemporary definitions of talent mobility run across all levels of organisations and a multitude of economic sectors. Sylvia Vorhauser-Smith, Senior Vice President of Global Research at PageUp, and an author, highlights that talent mobility is becoming more inclusive and that talent at all levels of the organisational hierarchy are now interested in overseas employment opportunities and assignments in the pursuit of accelerating their careers (Forbes, 2013).

Legal frameworks and organisational good practice in promoting values of equality and diversity

The sheer volume and scale of global talent mobility, coupled with recent developments and advancements in key talent mobility enablers – such as improved transportation and technologies – support the case for wider recognition of diversity in the workplace.

So, diversity in the workplace and increased cross-cultural work cannot be ignored and we would argue that, in fact, they should be embraced, due to the benefits a diverse talent workforce can bring to organisations and teams. The introduction of policy, good practice and regulatory frameworks is thus an important stepping stone to recognising and elevating diversity, inclusivity and the benefits of nurturing a cross-cultural workforce. These enablers of great diversity and cross-cultural workforce inclusion are starting to emerge on both an organisational and corporate level, alongside policy circuits and national-level policy.

One's ability to understand and navigate through the cross-cultural workforce also means that we should be aware that what might have been acceptable pre-2010 when the Equality Act was introduced, in 2010 (in a UK context) is no longer considered as such and different dimensions of equality and diversity have gained recognition.

POLICY INSIGHT

UK Equality Act 2010

The UK government's 2010 Equality Act was an important stepping stone in bringing in greater regulation to matters of diversity and equality in the workplace and in society at large. The Act legally protects people from discrimination in the workplace and in society. It sets out the different ways in which it is unlawful to treat someone in the UK. The Act replaced previous anti-discrimination laws with a single Act, making the law easier to understand and strengthening protection in some situations. The Act assumes the following characteristics as protected ones – age; disability; gender reassignment; marriage and civil partnership; pregnancy and maternity; race; religion or belief; sex; and sexual orientation. The Act also covers workforce and workplace matters of equality (Equality Act 2010).

Canada is another example where the country has developed and implemented an equality policy for its workforce. The Employment Equity Act 2018 aims to achieve equality in the workplace whereby 'no person shall be denied employment opportunities or benefits for reasons unrelated to ability and, in the fulfilment of that goal, to correct the conditions of disadvantage in employment experienced by women, Aboriginal peoples, persons with disabilities and members of visible minorities'. Canada's Act has also adopted a wider and more inclusive definition of how diversity and equality are protected in the workforce: 'employment equity means more than treating persons in the same way but also requires special measures and the accommodation of differences'. Canada's prime minister, Justin Trudeau, has also openly expressed his position on protecting diversity and inclusivity, both in the workforce of the country and in wider society.

Further examples of how diversity in the workplace is protected and embraced through legislation exist in countries such as Germany, France, Australia, Hong Kong and Singapore. Hence, as global talent, you need to have a well-rounded knowledge and awareness of the legal frameworks behind equality and diversity in the workplace. Developing an understanding of such frameworks and how they serve as recognition of the benefits of promoting a level playing field in the workforce, in terms of protected characteristics such as gender, race and (dis)ability, is also important.

Despite these current developments and recognition of the value of diversity in the workforce, there has been a backlash, perhaps on a national level, where we evidence countries' leaders going against the values of diversity and inclusiveness promoted by their own countries. Donald Trump, President of the USA, and Theresa May, Prime Minister of the UK, are two prime examples of this backlash. Donald Trump has been using social media to often express and promote his radical views on gender and race, while Theresa May has been caught up in using her PR machine to promote anti-immigration rhetoric.

One might argue that this anti-diversity rhetoric is not acceptable, particularly from world leaders who are often perceived as role models with millions of followers both on social media and in real life. Being a global talent with the ability to navigate the cross-cultural workforce then means having an understanding of different perspectives on ethics, equality and diversity that help you understand the complexities of the world we live in and the divergence in the views of different people.

Just as the cross-cultural workforce concept and matters of equality and diversity have gained the recognition of societies and governments across the world, there has been an emphasis on the interplay between diversity in the workplace and innovation, particularly in the corporate world where business organisations are the direct benefi-ciaries of global talent.

The link between diversity and innovation

There is a clear link between promoting diversity in the workplace and unlocking inno-vation in teams and organisations and you, as a global talent, should develop the ability to navigate through, make the most of and innovate by recognising the benefits of diver-sity in the office.

Recent research on workplace and workforce diversity outlines the many benefits that a diverse talent pool can bring to organisations and teams alike. In a seminal paper, 'The Multicultural Organization', Professor Simon Cox, of the University of Michigan, recog-nised the fact that modern organisations are becoming increasingly diverse in terms of gender, race, ethnicity and nationality. Cox (1991) went on to argue that this diversity in the workplace brings in certain benefits, including better decision making, higher creativ-ity and innovation, global exposure and a better distribution of economic opportunity.

Fast forward 22 years after the diversity–innovation argument made by Cox, and Sylvia Ann Hewlett, founder and CEO of the Center for Talent Innovation, and her team used a large-scale research project to provide 'compelling evidence that diversity unlocks inno-vation'. They uncovered six behaviours and, indeed, enablers that have the potential to unlock innovation: ensuring that everyone is heard; making it safe to propose novel ideas; giving team members decision-making authority; sharing credit for success; giving action-able feedback; and implementing feedback from the team (*Harvard Business Review*, 2013).

Following on from these two influential studies, there have been a number of other contributions from industry, research and academia that confirm the strong correlation between promoting diversity and innovation in the workplace. Now that you know the importance of embracing diversity in the workplace, we move on to the third section of this chapter where the importance of global talent's ability to navigate through a multi-generational workforce is discussed.

NAVIGATING A MULTI-GENERATIONAL WORKFORCE
The multi-generational workforce and implications for global talent

At the outset of this chapter, we touched on two key global workforce dynamics. Alongside a greater workforce mobility of talent internationally, another trend, which has also become a key driver of change in the world of work, is the increasing life expectancy of people around the world. Advancements in healthcare and lifestyle have led to improvements in longevity among the population on a global level. Longevity means that global talent, like you and other students in colleges and universities across the world, will be expected to have longer working lives than those of your parents.

In fact, a new, influential report by the World Economic Forum, *We'll Live to 100 – How Can We Afford It*, predicts that babies born in 2017 can expect to live to over 100 years old. In other words, these citizens of the world will live to see the year 2117 (WEF, 2017b). This global demographic trend is expected to have a profound impact on the workforce, which will become more multi-generational and diverse in terms of age and gender. That potentially means being a talent in a workforce where the age could range from 18 to 80.

There have been various definitions of the multi-generational workforce, which often simply refer to the presence of two or more generations in the workforce. Perhaps one of the earliest ones was put forward by Zemke et al. (1999) in their seminal work, *Generations at Work: Managing the Clash of Veterans, Boomers, Xers, and Nexters in your Workplace*. The authors discuss four different generational groups that form the multi-generational workforce – Veterans, Baby Boomers, Generation Xers and Generation Nexters (Zemke et al., 1999). This text brings to the fore contemporary definitions of the different generations in the workplace that have been adopted in practice in the past decade. We will discuss different generations in a bit more detail later in this chapter.

The working definition of a multi-generational workforce that this text puts forward highlights cross-generational complexities, includes some key characteristics of the concept and locates the place of global talent in it:

> Cross-generational workforce is a term that denotes a global workforce made up of five generations – traditionalists, baby boomers, Generation X, millennials and Generation Z – each of which has grown up in different economic, social and historical environments. This cross-generational workforce is an amalgam of diverse values, attitudes, priorities and behaviours in the workplace. Further, each of these five generations exhibits different abilities to learn, adapt, re-skill and up-skill.

The complexity of the cross-generational workforce reflected in this elaboration would mean that global talent should have a good understanding of this cross-generational landscape and the ability to navigate through the differences and commonalities across generations. They should make the most of this collective cross-generational wisdom and deliver impact organisationally and societally.

Five generations in the workforce and the place of millennials

Just three decades ago, we had only three generations in the workforce – traditionalists, baby boomers and Generation X. In 2018, we have five generations in the workforce, now including Generation Y or millennials, and Generation Z. This growth in the number of generations in work in such a short period of time, points to a trend of more and more people staying in the workforce till later in their years. Hence, you, as global talent, need to develop an awareness and understanding of the implications of global demographic trends, such as longevity, and develop an understanding of the different generations in the workforce in order to thrive within multi-generational teams and organisations.

We now go back to the five generations that form the global workforce in 2018 to discuss the key behavioural characteristics of these very different generations in more detail.

Traditionalists or *maturists* were born prior to 1945 and have experienced the Second World War, the Korean War and the Great Depression in the USA. Respect, security, moderate loyalty and obedience are among the key values exhibited by this generation in the workplace. Traditionalists have thrived in a work environment where hierarchical command and control were the norm and where the notion of 'one job, one employer' has largely defined their professional lives. When it comes to technology in the workplace, we can say that this generation is largely disengaged.

Baby boomers, born between 1945 and 1960, have lived through the Cold War and experienced the sexual revolution and civil rights movement. Core workplace values that this generation has been characterised by include power, achievement, challenge and ambition. Just like with traditionalists, baby boomers embraced job security. This generation is often seen as the early adopters of IT technology in the workplace, though the scale of penetration of technology has been uneven.

Generation X, who were born between 1961 and 1980, have been through the era of Thatcherism, the fall of the Berlin Wall and the moon landing. This generation is characterised by values in the workplace that relate to leadership, freedom, truth and independence. For Generation X, work–life balance is seen as a key priority. They are, however, often labelled as digital immigrants due to their limited exposure to technology in the workplace, which has largely been limited to email.

Generation Y or *millennials*, born between 1981 and 1995, have experienced global crises such as the 9/11 terrorist attacks and the global economic downturn. Millennial values in the workplace include safety, loyalty and flexibility. They are the first generation to embrace the gig economy, discussed in Chapter 2, which poses certain challenges for this generation to adapt to frequent career moves. Millennials are digital natives and entrepreneurs who have embraced and mastered the text message and social and professional media as a means of communication and getting work done.

Generation Z or *Gen 2020* were born after 1997 and have only recently joined the workforce. This generation has experienced not only the Arab Spring and Wikileaks but also the rapid penetration of technology and smartphones in every aspect of our personal and professional lives. Although this generation embraces the benefits of freedom and flexibility in the workplace, they also value security and stability. As career multitaskers, Generation Z are said to be mastering the adaptation that will help them move seamlessly between careers, projects and assignments.

CROSS-GENERATIONAL INSIGHT

Millennials in the spotlight

Millennials are projected to make up 35% of the global workforce by 2020 while the baby boomers, in contrast, will only occupy a 6% share. This shift in the make-up of the workforce makes it imperative to understand the millennial mindset.

(Continued)

(Continued)

A study by ManpowerGroup into 19,000 working millennials and 1,500 hiring managers, *Millennials Careers: 2020 Vision*, contends that this generation is both shaping and being shaped by the world of work, while, equally notably, redefining the employer–employee relationship (ManpowerGroup, 2016). The study highlights some of the challenges that millennials are faced with in the workforce:

As the offspring of parents whose jobs became increasingly less secure in the 70s, 80s and 90s, they entered the labour market during a global recession with record youth unemployment, faster-changing business cycles and increasing demand for new skills for which they are often told they lack the necessary education.

ManpowerGroup also found that most millennials expect to work longer than the generations before them and over half expect to work past age 65, while 20% expect to work over the age of 70 and this figure is likely to grow further. But millennials are also more likely than previous generations to have a strong view in favour of the need for continuous skills development to remain employable.

With the rise of the gig economy, employment insecurity and multiple careers, millennials are redefining job security as career security. While their loyalty to a specific organisation or employer is much lower than that of previous generations, their priority is to remain employable and employed, even if this means frequent shifts in career and juggling between two or more jobs or assignments at the same time.

Millennials and other generations that co-exist in the workplace are all very different. It is, therefore, key for global talent who can effectively navigate through the cross-generational workforce to be able to understand the key characteristics and values that define traditionalists, baby boomers, Generation X, millennials and Generation Z.

Building on this, Alistair Cox, CEO of the global recruiting firm Hays, highlighted that global workforce will become more and more multi-generational going forward. Hence, it is not unusual in 2018 to see a mix of baby boomers, Generation X, Generation Y and Generation Z all working together under one roof in organisations. Alistair Cox also emphasised the importance of global talent to understand different generations as 'each generation entering the workforce sees different challenges, has different aspirations and looks for different values and experiences from their working lives' (Hays, 2018).

Opportunities and challenges related to having five generations in the workforce

Having at least four generations in the workforce brings about a range of opportunities and challenges for talent, employers, teams and their organisations. Lynda Gratton, Professor of Management Practice at London Business School, highlights the opportunities that lie ahead:

> There is no doubt that we are facing an unprecedented opportunity. Society will have more people over the age of 70 and all the accumulated wisdom they bring. When four or even five generations are alive together, that creates a wonderful opportunity for inter-generational collaboration and cohesion. (WEF, 2017a)

She notes that society, government and employers should encourage the over-60s to engage in the workforce, and concludes that 'in a world of centurions, working into your 80s will be the norm' (WEF, 2017a). Lynda Gratton's perspective is mainly concerned with or related to society, but what would this mean in the world of work? For global talent to navigate through a four- or five-generational workforce, where age may well range between 18 and 80, this brings opportunities but also a number of challenges and considerations that one needs to take on board.

The Chartered Institute for Personnel Development (CIPD, 2014) contends that the opportunity for knowledge-sharing and pooling together different perspectives to be among the greatest benefits of an age-diverse workforce and workplace. The CIPD's *Managing an Age-diverse Workforce* study, however, concluded that the lack of shared interests and values is a challenge that presently hinders progress in integrating different generations in the workplace. Equally, for Stina Näslund, Human Resources Manager at the financial and professional service firm Equatex, the multi-generational workforce brings about many benefits. According to Näslund, 'different generations bring diversity, new ideas, varying levels of experience and suggestions for improvements to the workplace' (Equatex, 2017).

Having multiple, perhaps as many as five, generations in the workforce would mean a pool of talent with contrasting behaviours, personal and professional values, patterns of work and different abilities to learn, re-skill and up-skill in the workplace (Figure 3.1). This will have some important implications for both global talent employers and employees. Here we outline some of the key challenges that we believe the increasingly multi-generational workforce might pose to global talent.

Characteristics	Maturists (pre-1945)	Baby Boomers (1945–1960)	Generation X (1961–1980)	Generation Y (1981–1995)	Generation Z (Born after 1995)
Formative experiences	Second World War, Rationing, Fixed-gender roles, Rock 'n' Roll, Nuclear families, Defined gender roles — particularly for women	Cold War, Post-War boom, "Swinging Sixties", Apollo Moon landings, Youth culture, Woodstock, Family-orientated, Rise of the teenager	End of Cold War, Fall of Berlin Wall, Reagan / Gorbachev, Thatcherism, Live Aid, Introduction of first PC, Early mobile technology, Latch-key kids; rising levels of divorce	9/11 terrorist attacks, PlayStation, Social media, Invasion of Iraq, Reality TV, Google Earth, Glastonbury	Economic downturn, Global warming, Global focus, Mobile devices, Energy crisis, Arab Spring, Produce own media, Cloud computing, Wiki-leaks
Percentage in U.K. workforce*	3%	33%	35%	29%	Currently employed in either part-time jobs or new apprenticeships
Aspiration	Home ownership	Job security	Work-life balance	Freedom and flexibility	Security and stability
Attitude toward technology	Largely disengaged	Early information technology (IT) adaptors	Digital Immigrants	Digital Natives	"Technoholics" – entirely dependent on IT; limited grasp of alternatives
Attitude toward career	Jobs are for life	Organisational — careers are defined by employers	Early "portfolio" careers — loyal to profession, not necessarily to employer	Digital entrepreneurs — work "with" organisations not "for"	Career multitaskers — will move seamlessly between organisations and 'pop-up' businesses
Signature product	Automobile	Television	Personal Computer	Tablet/Smart Phone	Google glass, graphene, nano-computing, 3-D printing, driverless cars
Communication media	Formal letter	Telephone	E-mail and text message	Text or social media	Hand-held (or integrated into clothing) communication devices
Communication preference	Face-to-face	Face-to-face ideally, but telephone or e-mail if required	Text messaging or e-mail	Online and mobile (text messaging)	Facetime
Preference when making financial decisions	Face-to-face meetings	Face-to-face ideally, but increasingly will go online	Online — would prefer face-to-face if time permitting	Face-to-face	Solutions will be digitally crowd-sourced

Figure 3.1 Five generations infographic

(Source: Barclays, 2013)

The skilling, re-skilling and pace of learning of different generations in the workforce will become increasingly important going forward. Learnability is a global talent attribute that would need to be inculcated in every member of the workforce, regardless of whether they are 18 or 80, which may prove challenging as this would require additional resources and investment as well as the active involvement of traditionalists and baby boomers. You, as a global talent, should recognise this challenge and actively engage in initiatives that enhance your personal development and that of your colleagues, regardless of their age or organisational standing.

The diversity of workplace values and aspirations among talent representing different generations in the workforce introduces certain challenges for talent alignment in the organisation. Because the five generations have grown up in differing economic, social and historical environments, they are prone to contrasting pursuits and values in the workplace. You, as a member of Generation Z, may not always be able to find common ground with baby boomers, for example. As the five generations see the workplace from a different perspective, you, as a global talent, should be able to understand and be accommodative of different perspectives.

Different generations in the workforce have different degrees of autonomy and attitude towards hierarchy. We are likely to see a more hierarchical misbalance as millennials are gradually progressing into their career pathways. We already see millennials being managed or led by baby boomers, which often leads to communication and collaboration challenges between these two generations. Earlier in this chapter, we discussed the notion that millennials are more team- and collaboration-centric which is a work-related behaviour partly influenced by the penetration of technology in the workplace and the fact that this generation, as digital natives, are technology-savvy enough to embrace this opportunity.

This leads us to the challenge related to understanding and making use of technology in the workplace. Amid the exponential growth in technology adoption in the world of work, acquiring a digital native badge is now a necessity. This may pose challenges for the integration of baby boomers and Generation X into a more technological and digitally enabled workforce and workplace. Narrowing this cross-generational gap in technology adoption would mean the use of targeted interventions in skilling and re-skilling those generations.

If you aspire to become an HR specialist or head of a GT or HR department, then you would also need to consider how different generations in the workforce may influence key employment outcomes, including talent recruitment, engagement and retention – important concepts that we will discuss in the second part of this text. GT leaders and managers will be tasked with creating a more flexible work culture and with working towards building a sense of community that values the strengths of each generation in the workforce and enables inter-generational learning.

Generation U on the horizon

Amid these five dominant generations, there is a new generation on the horizon. Let us now give you a glimpse into the future, put our media hats on and throw at you a new generation – Generation U! Also referred to as 'Generation Unlimited', Generation U reflects technologically and digitally empowered children who live in a digital, content-rich and gamified world. They have access to all the content and information they need at their fingertips and use it to elevate their voice and message and to communicate with a wider audience.

This digitally empowered generation builds on the first digital natives, the millennials and their successors, Generation Z, to amplify the importance of media, technology, content and how they are being used and leveraged by the youngest among us; hence, why talent with a global skillset is expected to demonstrate attributes such as new media literacy and digital identity – something we covered in Chapter 1 of this text.

Dave Coplin, the Chief Envisioning Officer for Microsoft UK and an established thought leader in the UK, argues that Generation U is a generation of young people who are unlimited in their potential and who live in an environment that is changing faster than we anticipated (BBC, 2017).

This generation, according to Dave Coplin, is supported and surrounded by technology that knows no boundaries. In this fast-paced and disruptive environment, Generation U has the opportunity to develop the skills and attributes to solve tomorrow's global problems and challenges.

But what would Generation U or Generation Unlimited look like in the future? Let us throw at you the challenge of defining this emerging generation further. Watch Dave's video in the further reading and resources section of this chapter and discuss your vision and ideas with your peers in the classroom.

What we can certainly learn from Generation U and Dave Coplin is the importance of communication, the opportunities and challenges connected with it, and how we are now empowered through a technology that enables us to communicate across cultures and generations and get our message across. Therefore, communication is important and we would like to devote the next section of this chapter to communication seen through a cross-cultural and cross-generational lens.

Generation One in the workforce

Alongside Generation U, whose behaviour and characteristics have been influenced by technological innovations, there is another generation that has been subject to much discussion and has thus received a lot of attention – Generation One. The growth of this generation has been fuelled by the unprecedented growth in movement of people and talent mobility. Generation One refers to individuals who are first-generation immigrants in countries that are different from their country of birth.

One recent event and development that has put Generation One in the spotlight is the Syrian refugee crisis and Germany, whereby over 1 million Syrian refugees have been welcomed to the country in 2017 alone. Most of this lost generation fleeing the Syrian war are at an active working age and the majority of them are expected to join the German workforce. In fact, nearly one in five German residents is now a first- or second-generation immigrant.

Germany is a timely large-scale example of how the mobility of people caused by wars and geo-political instability puts the importance of recognising and including Generation One on the workforce agenda. The German government has taken steps to integrate this talent into the workforce, whereby over 20% of them are now engaged in the workforce. Yet more work needs to be done on workforce integration, including skilling and re-skilling, particularly as the country experiences skills gaps across vital sectors of its booming economy and Generation One are increasingly seen as an important solution to this challenge.

In the years to come, we are likely to see more Generation One talent in countries that experience negative demographic growth such as Japan, the UK and Germany alongside other countries needing a workforce to fill talent and skills gaps in some key sectors of their economies. This can be achieved as long as these countries provide an enabling environment to attract talent and provide opportunities for it to flourish.

Amid the rapid growth of talent mobility and that of Generation One, it is important for global talent to understand this generation, particularly from a cross-cultural perspective, to embrace the diversity that this generation brings to the workforce and optimise its value to the workplace and society at large.

THE IMPORTANCE OF CROSS-CULTURAL AND CROSS-GENERATIONAL COMMUNICATION

Developing your communication skills and effectively communicating across cultures and generations

The ability to appreciate and navigate through different cultures, across borders and between generations is essential in the modern workplace. This requires empathetic cross-cultural communication as key armourey in the global talent skillset toolkit. Take a moment to reflect on Chapter 1 where we discussed attributes, such as cross-cultural and cross-generational communication and understanding (Table 1.1), which are essential for global talent with a global skillset. So far, this chapter has demonstrated that the notion of a cross-cultural and cross-generational workforce is very powerful, yet equally very complex. A global talent's ability to understand, engage with and effectively communicate across cultures and generations in the workplace will be of key importance going forward.

The complexity of cross-cultural and cross-generational developments

The cross-cultural and cross-generational workplace is complex to say the least, and this complexity is exacerbated but its dynamic evolution. Enhanced mobility will only intensify this complexity which will require greater flexibility and agility in its navigation from global talent.

Your ability as a global talent to leverage technology and conversational tools and communicate effectively across cultures and generations is a necessity, not a choice, particularly if you want to succeed and thrive in this global workplace.

However, even big and well-established companies like Google fail to communicate across cultures and embrace diversity, equality and new expectations in the workplace. Here's just one example for you. Despite its strong commitment to diversity and inclusion, the profile of Google's workforce at the time of writing this text is 69% male and only 2% African American. Equally, women hold only 20% of technical jobs at the largest and most popular search engine in the world (Wong, 2017). The company was also recently involved in an anti-diversity polemic when the negative message of one of its employees leaked through a communication channel.

We think that the dynamics in communication we are going to experience have not yet been imagined. It is sometimes assumed that getting a LinkedIn profile or a Twitter account is enough for global talent to be able to demonstrate that they are good global communicators. What we are currently teaching in our communication models at universities has not begun to see the impact of interactions when a multi-generational workforce operates in a cross-cultural environment beyond the old barriers of language and space.

Knowing what we can do to succeed as global talent is important, but what is even more important is one's ability to anticipate and imagine what might actually become essential going forward because there is the possibility that this would eventually become law – just as the Equality Act in the UK did in 2010, which served as the beginning of a conversation on equality, diversity and inclusion, rather than a mere compliance requirement.

So, it's not just about navigating cultures and generations at work and being tolerant of them – those are prerequisites anyway – but also being open to new future interpretations. You, as a global talent, should be able to develop your intellectual curiosity in a way that will enable you to be more open to, inclusive and accommodative of different cultural and generational perspectives.

CASE STUDY 3.1

Global business approach to the changing workforce composition

How Facebook is making its workforce more diverse

Establishing effective strategies in order to manage diversity and the cross-cultural workforce enables businesses to respond to the changing workforce composition on a global level and scale up the competitiveness of their organisations.

But beyond management, leveraging diversity in the workplace has many other benefits. As was discussed in Chapter 3, a strong correlation exists between diversity and innovation. A more diverse workforce has the potential to bring innovation, according to a study commissioned by the New York-based Center for Talent Innovation.

Companies leveraging diversity and embracing their cross-cultural workforce are 45% more likely to report a growth in market share over the previous year, and 70% are more likely to report that their organisation captured a new market.

One of the largest technology-enabled companies in the world, Facebook, with a revenue of over $8 billion and a community of 2 billion users across its social media platforms, is actively seeking ways to make its workforce more diverse. Facebook recognises the benefits that diverse mindsets, perspectives and socio-cultural backgrounds can bring to the organisation.

(Continued)

(Continued)

Embedding an innovation-driven strategy for managing and leveraging diversity enables Facebook to gather ethnically, culturally, socially and sexually diverse perspectives and ideas from its workforce, in order to identify and develop products that better serve and respond to the needs of its global community of over 2 billion people.

Facebook's strategy for managing and leveraging diversity

Facebook has a total workforce of over 10,000 people. In terms of ethnicity, a total of 49% of its workforce is White and 40% Asian, followed by Hispanic (5%) and Black (3%). On a senior leadership level, employees of Asian, Hispanic and African backgrounds hold over a quarter or a total of 27% of Facebook's top positions.

The 2017 trends in Facebook's hiring rates demonstrate the company's ambition to capitalise on a diverse workforce. Facebook's strategy for recruiting and programming has contributed to an increase in representation for both Hispanic (from 4% to 5%) and Black people year on year (from 2% to 3%). With a global community of over 2 billion people, Facebook supports the case for a more diverse and inclusive company and recognises that diversity helps it build better products, make better decisions and better serve its community. The appointment of Facebook's first global director of diversity has contributed to the implementation of organisational policy and good practice aimed at workforce and workplace diversity.

Maxine Williams, Facebook's Global Director of Diversity, leads on the diversity agenda and cross-cultural integration of teams and individuals at Facebook. In her 2014 Facebook Newsroom update, 'Building a More Diverse Facebook', she highlighted the multifaceted contribution that talent with diverse cultural perspectives bring to the company (Williams, 2014):

At Facebook, diversity is essential to achieving our mission. We build products to connect the world, and this means we need a team that understands and reflects many different communities, backgrounds and cultures. Research also shows that diverse teams are better at solving complex problems and enjoy more dynamic workplaces. So at Facebook we're serious about building a workplace that reflects a broad range of experience, thought, geography, age, background, gender, sexual orientation, language, culture and many other characteristics.

The organisation is dedicated to valuing the impact that every individual is able to make. Facebook aims to create an environment where people can be their authentic selves and share their own diverse backgrounds, experiences, perspectives and ideas.

In her 2017 Facebook Newsroom update, 'Building a More Diverse, Inclusive Workforce', Maxine Williams stated that Facebook is already seeing the tangible impact of a more diverse Facebook – and highlighted the organisation's intentions to continue to find, grow and keep the best global talent regardless of their ethnic background. This statement of intent is evidenced through the range of programmes developed by Facebook to embrace the benefits of diversity and a cross-cultural workforce, and promote a culture of inclusivity, openness and understanding across employees of the organisation.

An insight into Facebook's diversity training programmes

Facebook has a strong focus on diversity and a recognition of the benefits that a cross-cultural workforce brings to the organisation. Facebook promotes this not only through its diversity vision and mission, but also through its training and immersion programmes and pilots.

Facebook tracks the results of a series of pilot training and immersion programmes, revises accordingly and then either expands successful programmes or kills unsuccessful ones. Commissioning pilot programmes is at the core of its strategy, which helps the company refine and improve the overall efficacy of interventions aimed at promoting diversity in the workplace.

Facebook's diversity training programmes aim to integrate the cross-cultural workforce for the benefit of the organisation and individuals themselves, and the following offers a glimpse into some of the approaches that Facebook uses.

Managing Unconscious Bias is one of Facebook's most successful programmes piloted back in 2015, which promotes the development of inclusive culture in the organisation – one which is supportive of diversity (Williams, 2015). Through this programme, Facebook encourages its own employees to challenge and correct bias as soon as they see it – both in others and in themselves. It is designed to surface biases that people might not even realise they have, and provides Facebook's workforce with the tools to identify and interrupt biased behaviour as it occurs. After identifying key biases and developing a personal understanding of their possible biases, Facebook's employees work together through real-world examples to address them. At the time of writing this case, the entire Facebook leadership team has taken the programme and the company is rolling it out to its teams across the world, whereby 50% of its entire workforce has taken it.

In 2017, Facebook introduced two other internal programmes aimed at capitalising on diversity within its workforce – Managing Inclusion, which trains managers to understand the issues that affect marginalised communities; and Be the Ally, which gives everyone the common language, tools and space to practise supporting others in the organisation (Williams, 2017).

(Continued)

(Continued)

Further case study resources

Facebook (2017). Update. Available at: https://fbnewsroomus.files.wordpress.com/2017/08/fb_diversity_2017_final.pdf [Accessed 4 April 2018].

Williams, M. (2014). Diversity Press Release 2014. Available at: https://newsroom.fb.com/news/2014/06/building-a-more-diverse-facebook [Accessed 4 April 2018].

Williams, M. (2015). Diversity Press Release 2015. Available at: https://newsroom.fb.com/news/2015/06/driving-diversity-at-facebook [Accessed 4 April 2018].

Williams, M. (2016). Diversity Press Release 2016. Available at: https://newsroom.fb.com/news/2016/07/facebook-diversity-update-positive-hiring-trends-show-progress [Accessed 4 April 2018].

Williams, M. (2017). Diversity Press Release 2017. Available at: https://newsroom.fb.com/news/2017/08/facebook-diversity-update-building-a-more-diverse-inclusive-workforce [Accessed 4 April 2018].

REFLECTIVE EXERCISE

The world's workforce in 2025 and 2050 quiz

The global workforce in 2025 and 2050 will be very different from that in 2018, due to emergent global trends predicted to reshape the profile and composition of manpower. Trends such as global talent mobility, increased focus on diversity and cross-cultural teams, coupled with four generations of workers, will contribute to this global workforce and workplace transformation. Chapter 3 demonstrated that greater workforce mobility contributes to the development of a cross-cultural workforce. The multi-generational workforce is influenced by a higher workforce life expectancy. The chapter discussed the forthcoming dominance of the millennial workforce and provided insight into a global business approach to the changing workforce composition.

> **Reflective exercise:** Having read this chapter and the Economist Intelligence Unit's 'What's Next? Future Global Trends Affecting Your Organisation' White Paper, take the following quiz, which will help you test your knowledge of the global trends reshaping the global workforce of the future (the EIU White paper can be accessed here: http://futurehrtrends.eiu.com/report-2015/cultural-differences-inevitability-in-a-global-economy).

Question	Response
1: In its Annual Millennial Survey, the global accountancy firm Deloitte predicted that the millennial generation would make up 75% of the global workforce by 2025.	True/False
2: The EIU's *What's Next?* White Paper provided five driving forces behind a globalised workforce. Which of the following driving forces does not belong to the five driving forces behind a globalised workforce provided by the White Paper? (A) Expansion of transnational companies (B) Free movement of goods and services (C) Rapid ageing of the workforce (D) Technological advancement (E) Labour migration	A B C D E
3: The retired workforce is growing in size on a global level where, for example, in Japan the number of elderly people as a share of those of working age is predicted to rise to 72% by 2050.	True/False
4: The EIU's *What's Next?* White Paper provided a number of key challenges for human resource management and global business strategy going forward. The White Paper provided five driving forces behind a globalised workforce. Which of the following challenges does not belong to the key challenges for human resource management and global business strategy provided by the White Paper? (A) Adapting hiring and retention strategies to prepare for tomorrow's changing workforce (B) Preparing a new set of globally prepared leaders (C) Developing a strategy to integrate older workers into the workforce (D) Balancing corporate and societal cultures while promoting diversity (E) Preparing for the complexities of hiring, managing and integrating a global workforce	A B C D E
5: The US Department of Labour predicts that, by 2050, immigration and inward talent mobility will have increased the US population by 80 million people.	True/False
6: Diverse cultural backgrounds within the workforce can bring to a company some common benefits, such as in-depth local knowledge of different markets and the increased probability of successful operations in a range of locations, as well as an appreciation of different ways of doing business.	True/False

(Continued)

(Continued)

7:	The EIU's *What's Next?* White Paper predicts that, by 2030, Europe's working-age population at 15–64 years old is likely to increase by only 9.1%.	True/False
8:	The Center for Talent Innovation's Two-Dimensional (2D) Diversity Model named Inherent Diversity as one of the dimensions of the model. Which of the following elements does not belong to those featured in the Inherent Diversity dimension of the 2D Diversity Model? (A) Socio-economic background (B) Gender (C) Race (D) Cultural fluency (E) Religious background	A B C D E
9:	The Center for Talent Innovation's Two-Dimensional (2D) Diversity Model named Acquired Diversity as one of the dimensions of the model. Which of the following elements does not belong to those featured in the Acquired Diversity dimension of the 2D Diversity Model? (A) Global mindset (B) Nationality (C) Cultural fluency (D) Cross-functional knowledge (E) Language skills	A B C D E
10:	An inherently diverse workforce can serve as a source of innovation as diverse individuals are better attuned to the unmet needs of consumers or clients like themselves. Their insight is critical to identifying and addressing new market opportunities for organisations.	True/False

Answers

Q1:   True

Q2:   Option C – rapid ageing of the workforce is not among the five driving forces behind a globalised workforce provided by the White Paper.

Q3:   True

Q4:   Option C – developing a strategy to integrate older workers into the workforce does not belong to the key challenges for human resource management and global business strategy provided by the White Paper.

Q5:   True

Q6:   True

Q7:   False – by 2030, Europe's working-age population at 15–64 years old is projected to actually decrease by 9.1%.

Q8:   Option D – cultural fluency is not an element of the Acquired Diversity dimension of the 2D Diversity Model developed by the Center for Talent Innovation.

Q9:   Option B – nationality is not an element of the Inherent Diversity dimension of the 2D Diversity Model developed by the Center for Talent Innovation.

Q10:   True

Further reading and resources

BBC (2017). *The Envisioners founder Dave Coplin: Generation U.* Video. Available at: www.bbc.co.uk/academy/en/articles/art20171218165328266 [Accessed 2 February 2018].

Financial Times Lexicon (2018). *Definition of globalisation.* Available at: http://lexicon.ft.com/term?term=globalisation [Accessed 1 February 2018].

World Economic Forum (WEF) (2017). *Everything you thought you knew about millennials is wrong.* Available at: www.weforum.org/agenda/2017/01/everything-you-thought-you-knew-about-millennials-is-wrong [Accessed 2 February 2018].

REFERENCES

Barclays (2013). *Talking about my generation: Exploring the benefits engagement challenge.* Available at: https://wealth.barclays.com/global-stock-and-rewards/en_gb/home/research-centre/talking-about-my-generation.html (Accessed 28 March 2018).

BBC (2017). *The Envisioners founder Dave Coplin: Generation U.* Available at: www.bbc.co.uk/academy/en/articles/art20171218165328266 [Accessed 2 February 2018].

Business Dictionary (2018). *Workforce diversity.* Available at: www.businessdictionary.com/definition/workforce-diversity.html [Accessed 1 February 2018].

Chartered Institute for Personnel Development (CIPD) (2014). *Managing an age-diverse workforce: Employer and employee views.* London: CIPD.

Chartered Institute for Personnel Development (CIPD) (2016). *Moving the employee well-being agenda forward.* London: CIPD.

Cox Jr, T. (1991). The multicultural organization. *The Executive,* 34–47.

Employment Equity Act (2018). *Employment Equity Act* (last amended on 12 December 2017). Available at: http://laws-lois.justice.gc.ca/PDF/E-5.401.pdf [Accessed 1 February 2018].

Equality Act (2010). *Equality Act 2010: Guidance.* Available at: www.gov.uk/guidance/equality-act-2010-guidance#equalities-act-2010-legislation [Accessed 1 February 2018].

Equatex (2017). *The benefits of multi-generational workforces.* Available at: www.equatex.com/en/article/benefits-of-multi-generational-workforces [Accessed 2 February 2018].

Forbes (2013). *Global mobility: A win-win for you and for your employer.* Available at: www.forbes.com/sites/sylviavorhausersmith/2013/10/31/global-mobility-a-win-win-for-you-and-your-employer/#5af5147a7c16 [Accessed 1 February 2018].

Harvard Business Review (2013). *How diversity can drive innovation.* Available at: https://hbr.org/2013/12/how-diversity-can-drive-innovation [Accessed 1 February 2018].

Harvard Business Review (2017). *How to successfully work across countries, languages, and cultures.* Available at: https://hbr.org/2017/08/how-to-successfully-work-across-countries-languages-and-cultures [Accessed 1 February 2018].

Hays (2018). *Generation Y: What makes them tick?* Available at: https://social.hays.com/2014/01/03/generation-y-at-wor [Accessed 2 February 2018].

International Labour Organisation (ILO) (2014). *World of work report.* Available at: www.ilo.org/global/research/global-reports/world-of-work/2014/lang--en/index.htm [Accessed 1 February 2018].

Jayakumar, U. (2008). Can higher education meet the needs of an increasingly diverse and global society? Campus diversity and cross-cultural workforce competencies. *Harvard Educational Review,* 78(4), 615–51.

ManpowerGroup (2016). *Millennial careers: 2020 vision.* Available at: www.manpowergroup.com/millennials [Accessed 2 February 2018].

Migration Watch UK (2017). *Employment and welfare: Main points.* Available at: www.migrationwatchuk.org/briefing-papers/category/3 [Accessed 20 February 2018].

Organisation for Economic Co-operation and Development (OECD) (2015). *Indicators of immigrant integration 2015: Settling in.* Available at: www.oecd.org/els/mig/Indicators-of-Immigrant-Integration-2015.pdf [Accessed 1 February 2018].

PricewaterhouseCoopers (PwC) (2016). *Recent talent trends forcing strategic approaches: How enhanced mobility is at the core*. Available at: www.pwc.com/gx/en/people-organi sation/pdf/recent-talent-trends-forcing-strategic-approaches.pdf [Accessed 1 February 2018].

Slalom (2017). *Adapting to the multigenerational workforce*. Available at: www.slalom.com/ thinking/adapting-to-the-multigenerational-workforce [Accessed 1 February 2018].

Wong, J. C. (2017). *Segregated Valley: The ugly truth about Google and diversity in tech*. Available at: www.theguardian.com/technology/2017/aug/07/silicon-valley-google-diversity-black-women-workers [Accessed 2 February 2018].

World Economic Forum (WEF) (2017a). *What happens when we all live to be 100?* Available at: www.weforum.org/agenda/2017/01/what-happens-when-we-all-live-to-be-100 [Accessed 1 February 2018].

World Economic Forum (WEF) (2017b). *We'll live to 100: How can we afford it?* Available at: www3.weforum.org/docs/WEF_White_Paper_We_Will_Live_to_100.pdf [Accessed 1 February 2018].

World Health Organisation (WHO) (2018). *50 Facts: Global health situation and trends 1955–2025*. Available at: www.who.int/whr/1998/media_centre/50facts/en [Accessed 1 February 2018].

Zemke, R., Raines, C. and Filipczak, B. (1999). *Generations at work: Managing the clash of Veterans, Boomers, Xers, and Nexters in your workplace*. New York: AMACOM.

4

THRIVING IN THE 4IR: WORKPLACE AUTOMATION AND ARTIFICIAL INTELLIGENCE

Chapter contents

Global workplace dynamics

- The 4th Industrial Revolution
- The role of the 4th Industrial Revolution in reshaping the workplace
- Key developments and workplace implications

Workplace automation and global talent

- Workplace automation and robotics
- The effects of automation in the run-up to 2030, according to the evidence
- The impact of workforce automation on organisational practice
- Global talent attributes, skills and abilities to stay ahead of automation and robots

Artificial intelligence and global talent

- Artificial intelligence as a game changer
- Artificial intelligence as a workforce opportunity and challenge
- Global talent attributes, skills and abilities for staying ahead of AI

WEF projections for the 4IR and implications for talent

- The current state of 4IR and its influence on the workforce and the workplace
- The place of global talent in a post-4IR world

Case study 4.1: Robotics and AI replacing the workforce in Chinese companies

Case study 4.2: The Chinese perspective

WEF World of Work Video Quiz

Learning objectives

After reading this chapter, you will be able to:

- understand preceeding industrial revolutions, the 4th Industrial Revolution and its defining features and developments
- identify key characteristics of automation and artificial intelligence and their impact on talent
- critically analyse key implications of the 4th Industrial Revolution.

GLOBAL WORKPLACE DYNAMICS
The 4th Industrial Revolution

The 4th Industrial Revolution (4IR) or Industry 4.0 has been one of the most widely used and prolific terms in recent times, not only in the world of work but also in society and media more generally. In fact, Google registered over 100,000 searches of the term '4th Industrial Revolution' in 2017 alone. Before discussing the 4IR in depth, we provide a historical insight into the transition from Industry 1.0 to Industry 4.0 from a historical perspective.

The first Industrial Revolution or Industry 1.0 was seen in 1784 and was fuelled by advancements in mechanical production equipment driven by water and steam power. Water and steam power were used as a means of introducing mechanisation to a range of industries and sectors at the time, such as transport and agriculture. 1744 saw the invention of the first mechanical loom designed by British inventor Edmund Cartwright. Industry 1.0 took British manufacturing into factories as it set the foundations of organisational hierarchy (Figure 4.1).

Industry 2.0 or the second Industrial Revolution emerged in 1870 and was enabled by the invention and use of electrical energy and the division of labour that both contributed to mass production. Machinery production and food processing are industries and sectors of the economy that have significantly benefited from Industry 2.0. Richard Garrett and sons invented assembly lines in their factory in 1870, which enabled the introduction of mass production. Industry 2.0 led to the birth of middle-class professions including engineering, banking and teaching.

In 1969, the world experienced the third Industrial Revolution or Industry 3.0, enabled by the development and adoption of advanced electronics and Information Technologies (IT). This led to further automation of production and provided opportunities for expansion in the scale and scope of sectors closely linked to manufacturing. 1979 saw the invention of the first programmable logic controller invented by American electrical engineer, Richard Morley. Following advancements in manufacturing and production, many jobs performed by talent started to become more service-driven.

Industry 4.0 is said to be built on the previous revolutions and is characterising the second decade of the 21st century through the introduction of cyber-physical systems and related innovations and developments in technology more broadly, including cloud computing, the Internet of Things (IoT), Big Data, artificial intelligence (AI), automation and robotics. This revolution is, according to Klaus Schwab, founder and executive chairman, World Economic Forum, 'characterised by a fusion of technologies that is blurring the lines between the physical, digital, and biological spheres' (Schwab, 2016).

Navigating the next industrial revolution

WORLD ECONOMIC FORUM

Revolution	Year	Information
1	1784	Steam, water, mechanical production equipment
2	1870	Division of labour, electricity, mass production
3	1969	Electronics, IT, automated production
4	?	Cyber-physical systems

Figure 4.1 The four industrial revolutions

(Source: WEF, 2016)

The role of the 4th Industrial Revolution in reshaping the workplace

So why is the 4IR different from the previous industrial revolutions? Schwab highlighted that 4IR is projected to have a profound impact on businesses, government and people more generally. He emphasised the transformative nature of Industry 4.0 on the world of work and how we develop as global talent (Schwab, 2016):

> The Fourth Industrial Revolution, finally, will change not only what we do but also who we are. It will affect our identity and all the issues associated with it: our sense of privacy, our notions of ownership, our consumption patterns, the time we devote to work and leisure, and how we develop our careers, cultivate our skills, meet people, and nurture relationships.

Schwab's perspective highlights the sheer scale and pace of anticipated change brought by the 4th Industrial Revolution and the fact that 4IR is projected to impact most, if not all, sectors of the economy, alongside individuals, organisations, cities, countries and society at large.

In 2016, during the WEF in Davos, Switzerland, a new report was launched, *The Future of Jobs*, which highlighted the current and future impact of 4IR in reshaping the workforce and workplace as we know it (WEF, 2016). The underpinning research by WEF reveals the potential magnitude of 4IR and developments in technology by industry and geography, which is predicted to shake up traditional employment hierarchies, job functions and levels, skills and attributes.

WEF predicts that by 2020, more than one third, or 35%, of the skills that are considered important in today's workforce and workplace will have changed considerably. Major disruptions will transform the way we work and the future workforce will need to align its skillsets to keep pace with such disruptions. We would strongly recommend you explore this report, which is listed in the further reading and resources section of this chapter.

Following the launch of this research, there has been a plethora of events, fora, reports and further publications into the future of jobs and the role of 4IR in reshaping the world of work. A 2017 study by the McKinsey Global Institute estimated that approximately half the activities people are currently paid to do globally, could be automated by 2055 by using technology that is available at present. Its study also concluded that 'While few occupations are fully automatable, 60 percent of all occupations have at least 30 percent technically automatable activities' (McKinsey, 2017a).

Key developments and workplace implications

The 4IR is linked with key innovations and developments, predominantly linked to advances in technology and its wide-reaching influence and impact on people, organisations, sectors of the economy and society. The most important area of these innovations and developments is the introduction of artificial intelligence (AI), automation and advances in robotics.

AI can be simply defined as computational models of human behaviour. On the other hand, it is the study of how to make computers do and think about things in the same way that humans do and think about them. Automation, in contrast, is a piece of technology like robots whose primary focus is the performance of repetitive tasks by following set parameters or rules. Human beings are, nevertheless, complex and may not necessarily follow rules when making decisions – this makes AI far more complex than automation, which, in fact, is now everywhere around us! Although both AI and automation processes are driven by data, there are some fundamental differences between the two and we will discuss these in the second and third parts of this chapter and back them up with some concrete examples from practice.

Occasionally, it is assumed that AI, robotics and automation are corporate-driven, private sector constructs that will only impact a certain segment of the economy and society. The 4IR developments are not exclusive to large corporations as their costs of implementation are gradually being reduced, though they still require extensive investment depending on the sector.

The opportunities and challenges associated with the deployment of AI, automation and robots are projected to have wide-reaching implications. Therefore, even some well-established public and possibly under-funded sectors (for example, in the UK the National Health Service (NHS) and city councils) are looking at the opportunities provided by AI and automation. We will discuss this in detail in the next section of this chapter.

This large-scale disruption in the world of work provides a variety of stakeholders, with an interest in skilling, up-skilling and re-skilling talent, an opportunity to work together more closely and more collaboratively to help shape the next generation of talent and respond to the changing dynamics and needs of today's and tomorrow's working environment.

WORKPLACE AUTOMATION AND GLOBAL TALENT

Workplace automation and robotics

Back in 1983, David Collier, Associate Professor of Business Administration, University of Virginia, USA, studied the automation of 10 service industries and discussed the implications of the simultaneous automation of goods and services – a transformative process which he labelled a 'service sector revolution' (Collier, 1983). He argued that automation is not exactly a new trend as, in fact, automation in the financial services sector can be traced back to the 1930s through the introduction of mechanical machines sorting cheques in banks.

In his popular publication, *The Service Sector Revolution: The Automation of Services* (1983), David Collier defined workplace automation as 'any single or multiple functional machine or group of machines that performs a predetermined or reprogrammable sequence of tasks'. He identified six categories of automation:

- *fixed sequence robots* – machines which perform successive steps of a given operation repetitively by following set information or instructions that cannot be easily changed
- *variable sequence robots* – machines which perform successive steps of a given operation repetitively by following set information or instructions that can be altered
- *playback robots* – enables machines to produce operations from memory that have been previously executed by a human workforce
- *numerical controlled robots* – machines that perform a given task commanded by numerical data and following a defined sequence, conditions and position
- *intelligent robots* – machines with sensory perception detecting changes in the work environment and armed with decision-making abilities
- *totally automated systems* – a system of machines performing a set of physical and intellectual tasks required to produce a product or deliver a service. (Collier, 1983)

Building on Collier's contributions and looking back at the past three decades, concerns about the effects of automation have also been captured in works such as *The Jobless Future* (Aronowitz and DiFazio, 1994) and *The End of Work* (Rifkin, 1995), alongside numerous other scientific and non-scientific outlets. Automation as a concept and practice may have emerged in the early 20th century but it has only recently attracted significant attention from industry, governments, futurists and global talent due to the technological innovations and advancements that enable automation to expand in scale and scope.

In a recent work report that discusses workplace automation in the context of 4IR more broadly, Janet Johansson, a researcher at Mälardalen University in Sweden, defined the process of automation through the perspective of workforce and workplace efficiency (Johansson, 2017):

the use of computers or machines to control a particular process in order to increase efficiency. Generally, this means a faster, human-free way of doing something. Automation is the use of technology to improve less efficient human tasks.

Automation thus provides opportunities to introduce improvements in the way jobs and tasks are carried out, and, equally, to reduce the need for human intervention. After Collier (1983), we can conclude that automation and automated programmes and hardware use various control systems and follow pre-programmed rules and scenarios. This means that you would usually need to 'instruct' your hardware or software robot as regards what tasks should be accomplished and, importantly, set the parameters of these tasks so that they can be performed autonomously. The reduced or minimal human intervention is one of the core defining features of automation, also in line with Johansson's definition of the term.

But what does automation mean in the context of global talent? The working definition of workplace automation that this text puts forward is focused on the interplay between automation and you, as global talent:

> Workplace automation in the context of global talent is a complex, advanced technological process related to the automation and robotisation of processes, functions, tasks and jobs, either partly or fully, that have previously been carried out by human talent. Workplace automation has the potential to create an environment where both automation features and global talent co-exist in a way that the former enables the latter to focus on more strategic and complex tasks that require higher-level skills and interpersonal traits and abilities such as emotional intelligence, innovation and complex problem solving.

We see automation in a balanced way and as such we discuss here both the opportunities and challenges that this 4IR development provides to people and organisations. In placing yourself in such a context, you would need to reflect on the adaptivity, creativity and flexibility necessary to integrate future automation prospects. Let us illustrate this through an example from the marketing and communications industry. Let's imagine that you hold the role of digital communications officer and you are responsible for the social and professional media engagement and content development of your organisation. There are already automated systems, such as Hootsuite, that enable you to schedule and automate most, if not all, of your digital engagement across social and professional media platforms, including LinkedIn, Twitter and Facebook. This process of automating aspects of your job would ultimately mean that you would have more time to, for example, put on your creative hat and develop an innovative, high-impact digital campaign to boost your digital engagement and content development.

The effects of automation in the run-up to 2030

But alongside its benefits, automation and its advanced dimensions, which we will discuss later in this chapter, this 4IR feature is also set to challenge and reshape the landscape of work and thus often carry negative connotations. Building on its earlier report on automation, McKinsey Global Institute's late 2017 report, *Jobs Lost, Jobs Gained: Workforce Transitions in a Time of Automation*, provided insights into the number and types of jobs that might be created under different scenarios through to 2030, in a way that delivers a comparative discussion on the jobs that could be lost to automation (Figure 4.2).

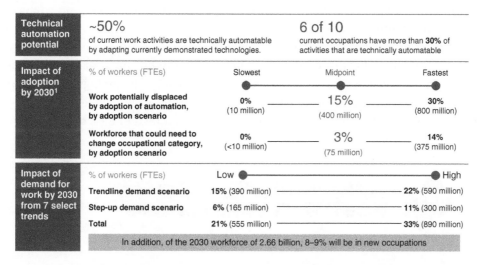

Figure 4.2 Impacts of automation

(Source: Exhibit from "Jobs lost, jobs gained: What the future of work will mean for jobs, skills, and wages", December 2017, McKinsey Global Institute, www.mckinsey.com. Copyright (c) 2018 McKinsey & Company. All rights reserved. Reprinted by permission.

The report highlighted that more than a fifth of the global labour force – 800 million workers – might lose their jobs due to the effects of automation. McKinsey Global Institute also concluded that at least one third of tasks could be automated in approximately 60% of jobs, which is projected to lead to substantial changes for employers and the world of work more widely. Amid the uncertainty and potentially negative implications for the global workforce, the report also provides a somewhat optimistic picture as it places a strong emphasis on the projected benefits of automation to economies and societies (McKinsey, 2017b):

> Automation technologies including artificial intelligence and robotics will generate significant benefits for users, businesses, and economies, lifting productivity and economic growth. The extent to which these technologies displace workers will depend on the pace of their development and adoption, economic growth, and growth in demand for work.

These notable developments in the 4IR have the potential to deliver wide-reaching implications and are, in fact, already impacting the world of work. *Work in Progress: Towards a Leaner, Smarter Public-Sector Workforce* by Reform UK, an influential think tank in the UK, estimated that almost 250,000 public sector workers in the UK could lose their jobs to robots over the next 15 years (Reform UK, 2017). Reform UK sees technology and automation disrupting jobs in three key areas: administration or operative roles involving repetitive and predictable functions; interactive or frontline roles that require personal interaction; and cognitive roles with a focus on strategic thinking and complex reasoning.

Another influential study includes the Citibank and University of Oxford's *Technology at Work: V2.0*, which has made even bolder predictions on the impact of 4IR and automation on the global workforce and workplace (Figure 4.3). Its findings suggest that 35% of jobs in the UK are at risk of being replaced by automation, while this figure in the USA is 47%. Across all OECD countries as a whole, a total of 57% of jobs can be automated (Citi, 2016).

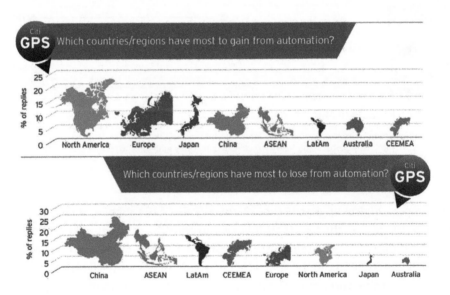

Figure 4.3   Countries set to gain and lose the most from automation

(Source: Citi, 2016)

Citibank and the University of Oxford have found that most of the jobs at risk of auto-mation are predominantly low-skilled ones in the manufacturing industries. As a global lead in manufacturing, China was projected to have a high risk of automation, perhaps as high as 77%. The study, nevertheless, concluded that, increasingly, job roles and positions that require higher-level skills and a degree of specialisation are also at risk of being replaced by automation and robots (Citi, 2016).

However, 4IR is not a figment of the academic imagination. It is a reality. Indeed it is already around us and used extensively in marketing, in customer service systems, in manufacturing plants using robotic arms, and so on. We will touch on diverse examples over the course of this chapter.

The impact of workforce automation on organisational practice

Recent developments and advances in automation ultimately result in the adoption of more robots in the workplace and this is projected to have a notable impact on industries and sectors of the economy. Robots in the workplace primarily focus on low-skilled, repetitive jobs and tasks. At the time of writing (2018), however, we are already seeing industrial robots that are able to carry out more specialist tasks that usually require higher-level skills and abilities. Despite advancements in robotics in the workplace, the relatively high cost of the development and deployment of automation and robotics is projected to slow down this transition.

Building on the first section of this chapter, we now go on to discuss how the NHS in the UK, a public-sector healthcare organisation that has been suffering from funding cuts, has already been exploring opportunities to automate its operations.

INDUSTRY INSIGHT

Automating the NHS and the robotic surgery arm

The National Health Service (NHS) has been the UK's national healthcare provider since 1948, providing pioneering healthcare services to over 65 million people. However, the organisation has been negatively impacted by the aftermath of the 2008 economic

(Continued)

(Continued)

downturn coupled with demographic trends in the UK where we now increasingly see a larger proportion of the ageing population (18% of the UK's population is aged 65 or over). The latter developments have put a strain on the NHS's long-term financial sustainability and its ability to continue to fulfil its vision, mission and objectives to deliver healthcare services in the UK. But this is set to change. The NHS may well be at the forefront of embracing opportunities for automation and the deployment of robots across a broad array of healthcare services, where surgery is just one example.

Kate Laycock, a doctor and researcher at the Reform think tank, highlighted that the number of tasks within an NHS job that can be automated, and thus the number of positions that are no longer required, differs by clinical role but the opportunities are significant. For example, Dr Laycock suggests that 29% of registered nurses and 35% of paramedics in the UK can be automated (Laycock, 2017). Even 13% of surgeons in the NHS can be automated, according to her research. This could ultimately lead to an estimated 114,462 frontline roles being automated with cost savings of over £4 million.

How is the NHS changing by adopting robotics and what are the implications for the healthcare profession? The deployment of robots in healthcare, once said to be a distant dream or labelled as science fiction, is already under way in the NHS. British scientists from Cambridge Medical Robots (CMR) have developed the world's smallest surgical robot, Versius, which has the ability to mimic the human arm and can be used to carry out a wide range of interventions, including hernia repairs, colorectal operations, prostate and ear, nose and throat surgery. Versius eliminates the need for traditional open surgery (CMR, 2018). CMR collaborates with a number of NHS and private hospitals to introduce the robots, and predicts that the global market for surgical robots will reach $20 billion by 2024 (Ellis, 2017).

Meanwhile, the NHS has signalled its intention to continue with the adoption of robots in surgery, after the NHS, in 2018, launched a search for companies to provide £300 million of robotics services to hospitals across the UK. It is argued that, if deployed in the NHS, robots could support complex surgical procedures, including heart disease and tumour surgeries, and provide a diagnosis for many common diseases (Curry, 2018).

This example of the NHS being on the brink of automation and robot adoption is something we thought we could not afford for at least another 10 years, but it is here now! It is no longer a matter of navigating this new disruptive world of work, nor of simply having the knowledge or awareness of what is happening in the world of work. A global talent's mindset, heartset and skillset will be key amid the 4IR – particularly the global skillset attributes such as learnability that we discussed in Chapters 1 and 2 in detail.

The NHS is a prime example of how specialist skills are being automated or robotised – and rightly so. Joshua Healyand his team from the Centre for Workplace Leadership at the University of Melbourne, Australia, point out that governments, industries and society at large still hold a more traditional view of automation in which automation replaces predominantly low-skilled, repetitive jobs such as those in farms and factories. Healy et al. (2017: 157) contend thereforce that:

> Newer forms of automation, driven by machine-learning technologies, are now beginning to encroach on more highly skilled 'cognitive' and 'non-routine' occupations, such as in accounting, medicine and the law. With accuracy that matches or betters human experts – and usually in much less time – machines can now comb through case files to identify legal precedents, or diagnose diseases in patients' medical scans.

Machine learning gives computers and robots the ability to learn without being specifically programmed to do so. Machine learning has greatly advanced automation and, as you can see, advanced automation contributes to automating aspects of industries, jobs and professions that have been perceived as automation-proof in the past, such as complex surgery interventions carried out by NHS surgeons. Automation and its advanced forms have penetrated other sectors such as technology, defence, retail and e-commerce.

In fact, three of the largest employers in the world, among which is the iPhone and iPad components developer Foxconn (the world's 10th largest employer), have embraced automation and have gradually started replacing their human workforce with robots. Foxconn has already replaced 60,000 workers with robots and retail giant Walmart and the US Department of Defence are set to follow suit (Williams-Grut, 2016). Alibaba, the Chinese multinational e-commerce, retail, internet, AI and technology conglomerate, has also adopted robots to improve productivity and precision in its smart warehouses and logistics hubs where robots already do 70% of the work.

What do all of theses statistics indicate? Even the most established of sectors and employers have come to understand and realise the need to respond to 4IR developments, including automation and robots. This response might be perceived as expensive and research and development oriented. However, as in the case of the NHS and other organisations transitioning to automation, the productivity and success rates are much better. Robotics and automation deployment thus becomes a necessity.

In the case of healthcare, in particular, the potential focus is on how technology has the ability to considerably improve our lives and scale up the impact of healthcare interventions. That being the driver, global talent would eventually need to find a way to cope with the negative effects of adopting AI, robotics and automation, which, among others, may well include redundancies and jobs losses. Later in this chapter, you will have the opportunity to explore the case of China and critically reflect on the effects of automation adoption in the manufacturing sector. All of this might sound scary but there are certain global talent skills and attributes that robots and automated systems are not good at and we will discuss them now.

Global talent attributes, skills and abilities to stay ahead of automation and robots

What attributes, skills and abilities would enable global talent to stay ahead of automation and robots? What does the 4IR mean for the profession? Do creativity and authenticity have a place in the skillset of global talent that will separate them out from robots? If you have asked yourself any of these questions, here's our response with the aid of some examples from industry.

Johan Aurik, a managing partner and the chairman at the global management consulting firm A.T. Kearney, highlights that each of the first three industrial revolutions brought change and disruption, and concluded that the fourth wave will be no different. He argues:

> Instead of focusing on the specific jobs that will appear or disappear, we should instead concentrate on the skills that will be needed, then educate, train and reskill the human workforce to leverage the new opportunities afforded by technology. (2017)

In which areas might people have an advantage over robots and automation? McKinsey (2017a) concluded that humans are better than robots in a number of strategic areas important for the modern workforce and workplace, including the spotting of new patterns, logical reasoning, creativity and innovation, coordination between multiple stakeholders or individuals, natural language understanding, navigating across diverse environments, as well as identifying, responding to and displaying social and emotional states.

Early career professionals, like some of our students, will probably ask us the question – where will we be trained and how will we be trained on the job? If we go back to the NHS example, if a surgeon is trained at the moment, they are usually trained to use their hands. If a robotic arm was, however, helping with operations, then that surgeon would need to be trained differently. Thus, the NHS and other large organisations may still be spending millions on training their workforce in the traditional way, when we can be skilling this talent from day one on the robotic arm.

However, if this robotic arm costs millions, the majority of training across hospitals would still follow a more traditional approach, often due to the lack of investment in talent development. Following conventional approaches to training would mean that the NHS would constantly need to up-skill and re-skill its workforce in order to stay in the profession.

There is, therefore, that big paradox and complexity around the adoption of AI technology and robotics – namely, do we train surgeons to work well with their hands or with the robotic arm, or both? How do we ensure that surgeons can do both when they are not trained from day one to do so? So, as a consequence, we anticipate seeing disproportionality between those operating the robotic arm and those operating with their own hands.

Global talent surgeons would need to be trained both ways wherever possible, at least until the time has come when a reduction in production costs and channelled government investment will enable the scale of robot adoption to accelerate.

There is one thing that you as a global talent should consider and this is the fact that the pace of adoption is different across different sectors and in different contexts. Hence, it is why you would need to develop future-proof attributes and reinvent your approach to work and learning in a world of work where global talent and robots both co-exist and work together.

Key global talent attributes that come into play in this rather complex environment of the varied and often fragmented adoption of automation and robots across different sectors and professions, are located at the interplay between technology and the key defining features of your profession. This includes your ability to stay abreast of the latest developments in your professional area, to adopt a visionary approach to see how technology reshapes different aspects of your profession and to be prepared to skill and up-skill accordingly.

Again, think about the concept of learnability that we discussed in Chapters 1 and 2,but this time reflect on it in the context of technological innovations and how they influence your sector and profession. Learnability alongside your ability to navigate through change in the workplace will help you stay employable and employed.

We should not, of course, forget the global talent attributes of creativity, authenticity and complex problem solving which set us apart from machines, and should find ways to nurture these key attributes regardless of our industry and profession.

ARTIFICIAL INTELLIGENCE AND GLOBAL TALENT
Artificial intelligence as a game changer

While 4IR developments, including automation and robots, are gradually making their way in to the modern workforce and workplace, there is a bigger agenda amid this fourth revolution. It has attracted a lot of attention in major global gatherings such as the World Economic Forum, United Nations and TEDx talks, and equally has become a headline in both scientific and popular outlets across the world.

The field of artificial intelligence (AI) research was founded more than 50 years ago. Professor Emeritus Marvin Minsky, a mathematician, computer scientist and pioneer in the field of artificial intelligence, has been named the father of AI by the Massachusetts Institute of Technology. He is an expert on the theory of artificial intelligence and his 1985 book, *The Society of Mind*, is thought to be a seminal work on intellectual structure and function, bringing to the fore an advanced understanding of intelligence and thought (MIT, 2015). However, very little progress has since been made on AI until recently.

At the 2018 World Economic Forum in Davos, Switzerland, Google's CEO Sundar Pichai made a bold statement, in which he suggested that 'AI is probably the most important thing humanity has ever worked on. I think of it as something more profound than electricity or fire' (WEF, 2018). Pichai highlighted the scale of AI, which can no longer be ignored, as well as the profound impact it will have on people, organisations and society. Google's CEO believes that AI is a response to many of the grand challenges that the world at large and our societies face today and the company is gearing up to open AI research centres in China and France.

But what does artificial intelligence really mean? AI can simply be defined as computational models of human behaviour – that is, programmes that behave externally like human beings. Or, according to *The Financial Times* (2018b), AI is the study of how to make computers do things in the way that humans do them, such as the process of taking in information and making decisions based on this information.

Peter Stone and his team at Stanford University in the USA, who have launched The One Hundred Year Study on Artificial Intelligence, emphasised the lack of a specific and widely accepted definition of AI, which they see as a branch of computer science (Stone et al., 2016). Stone, nevertheless, points out that Nils J. Nilsson's definition of AI is a widely accepted one (Nilsson, 2010: i): 'Artificial intelligence is that activity devoted to making machines intelligent, and intelligence is that quality that enables an entity to function appropriately and with foresight in its environment.'

How does this definition translate into practice? If we take technology and smartphones, the intelligent assistant Siri, who we use on our iPhones on a daily basis, is powered by artificial intelligence, though not as advanced as one might expect. Siri is, nevertheless, intelligent enough to help you with a range of tasks and research that you previously had to do yourself. Other examples include chat bots which are being used almost everywhere now by companies in the legal and conveyancing sector, transportation, retail and in virtually every large organisation's customer service portal or application.

INDUSTRY INSIGHT

Siri – the AI-enabled assistant

The Speech Interpretation and Recognition Interface, or simply Siri, is Apple's intelligent personal assistant, which, according to the company, helps iPhone users get things done. It enables users of Apple products to speak natural language voice commands in order to operate the mobile device and its applications. Siri's AI integration means that its software is able to learn and adapt to its user's individual language usages, preferences and searches – this is enabled with the use of the digital assistant over time.

Siri supports a range of user commands, including performing phone actions, checking information, scheduling events and reminders, handling device settings, searching the internet and finding information on virtually anything. It is also able to engage with applications for iOS – Apple's native operation system. Siri is powerful enough to work across multiple iPhone and iPad applications as needed in order to complete the tasks that have been set originally. The AI-enabled personal assistant has over 500 million users, at the time of writing.

Whilst the field of AI is far more complex than this, our focus in this chapter is on the implications and impacts that AI brings to the world of work that you, as a global talent, should be able to understand and make the most of. Nevertheless, we do provide further resources for those of you who are keen to gain a broader understanding of the essence of AI and its far-reaching impact and implications.

Designed to simulate human thinking, AI is far more powerful than automation and has its focus on the replication and advancement of cognitive and behavioural functions performed by humans. This text puts forward a definition of artificial intelligence that is centred around the interplay between this 4IR development and global talent:

Artificial intelligence in the context of global talent is a technological innovation that influences processes related to the advancement of cognitive and behavioural functions and roles that have previously been carried out by talent. Advances in AI enable these behavioural functions and roles to be replicated by computers, robots and other AI-enabled hardware and software. AI's interplay with global talent creates an environment where they can complement one another and where talent have the opportunity to advance their productivity and practice through the adoption of AI-enabled technologies.

Our definition is in line with a recent PricewaterhouseCoopers (2017) study, *Workforce of the Future: The Competing Forces Shaping 2030*, which also emphasised the potential benefits of the interplay between AI and talent:

> AI could create a world where human abilities are amplified as machines help mankind process, analyse, and evaluate the abundance of data that creates today's world, allowing humans to spend more time engaged in high-level thinking, creativity, and decision-making.

AI is generally seen as a positive outcome of the 4IR, one that introduces a range of opportunities to improve processes and practices in the world of work but which also contributes to improvements in the state of society. Of course, we have all come across news and reports warning humanity of the potential pitfalls of AI adoption in the world of work and the implications for jobs being lost or created as a result. From our perspective, AI can bring about both opportunities and challenges in the world of work. We now go on to critically reflect on both perspectives in the next section.

Artificial intelligence as a workforce opportunity and challenge

The single most prominent challenge posed by AI and echoed by numerous organisations, events and publications is that, as with automation and robots, this 4IR innovation can fundamentally reshape the world of work and thus have wider implications for both global talent and employers. Building on the NHS case we provided earlier in this chapter, AI is seen as a challenge because this might lead to the displacement of jobs and talent on a global level, in both developing and developed countries.

McKinsey Global Institute suggested in its late 2017 report that up to 375 million workers around the world may need to switch jobs and learn new skills as a result of the wide-reaching impact of AI adoption in the workforce and workplace (McKinsey, 2017b). Meanwhile, up to one third of the workforce in the USA and Germany, 100 million of

China's workforce alone and nearly half of Japanese employees, will have to learn new skills or change jobs because of advances in AI.

We are already starting to see real examples of AI impacting industries and talent. A prime example is China, which will be discussed further later in this chapter, however many other countries and sectors across the world are also influenced by this 4IR development.

Take Japan, for example. The Japanese insurance company, Fukoku Mutual Life Insurance, is replacing some of its global talent claims workers with IBM Watson Explorer, a cognitive exploration and content analysis platform that is AI-enabled. IBM Watson Explorer will use AI to scan hospital records and other relevant documentation to estimate insurance payouts for claims made to the company. Watson AI is expected to improve productivity in the organisation by 30% (Gershgorn, 2017).

Not only are advanced economies like Japan, the UK and the USA seeing the transformation in their workforce influenced by AI, developing countries such as India are also starting to feel the pinch of AI adoption and workplace automation. According to Pranjal Sharma, a contributing editor at Businessworld and a WEF advisory board member, the 4IR is now well under way in India. Sharma (2017) provides examples of AI adoption in the financial services sector where some banks in India, including Canara Bank, are already using chatbots and even humanoid robots.

Sharma (2017) emphasised that the uncertainty that AI adoption creates in India is more widely felt where Indian society and talent fear job losses which are attributed to the spread of AI-enabled innovations, including automation and robots:

> There is much that India has to be worried about too. An over-reliance on automation will shrink job creation. Automation and robotics in industrial manufacturing suits countries with low productive populations. But it does not suit countries like India, where 12–13 million people enter the job market every year.

Artificial intelligence, alongside advances in robotics and automation, thus creates some challenges and ethical dilemmas for society at large. Some communities of scholars and industry practitioners indeed refer to AI, automation and robots as 4IR disruptions that will lead to large-scale unemployment on a global level. What would employment look like in the not too distant future then? Would there be any? In response, some experts have proposed the idea of robot taxation and the introduction of a universal basic income for people as a means of introducing equal opportunities for people amid the effects of AI adoption in the world of work. Universal basic income trials in Finland and Canada are now well under way (Galeon and Marquart, 2016) and we shall be closely watching how this concept develops in practice and what the key implications might look like. So would the roll-out of universal basic income replace the need to work? Would global talent work in tandem with robots and AI-enabled systems? The answers to these questions are complex but we offer our personal insights into them in the next section of this chapter.

Alongside this perceived challenge, AI is seen as an opportunity because, if we are to get some inspiration from the Google CEO's words, innovations that have emerged as a result of 4IR, such as AI and robots, can contribute to improving the state of the world alongside delivering wider impacts and benefits to society, organisations and individuals. We discuss some of these key benefits here.

Increased productivity is certainly one of the key opportunities to be seized. McKinsey Global Institute found that AI and the adoption of automated systems are estimated to contribute to productivity growth on a global basis by as much as 0.8 to 1.4% annually (McKinsey, 2017a). The opportunities for increasing productivity through AI are all-encompassing and include most sectors of the economy and society. If we take the public sector and healthcare as an example, Reform UK's study emphasised the potential to use AI and automation to increase productivity. This, as a result, would enable 'skilled practitioners to focus on activities that require currently non-automatable skills' (Reform UK, 2017).

Savings and resource optimisation to key sectors is another opportunity following the adoption of AI that leads to a better distribution of budgets and investment in times of reduced public sector budgets and volatile global economy. AI can bring about public sector savings in times of austerity. For example, the same Reform UK's study found that AI-enabled chatbots could replace up to 90% of Whitehall's administrators, as well as tens of thousands of healthcare talent currently employed by the NHS and doctors' surgeries, leading to a cumulative saving of £4 billion a year.

The creation of new jobs – historical data is able to demonstrate that technology has created large employment and sector disruptions, but also creates new jobs (Figure 4.4). The penetration of 4IR innovations alongside rising incomes and consumption, particularly in emerging economies, may lead to the creation of up to 130 million new jobs in healthcare and 50 million new jobs in technology as we head towards 2030, as concluded by McKinsey Global Institute. We should, nevertheless, note that the population on earth in 1850 was 1.2 billion, while in 2018 it is over 7.5 billion people. This rapid growth will ultimately create demand for more employment opportunities, which may lead to further growth in global unemployment levels in the era of AI, if not addressed by governments and policymakers.

Scaling up the knowledge economy through AI and other key 4IR innovations can also bring about benefits. AI can support further innovation and advancements in the knowledge economy where robots and global talent co-create innovations and

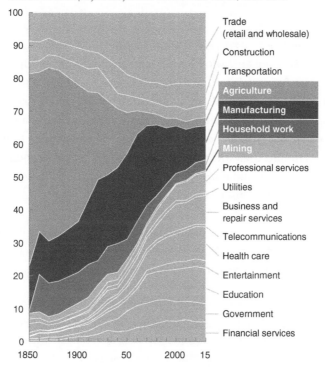

Large-scale sector employment declines have been countered by growth of other sectors that have absorbed workers

Share of total employment by sector in the United States, 1850–2015

Figure 4.4   History and job creation

'know-how' that use the strengths of both worlds – the virtual one and the human one – to develop or deliver a new product or service. According to Ian Smith, General Manager at Invu, intelligent automation and AI can collectively lead to improvements in the interplay between machines and human talent: 'intelligent automation is all about building better workers, both human and digital, by embracing and working alongside intelligent technologies' (Smith, 2017).

Generally, high levels of AI and robot adoption are also projected to contribute to an improved work–life balance and wellbeing of the workforce. Alongside the many challenges and opportunities associated with AI, global talent will be better placed to respond to them by developing the right attributes, skills and abilities that would enable them to stay ahead of AI.

Global talent attributes, skills and abilities for staying ahead of AI

During the 2018 World Economic Forum, Jack Ma, the founder and executive chairman of Alibaba Group, provided his perspective on the future of work and skills that would give talent a competitive advantage over AI (Flashman, 2018). He emphasised the importance of introducing future-proof interventions that will enable talent to thrive in the age of AI. Ma concluded that global talent, and students like you, should be taught and be able to develop soft skills, including independent thinking, values and teamwork. He also believes that humans will not be in a position to compete with AI-enabled machines and that they need to shift their focus to the development of unique and individual skills and abilities instead. We would encourage you to see the full video of Jack Ma during the 2018 World Economic Forum, which can be found under the further reading and resources section of this chapter.

AI will be a big part of our future, according to another perspective provided by Alistair Cox, CEO at global recruiting firm Hays, who also highlights that 'softer' skills, attributes and abilities would help global talent withstand disruption in the workplace triggered by the 4IR (Cox, 2018):

> the human element will still be required, probably even more so, since it remains incredibly difficult for any machine to analyse the soft skills that remain so crucial to modern business. I'm yet to see an algorithm that can read things like humour, temperament or enthusiasm as effectively as a person can.

Just like in the case of automation and robots, AI will require global talent to develop a range of interpersonal skills and attributes, or heartset attributes. If you go back to Chapter 1, you will be reminded of our discussion of the attributes that global talent with a global heartset should be able to develop and demonstrate. Alongside these attributes, we strongly believe that creativity and imagination are both soft skills and core attributes that have to be nurtured in global talent, regardless of their field of specialisation or job title.

Further, sensing emotions and most global heartset attributes that are core-defining features of humans and the human experience cannot be replicated by AI nor automated. To quote Anna Powers – advisor, consultant and Global STEM Leadership Prize recipient – 'in the age of AI human creativity will have more premium than ever before'. Powers (2017) also goes on to suggest that AI cannot be creative as its key strength lies in its ability to replicate and automate behaviour and decisions based on set algorithms and data that are fed into the programme:

Although it [AI] can replicate behaviour, it does not have imagination, because it is just a sorting algorithm with advanced functional optimization and regression techniques. The human mind, on the other hand, is rapidly creative and imaginative. Humans are able to think of stories and imagine things which we then bring to life.

We now go on to explore some of the key implications of AI and actions that need to be taken forward by policymakers, employers and educators alike to ensure that global talent are future-ready.

WEF PROJECTIONS FOR THE 4IR AND IMPLICATIONS FOR TALENT

The current state of 4IR and its influence on the workforce and the workplace

Despite current 4IR-driven advancements and developments, the scale and pace at which automation and AI are penetrating our lives, and impacting different sectors of the economy and different countries around the world, are very different. Let's imagine that in 2025 a hospital, which is part of the NHS network of hospitals in the UK, is doing 80% of its operations using robotics. Yet the scale of AI and robot adoption in many other healthcare organisations, particularly in countries in Africa, Latin America and Southeast Asia, may not even have touched 5% by then. AI is not evenly distributed, and may not be so for quite some time due to the high cost of adoption.

Further resources would also need to be channelled into skilling, up-skilling and re-skilling global talent. The case for re-skilling and up-skilling has a completely new dimension to it in an AI and automation era. In the past, people would have been sent to brush up their knowledge but the current AI landscape introduces a considerable degree of complexity into developing an employable and productive workforce. How do we create an environment in which innovative and AI-driven workforce practices can be developed and nurtured among the many and not the few? This is a question that all of us, including government, educators, policymakers and employers, would need to dive into in order to come up with practical responses and solutions.

Towards a Reskilling Revolution: A Future of Jobs for All, a 2018 insight report by the WEF in collaboration with the Boston Consulting Group (BCG), amplifies the case for re-skilling across a number of sectors of the economy to boost productivity and provide employment opportunities, including the transition from old jobs amid recent 4IR developments and disruptions (WEF and BCG, 2018).

The report also highlights the opportunities to align workforce skills development efforts with requirements of the world of work, including the WEF's big data-driven approach to discovering re-skilling pathways and job-transition opportunities – something that we will cover in the third part of this text. Making a reasonable investment in re-skilling and up-skilling global talent is, nevertheless, seen as a key barrier to progressing with this important agenda. Channelling resources in re-skilling has the potential to support the transition of talent into new employment opportunities (WEF and BCG, 2018): 'with adequate reskilling, 95% of the most immediately at-risk workers would find good-quality, higher-wage work in growing job families ... without reskilling, only 2% of workers would have an optimal opportunity to transition to new jobs'.

The key recommendations of the report in terms of re-skilling global talent include the need to engage in lifelong learning and regular re-skilling. A change in the current mindset is needed, according to WEF and BCG, where talent 'become creative, curious, agile lifelong learners, comfortable with continuous change' (WEF and BCG, 2018). WEF and BCG also advocate the development of a platform that enables proactive collaboration between talent, organisations, communities and governments to deliver progress in up-skilling and re-skilling talent.

Collaboration is important but many questions should be considered amid this rather complex transition into the world of work. As Sarah O'Connor, a *Financial Times* employment correspondent on the world of work, comments (*Financial Times*, 2018a):

> But beneath the smooth and sensible statements about collaboration, there are knotty questions we have to face. Who will pay for this retraining? How do we make sure it reaches the people who need it most? And what happens when the problem isn't just the supply of skills in a local economy, but the demand for them?

Indeed, the reality in 2018 is that we are left with more questions, rather than answers to such questions as how the global employment landscape is likely to change as a result of the 4IR and the implications of this transition for global talent. In fact, as making predictions is currently our best bet, we can tell you that there are at least eight key scenarios of what the future of work might look like. If you are a global talent with a key interest in how the world of work is transitioning, we would encourage you to put *Eight Futures of Work: Scenarios and their Implications* on your reading list. In this report, the WEF provides eight avenues for what the future of work might look like by 2030.

The place of global talent in a post-4IR world

Undoubtedly, the future of work holds various interpretations as to what might happen in 2030 and beyond, and some even argue that the way we define employment, the purpose of work and one's job, tasks, roles and responsibilities is too narrow, particularly now in 'the age of machines' where we have AI, robots and automation. As argued by Rutger Bregman, TEDx speaker and correspondent at *De Correspondent* in the Netherlands, society should radically rethink its definition of work, which according to him is incredibly narrow (Bregman, 2017).

Amid 4IR developments, a multitude of future work scenarios and calls to rethink the very definition and purpose of work, we can safely conclude that what employment will consist of in 2030 is likely to be very different from what it does in 2018! While some futurists predict that we may not even need to work in the foreseeable future should universal basic income go mainstream, thanks to a large-scale adoption of AI-powered scalable solutions, the taxation of robots, and high productivity and output, we believe that this is a long shot due to the fragmented and uneven distribution of the benefits brought by the 4IR.

What is more realistic as a prediction towards 2030 is that we will see people spending fewer hours at work and in more specialist roles that complement the work of robots, AI and automation systems, in order to coordinate and improve the outputs of 4IR innovations in the workforce and workplace. Therefore, a partnership between global talent and robots in the workplace is what we envisage as we approach 2030.

So, don't panic! Global talent will still be in demand, in fact even more than before, and critical attributes such as creativity, imagination, authenticity and emotional intelligence, as we discussed earlier in this chapter, will be paramount to the AI-enabled future world of work.

CASE STUDY 4.1

Robotics and AI replacing the workforce in Chinese companies

The rise of automation and robotics

The Future of Jobs, an influential 2016 report by the World Economic Forum, predicted that by 2020 more than one third (35%) of the skills that are considered important in

(Continued)

(Continued)

today's workforce will have changed considerably. Major disruptions will transform the way we work and the future workforce will need to align its skillset to keep pace with such disruptions. The report predicted that some jobs will be wiped out while others will be in high demand. All in all, the World Economic Forum predicts that around five million jobs will be wiped out by 2020 (WEF, 2016).

Building on this, Reform, a London-based think tank, recently predicted that up to 250,000 public sector workers could lose their jobs due to advances in robotics over the next 15 years (Reform UK, 2017). It is nevertheless expected that advances in robotics and automation to increase productivity will enable skilled practitioners to focus on activities that require currently non-automatable skills.

This evidence points to the implications of Industry 4.0 and its emergent dimensions such as automation and robotics on the world of work, specifically the impact that such technological advances will have, or are already having, on the workforce and the need for up-skilling and re-skilling.

Processes related to workforce automation and the replacement of manpower with robots, are now developing in the world of practice, where evidence is provided by both developed and developing countries. One such case is China, where the bulk of jobs are located in the manufacturing sector. The latter provides plenty of opportunities for automation, particularly of repetitive tasks and operations in Chinese factories, at a time when robots are evolving to take on more specialist functions.

In 2014 alone, China was the largest market for industrial robotics where 60,000 robots were sold. This section provides a case study of a Chinese company and its approach to the adoption of automation through robotics.

CASE STUDY 4.2

The Chinese perspective – Changying precision technology company, Dongguan

The first unmanned factory in Dongguan, a city in southeastern China's Guangdong province, gives us a glimpse of what the future of manufacturing might look like, where all functions and processes are operated by computer-controlled robots.

Changying Precision Technology Company in Dongguan, known as the 'world factory', focuses on the production of mobile phones and smartphone modules. In 2015, the company replaced 90% of its human workforce with robots, including automated and robotised production lines (Javelosa and Houser, 2017). The company invested in 60 robot arms operating across 10 production lines around the clock.

This process of automation of production led to a staggering 250% increase in productivity and a significant 80% drop in defects in products. In the past, Changying Precision Technology Company's factory employed 650 workers engaged in different operations related to the production of mobile phones (Javelosa and Houser, 2017).

Following this initial investment in the automation of production, only 60 out of the 650 workers are still employed by the company. A team of three workers is assigned to check and monitor the production line, and the remaining manpower has a responsibility for monitoring computer control systems. According to Luo Weiqiang, General Manager at Changying Precision Technology Company, the number of individuals employed by the company could drop to just 20 (People's Daily Online, 2015): 'A robot arm can replace six to eight workers, now there are 60 workers and the number will be reduced to 20 in the future.'

Future perspectives

A World Economic Forum Agenda article argued that robots have been taking our jobs for 50 years, but there is a logical reason as to why we should be worried about the future influence of automation and robotics on the future world of work (Morgan, 2017). Jeff Morgan, a manufacturing research engineer at Trinity College Dublin, contends that Industry 4.0 will contribute to the production of smarter robots that are capable of adapting to different tasks with little or no input from the human workforce.

This opportunity in the future of robotics is particularly relevant to the manufacturing sector, such as the Chinese mobile company discussed above, with its challenge to re-skill and up-skill the manpower.

According to Morgan, robots have been around for over 50 years but they evolve to assume more functions and roles that were previously fulfilled by the human workforce (Morgan, 2017):

> In the manufacturing industry, where robots have arguably made the most headway of any sector, this will mean a dramatic shift from centralised to decentralised collaborative production. Traditional robots focused on single, fixed, high-speed operations and requiring a highly-skilled human workforce to operate and maintain them. Industry 4.0 machines are flexible, collaborative and can operate more independently, which ultimately removes the need for a highly-skilled workforce.

(Continued)

(Continued)

China is a good example of the potential implications of Industry 4.0 adoption and robotics on a large scale due to the country's over-reliance on its booming manufacturing sector. The latter offers a high degree of automation opportunities once the initial robotics and automation investment is returned.

In the short to medium term, China is therefore likely to face challenges as to how to position its 770 million-strong workforce, which is the largest in the world. A range of up-skilling and re-skilling interventions are likely to be needed, alongside diversifying the economy with other sectors in the knowledge economy or advanced services that require higher levels of skills that are not currently automatable.

Further case study resources

Javelosa, J. and Houser, K. (2017). *This company replaced 90% of its workforce with machines: Here's what happened.* Available at: www.weforum.org/agenda/2017/02/after-replacing-90-of-employees-with-robots-this-companys-productivity-soared [Accessed 4 April 2018].

Morgan, J. (2017). *Robots have been taking our jobs for 50 years, so why are we worried now?* Available at: www.weforum.org/agenda/2017/07/robots-have-been-taking-our-jobs-for-50-years-so-why-are-we-worried-now [Accessed 4 April 2018].

People's Daily Online (2015). *First unmanned factory takes shape in Dongguan City.* Available at: http://en.people.cn/n/2015/0715/c90000-8920747.html [Accessed 4 April 2018].

REFLECTIVE EXERCISE

WEF world of work video quiz

In a Davos 2017 Issue Briefing video (at www.youtube.com/watch?v=QP8N3vMDq2I) focused on jobs and the 4IR, Erik Brynjolfsson (director, MIT Initiative on the Digital Economy, MIT – Sloan School of Management, USA) and Suzanne Fortier (principal and vice chancellor, McGill University, Canada) discuss the implications of advancements in technology and the 4IR on the world of work. They discuss how individuals and organisations should adapt to manage this transition in global labour markets influenced by technology and the 4IR and bring into the spotlight their perspective on where things will be heading in the next 3–5 years and in the longer term.

Reflective exercise: Having watched the 'Davos 2017 Issue Briefing: Jobs and the Fourth Industrial Revolution' video on YouTube, write a 500-word essay, or discuss with other students from your course, the implications of technology and the 4IR on the future world of work by attempting to answer the following questions.

Question	Response
1: What are the implications for the future workforce and workplace as a result of recent advances in technology and the 4IR?	
2: What would be some of the skills, attributes and competencies projected to be in high demand, due to the influence of the 4IR on the world of work?	
3: What would be some of the challenges and opportunities for labour markets in advanced and emerging economies brought about by advances in technology and the 4IR?	

Further reading and resources

McKinsey Global Institute (2017). *Jobs lost, jobs gained: Workforce transitions in a time of automation.* Available at: www.mckinsey.com/mgi/overview/2017-in-review/automation-and-the-future-of-work/jobs-lost-jobs-gained-workforce-transitions-in-a-time-of-automation [Accessed 3 February 2018].

World Economic Forum (WEF) (2016). *The future of jobs.* Available at: http://reports.weforum.org/future-of-jobs-2016 [Accessed 3 February 2018].

World Economic Forum (2018). *Eight futures of work: Scenarios and their implications.* Available at: www.weforum.org/whitepapers/eight-futures-of-work-scenarios-and-their-implications [Accessed 6 February 2018].

World Economic Forum (2018). *Meet the leader with Jack Ma.* Video. Available at: www.youtube.com/watch?v=4zzVjonyHcQ [Accessed 6 February 2018].

World Economic Forum (2018). *Putting jobs out of work.* Video. Available at: www.weforum.org/events/world-economic-forum-annual-meeting-2018/sessions/a0Wb000000AIH6EEAV [Accessed 6 February 2018].

REFERENCES

Aronowitz, S. and DiFazio, W. (1994). *The jobless future: Sci-tech and the dogma of work.* Minneapolis, MN: University of Minnesota Press.

Aurik, J. (2017). *The rise of the machines: Lessons from history on how to adapt.* Available at: www.weforum.org/agenda/2017/01/the-rise-of-the-machines-lessons-from-history-on-how-to-adapt [Accessed 3 February 2018].

Bregman, R. (2017). *A growing number of people think their job is useless: Time to rethink the meaning of work.* Available at: www.weforum.org/agenda/2017/04/why-its-time-to-rethink-the-meaning-of-work [Accessed 6 February 2018].

Cambridge Medical Robots (CMR) (2018). *Versius surgical robotic system.* Available at: https://cmedrobotics.com/versius [Accessed 5 February 2018].

Citi (2016). *Technology at Work v2.0: The future is not what it used to be.* Citi/Oxford Martin School. Available at: www.oxfordmartin.ox.ac.uk/downloads/reports/Citi_GPS_Technology_Work_2.pdf [Accessed 5 February 2018].

Collier, D. A. (1983). The service sector revolution: The automation of services. *Long Range Planning*, 16(6), 10–20.

Cox, A. (2018). *AI will be a big part of our future – but what does that mean for businesses searching for talent?* Available at: www.hays.co.uk/blog/AI-will-be-a-big-part-of-our-future/index.htm [Accessed 6 February 2018].

Curry, R. (2018). *NHS publishes £300m contract for new surgery robots.* Available at: www.telegraph.co.uk/business/2018/01/27/nhs-publishes-300m-contract-new-surgery-robots [Accessed 5 February 2018].

Ellis, R. (2017). *UK scientists create world's smallest surgical robot to start a hospital revolution.* Available at: www.theguardian.com/society/2017/aug/19/worlds-smallest-surgical-robot-versius-keyhole-hospital-revolution [Accessed 5 February 2018].

Financial Times (2018a). *Our robot era demands a different approach to retraining.* Available at: www.ft.com/content/c4bde676-0027-11e8-9650-9c0ad2d7c5b5 [Accessed 30 January 2018].

Financial Times (2018b). *Definition of artificial intelligence.* Available at: http://lexicon.ft.com/Term?term=artificial-intelligence [Accessed 3 February 2018].

Flashman, G. (2018). *Jack Ma on the IQ of love – and other top quotes from his Davos interview.* Available at: www.weforum.org/agenda/2018/01/jack-ma-davos-top-quotes/ [Accessed 6 February 2018].

Galeon, D. and Marquart, S. (2016). *Finland isn't alone in trialling a universal basic income, Canada is trying it as well.* Available at: www.weforum.org/agenda/2016/11/can-a-universal-basic-income-work-another-country-is-giving-it-a-go [Accessed 6 February 2018].

Gershgorn, D. (2017). *Worried about AI taking your job? It's already happening in Japan.* Available at: www.weforum.org/agenda/2017/01/worried-about-ai-taking-your-job-its-already-happening-in-japan?utm_content=bufferb5b03&utm_medium=social&utm_source=twitter.com&utm_campaign=buffer [Accessed 5 February 2018].

Healy, J., Nicholson, D. and Parker, J. (2017). Guest editors' introduction: technological disruption and the future of employment relations. *Labour & Industry: A Journal of the Social and Economic Relations of Work,* 27(3): 157–64.

Johansson, J. (2017). *Challenges and opportunities in digitalized work and management: Case study 8.* Västerås: Mälardalen University Sweden.

Laycock, K. (2017). *Automation in the NHS.* Available at: www.reform.uk/reformer/automation-in-the-nhs [Accessed 5 February 2018].

McKinsey Global Institute (2017a). *A future that works: Automation, employment and productivity.* Available at: www.mckinsey.com/~/media/McKinsey/Global%20Themes/Digital%20Disruption/Harnessing%20automation%20for%20a%20future%20that%20works/MGI-A-future-that-works_Executive-summary.ashx [Accessed 3 February 2018].

McKinsey Global Institute (2017b). *Jobs lost, jobs gained: Workforce transitions in a time of automation.* Available at: www.mckinsey.com/~/media/McKinsey/Global%20Themes/Future%20of%20Organizations/What%20the%20future%20of%20work%20will%20mean%20for%20jobs%20skills%20and%20wages/MGI-Jobs-Lost-Jobs-Gained-Report-December-6-2017.ashx [Accessed 3 February 2018].

Massachusetts Institute of Technology (MIT) (2015). *Marvin Minsky, 'father of artificial intelligence', dies at 88.* Available at: http://news.mit.edu/2016/marvin-minsky-obituary-0125 [Accessed 3 February 2018].

Nilsson, N. J. (2010). *The quest for artificial intelligence: A history of ideas and achievements.* Cambridge: Cambridge University Press.

Powers, A. (2017). *The most important skill in the age of artificial intelligence (AI).* Available at: www.forbes.com/sites/annapowers/2017/12/31/the-most-important-skill-in-the-age-of-artificial-intelligence-ai/#7634f70b3264 [Accessed 6 February 2018].

PricewaterhouseCoopers (PwC) (2017). *Workforce of the future: The competing forces shaping 2030.* Available at: www.pwc.com/gx/en/services/people-organisation/workforce-of-the-future/workforce-of-the-future-the-competing-forces-shaping-2030-pwc.pdf [Accessed 6 February 2018].

Reform UK (2017). *Work in progress: Towards a leaner, smarter public-sector workforce.* Available at: www.reform.uk/wp-content/uploads/2017/02/Work-in-progress-Reform-report.pdf [Accessed 5 February 2018].

Rifkin, J. (1995). *The end of work: The decline of the global workforce and the dawn of the post-market era.* London: Penguin Books.

Schwab, C. (2016). *The Fourth Industrial Revolution: What it means, how to respond.* Available at: www.weforum.org/agenda/2016/01/the-fourth-industrial-revolution-what-it-means-and-how-to-respond [Accessed 3 February 2018].

Sharma, P. (2017). *What the Fourth Industrial Revolution means for India.* Available at: www.weforum.org/agenda/2017/10/kranti-nation-india-and-the-fourth-industrial-revolution [Accessed 6 February 2018].

Smith, I. (2017). *The difference between artificial intelligence and intelligent automation.* Available at: https://realbusiness.co.uk/tech-and-innovation/2017/06/20/difference-artificial-intelligence-intelligent-automation [Accessed 3 February 2018].

Stone, P., Brooks, R., Brynjolfsson, E., Calo, R., Etzioni, O., Hager, G., et al. (2016). *Artificial intelligence and life in 2030: One hundred year study on Cox artificial intelligence.* Available at: http://ai100.stanford.edu/2016-report [Accessed 5 February 2018].

Williams-Grut, O. (2016). *3 of the world's 10 largest employers are now replacing their workers with robots.* Available at: http://uk.businessinsider.com/clsa-wef-and-citi-on-the-future-of-robots-and-ai-in-the-workforce-2016-6 [Accessed 5 February 2018].

World Economic Forum (WEF) (2016). *The future of jobs.* Available at: http://reports.weforum.org/future-of-jobs-2016 [Accessed 3 February 2018].

World Economic Forum (WEF) (2018). *AI will be bigger than electricity or fire – Google CEO.* Available at: www.weforum.org/agenda/2018/01/google-ceo-ai-will-be-bigger-than-electricity-or-fire [Accessed 5 February 2018].

World Economic Forum (WEF) and Boston Consulting Group (BCG) (2018). *Towards a reskilling revolution: A future of jobs for all.* Available at: www3.weforum.org/docs/WEF_FOW_Reskilling_Revolution.pdf [Accessed 6 February 2018].

PART II

Organisations as Hubs
for Global Talent

5
ORGANISATIONAL FOUNDATIONS FOR GLOBAL TALENT

Chapter contents

From people to talent management

- Organisations and people management
- Functional organisations versus people organisations

Talent in organisational vision and mission

- Vision and mission in organisations
- The importance of developing a talent-driven vision and mission
- Embedding talent in people and HR strategy
- The place of global talent in shaping future organisational strategies

Promoting an organisational culture informed by global talent

- Organisational culture and global talent
- The importance of a supportive environment for global talent
- Enablers of a talent-driven organisational culture

Global talent as a competitive advantage in organisations

- The role of talent in shaping competitive organisations
- Talent as a 'currency' for organisational competitiveness

Case study 5.1: Sony Japan

Organisational vision, mission and culture shaped by a global talent quiz

Learning objectives

After reading this chapter, you will be able to:

- understand the role of developing a talent-driven organisational vision and mission
- reflect on the importance of developing an organisational culture shaped by global talent
- gain insights into the role of global talent as a source of competitive advantage in organisations.

FROM PEOPLE TO TALENT MANAGEMENT

Organisations and people management

Talent management is often considered to be a subset of the human resource or organisational development function of an organisation and as such its discussion in management texts can often be relegated to the section on people or human resource management. Talent management is the central purpose of this book and that placement continues as we shift our focus to people management strategies that support the development and management of talent in organisations.

Our contention is that global talent ought to be at the heart of the organisation's foundations, and only then can it be a source of competitive advantage; anything less than that is merely people management, not talent management. What we frame as talent management, therefore, as per Figure 5.1, is perhaps, one may argue, only possible at the outset of an organisation's life but we will, through our discussion in this chapter, illustrate that while talent management may be more natural for a start-up or SME, even large corporates can renew themselves and evolve as global talent-oriented organisations. The typical five-year strategic and business planning cycles are natural avenues for this. For forward-thinking organisations, it is common to be looking at 10–20 year horizons, but we will argue that even then the integration of global talent into their fabric is not as elusive as it may seem.

Functional organisations versus people organisations

In determining the talent orientation it is important for organisations to place their people as opposed to its functions at its core. Figure 5.1 provides a visualisation of such a paradigm shift.

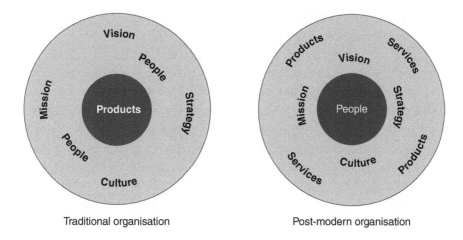

Figure 5.1   Traditional organisations versus post-modern organisations

The traditional organisation often features a product, service or experience at its organisational core while its vision, mission, culture and people or human capital tend to inhabit a secondary place or consideration (Figure 5.1). The post-modern organisation, we argue, would place talent at its heart followed by its products, services or experiences.

So, for us the left side of Figure 5.1 represents what we would call a 'functions-oriented organisation' with the image on the right representing a people organisation, where people are at the heart of what the central organisational purpose is. Typically, small and medium-sized enterprises (SMEs) and start-up ventures start off as people-centred organisations, often transitioning as they grow to be more product or functions centric.

For the purposes of this chapter, we use people organisations and talent-driven organisations interchangeably. What we mean by both, broadly, is that the organisation has established a vision, mission, strategy and culture that is shaped by the centrality of its people, its global talent.

TALENT IN ORGANISATIONAL VISION AND MISSION
Vision and mission in organisations

Developing a vision and a mission that are informed by global talent is an essential first step for organisations in building its talent base. Crafting and implementing a compelling and forward-thinking vision and mission serve to support the very purpose of such an organisation and its strategic objectives.

An organisational vision serves to provide insight into the future state of organisations, one that clarifies a future positioning and the development trajectory to go with it. This is often captured by organisations in a statement of their vision which, according to the Society for Human Resource Management, serves as a crucial guiding and motivational framework for organisations and their employees (SHRM, 2018): 'An effective vision statement is inspirational and aspirational. It creates a mental image of the future state that the organization wishes to achieve. A vision statement should challenge and inspire employees.'

The vision statement of a talent-driven organisation is also inspirational and provides answers to questions that focus on the interplay between talent contribution and organisational growth and success. Some of these questions may include 'What would our talent-driven organisation look like 10 years from now?' and 'How will our focus on talent orientation make us industry leaders by 2030?'

Building on this, an organisational mission and a statement of its mission serve to communicate the purpose and direction of an organisation to employees, customers, vendors and other stakeholders. Business and recruitment consultant, Bridget Miller, highlights that the mission statement serves to put the vision of an organisation into practice (Miller, 2014):

> Like the vision, the mission also tells everyone the organisation's purpose – what does the organisation exist to do? What are the objectives? It goes beyond the vision, however, by making a clearer delineation of company goals and how the vision will be accomplished.

A talent-driven mission statement in people organisations provides an insight into why the organisation exists and how it delivers the products, services and experiences through the global talent it employs and anticipates employing in the future.

What would talent-driven vision and mission statements of organisations convey in practice? Table 5.1 gives you an insight into a selection of vision and mission statements that position talent at the core of some well-known organisations.

What can we learn from these statements? Table 5.2 suggests that these organisations often craft their people-driven vision and mission through statements that promote organisational values, impact and goals related to talent. But, even more importantly, talent are often seen as carriers of their core purpose and objectives.

Developing an organisational vision and mission is a complex process that lays the foundations of the organisation and runs alongside its future identity development and evolution. It tackles the central questions of 'why' and 'what' – 'Why is this organisation necessary?' and 'What does it stand for?'. For a people-centric organisation, crafting a talent-first vision and mission is integral to the foundations of the organisation, and delivering an employee value proposition is a core design principle for such organisations, not an afterthought.

Table 5.1   Global talent-driven organisational vision and mission statements

Organisation (profile)	Sector	Vision and mission statements
Tesla, the world's largest producer of electric cars	Private	'Tesla's mission is to accelerate the world's transition to sustainable energy. We hire the world's best and brightest people to help make this future a reality.' (Tesla, 2018)
Ministry of Trade and Industry, Singapore	Public	'A leading global city of enterprise and talent, a vibrant nation of innovation and opportunity.' 'Our vision is for Singapore to be a leading global city with a dynamic economy, world-class enterprises and innovative and productive SMEs. Singapore will offer a conducive environment for entrepreneurs and enterprises to tap its diverse opportunities, and provide good jobs which are attractive to talent at all levels.' (Ministry of Trade and Industry, Singapore, 2018)
WPP, world's largest communication services group	Private	'WPP exists: To develop and manage talent; to apply that talent, throughout the world, for the benefit of clients; to do so in partnership; to do so with profit.' (WPP, 2018)
County of San Mateo, CA, HR Department	Public	'Through strategic partnerships and collaboration, the Human Resources Department recruits, develops and retains a high performing and diverse workforce and fosters a healthy, safe, and productive work environment for employees, their families, departments, and the public in order to maximize individual and organizational potential and position San Mateo County as an employer of choice.' (County of San Mateo, 2018)
Facebook	Private	'People first. That's how we see it at Facebook. Our people are all part of one large family who embrace each other's authentic selves. We hire the right people for the job and help them find a team where they can make the biggest impact.' (Facebook, 2018)

(Continued)

Table 5.1   (Continued)

Organisation (profile)	Sector	Vision and mission statements
University of Nottingham	Public	'Our vision is to: Enable and drive the delivery of the University plan through people; Attract and develop a highly talented and motivated international workforce; Create a culture in which our people thrive.' (University of Nottingham, 2018)
Astra Zeneca, one of the world's largest pharmaceutical companies	Private	'We are focused on developing a talented, science-led and patient-focused workforce that is committed to the pursuit of our purpose and values, and that is agile and high-performing. Our vision of a great place to work is one in which all our employees are engaged and inspired by a clear shared purpose and a compelling strategy; where they are encouraged to perform and develop to their full potential; and where they are supported by the right organisational design, culture, technology and processes.' (Astra Zeneca, 2015)
GISDA, youth charity headquartered in the UK	Non-profit	'GISDA is a people-led organisation which values its staff, trustees and stakeholders. We believe that people are the best asset of any organisation. Our staff and trustees are passionate about supporting the young people we work with and aim to change their lives for the better.' (GISDA, 2018)

The importance of developing a talent-driven vision and mission

Why is an organisational vision and mission that is talent centric as important? For Whitney Ohmer, a talent and organisational development consultant, the development of a talent vision is a powerful tool that helps lead and guide people-driven organisations and their employees (Ohmer, 2017). A well-crafted vision and mission for global talent, according to Ohmer, keeps organisations focused on matters that are really important to them, such as the ability to deliver value, develop a product or create an impact for people, communities and other organisations.

Organisations and employees, alongside policy, business and civic communities outside these organisations all benefit from a shaping of an organisational core that is informed by global talent.

For people-led organisations, the importance of developing vision and mission statements that are informed by global talent is paramount. People are a key source of competitive advantage for organisations. A vision and mission for global talent provide a guiding framework for CEOs, talent managers and employees in developing a talent-driven culture.

Developing a vision and mission that are shaped by global talent also provides recognition of the role and importance of this talent at an organisational level. This process helps people-led organisations focus on what matters so that they do not lose sight of the innovation, transformation and growth opportunities provided by talent in their teams and departments.

Visions and missions that have been informed by global talent are also important for current and prospective employees in organisations. They guide the day-to-day activities of employees and demonstrate the organisation's values and its position on talent to prospective recruits who may well be attracted to an organisation's values and culture.

They are also important for outside organisations. Policy, business and civic communities, which may not be directly related to these organisations, also benefit from having access to an organisation's vision and mission that are informed by global talent.

Individual and collective efforts that ultimately lead to the development of a global talent driven organisation can elevate the role of people and shape the identity of that organisation. The development and execution of a talent-driven organisational vision and mission nevertheless depends on some key enablers, which we now go on to discuss in detail.

Embedding talent in people and HR strategy

The development and implementation of a vision and mission in organisations that are informed by global talent will depend on the integration of key organisational elements, building blocks or enablers. They include resources, projects, planning and organisational culture at large.

A people strategy that is at the heart of organisational business strategy has the potential to shape talent-driven organisations, according to Julia Howes, principal at Mercer – the world's largest human resources consulting firm. Howes highlights that when we are in the midst of the 4th Industrial Revolution, the need for a shift from business strategy to people strategy will be greater than ever before (Mercer, 2017):

> Forward-thinking leadership teams are creating their people strategy as an integral part of their strategic business planning process, no longer left to HR to determine in isolation. These organisations shape their plans to meet their workforce needs, knowing that their most important competitive advantage is the ability to attract and retain the right people.

A people strategy, according to Andrew Mayo, professor of Human Capital Management is an essential component of business and strategic planning that has the potential to deliver real value to organisations (Mayo, 2009).

Developing a people strategy is also central to the crafting and promotion of a culture that has been informed by global talent in organisations. We discuss the interplay between people strategy and organisational culture for global talent later in this chapter. Alongside a people strategy that is aligned with the core business strategy of the organisation, leadership is a key enabler for global talent centricity in organisations.

Notable authors in the field of global talent strategy and management, such as Douglas Ready from MIT's Sloan School of Management, Linda Hill, Professor of Business Administration at Harvard Business School, and Robert Thomas, Managing Director of Accenture Strategy, all highlight that the development and implementation of a vision and mission that are informed by global talent depend on leadership. Highly engaged leadership, according to them, helps build a game-changing talent strategy – a conclusion that has been drawn from their study into BlackRock, the world's largest asset management firm (*Harvard Business Review*, 2014).

Well-known talent practitioner and academic Professor Paul Turner, who has held a number of professorial positions at universities in Leeds, Birmingham, Nottingham and Cambridge and is former HR director at Lloyds Bank, provides a similar perspective on the importance of leadership. Turner compellingly proposes the deployment of talent management and leadership to achieve competitive advantage in organisations in his book, written with Danny Kalman, *Make Your People Before You Make Your Products* (Turner and Kalman, 2014).

Together with activating these enables the development of a people strategy probably remains by far the most widely adopted approach to supporting a talent-driven vision and mission in practice. Through an industry insight, we put into the spotlight Mercer's 10 questions, which organisations and their leadership teams can critically reflect on in order to develop their people strategies. You, as either global talent yourself or someone who manages talent, should be able to critically reflect on these questions, which seek to place people at the heart of the business.

INDUSTRY INSIGHT

Mercer's 10 questions for future-proofing talent-driven organisations

1. Across value chains within your business, how are changes in technology and business models likely to affect work styles, jobs and skills?
2. What is the gap between current capabilities and job types, and those of the future? Which will disappear? Which will appear? Which will change?
3. Which roles are strategic and core to the business? Which are candidates for non-traditional work forms such as automation?
4. Which skills do people need that they do not have today? What is your plan for up-skilling and re-skilling them?
5. How well does your current learning approach meet future content and delivery needs, and what role does leadership play?
6. In which areas is it sensible and desirable for work to be done 'outside' your physical or legal borders? Where are emerging talent pools for these kinds of task located? Who are they?
7. What characteristics do future leaders need to display? What is the desired mix of technical and behavioural skills in your leaders?
8. How do you cultivate the right employer value proposition (EVP) for your people? What is the right mix of reward and non-reward benefits (such as flexible working, health benefits and competitive pensions) that will attract, motivate and retain different talent segments?
9. Is your culture driving the right behaviours and do you have the right culture to manage the changes ahead?
10. How do you ensure people can thrive at work? Are they enabled to excel in their work and their career? Are they healthy, energised and productive?

The place of global talent in shaping future organisational strategies

The industry insight by Mercer highlights a recent trend in organisations to shift to people and social capital-centric organisational strategies. So, where is the place of global talent in shaping the future of organisational planning and strategising? There is evidence from the world of business and practice to suggest that talent is firmly embedded in the organisational planning and strategising of the future. In fact, in Fortune 500 organisations and other businesses, total human capital-related investments now account for as much as 70% of all operating expenses and many of those organisations have taken steps to align talent with their business strategy (Korn Ferry Institute, 2014).

People-centric strategies are important as they provide a competitive advantage to organisations through talent. The contribution of talent in the form of knowledge, expertise and strategic human capabilities provides a platform for these organisations to grow, innovate and improve their standing in the highly competitive global marketplace.

The opportunities provided by people strategies in organisations, coupled with the complexity and uncertainty of an organisational environment, require new ways of thinking in shaping organisational policy and practice that are targeted at people, not products, services or experiences. It is people, human capital or talent that go on to create, innovate and deliver these products, services and experiences in organisations.

The development of a people strategy that is informed and guided by a vision and mission for talent development and management contributes to the shaping of an organisational culture that is informed by global talent, and we discuss this in the next section of this chapter.

PROMOTING AN ORGANISATIONAL CULTURE INFORMED BY GLOBAL TALENT
Organisational culture and global talent

We discussed the role of crafting and implementing a vision and mission in organisations, which is supported by a people strategy. The penetration, success and impact of this strategy on individuals, teams and organisations at large, nevertheless, depends on the development of an enabling organisational culture in which talent can thrive.

'Culture is the DNA of the company', said Rachel McCarthy, Senior Vice President of Talent at JetBlue – a company that has been voted among the top 25 best places to work in the USA (Indeed, 2017). JetBlue's people-first culture is key to the company's success. Values such as equality, diversity, caring, integrity, passion and fun have guided the company for the past 17 years and this set of values embodies the organisational culture and demonstrates what the company stands for. So, if we apply Rachel McCarthy's statement to talent-driven organisations, we may well argue that a culture that is informed by global talent is the DNA of people-led companies.

The development of this people-led organisational DNA and, indeed, the promotion of a culture shaped by global talent implies that the organisation embeds and embodies talent development and management in all its activities and creates environments in which people thrive.

The importance of a supportive environment for global talent

The development of an enabling, diverse, inclusive, collaborative culture for global talent to thrive in is often achieved through organisational policies and good practice. Organisational culture that puts people first is supported by a range of enablers, values and other factors at play to support the vision, mission and objectives of people-driven organisations.

Tesla, the largest producer of electric cars, has a talent-driven organisational policy whose focus is on openness and inclusivity. Global talent define these as key enablers of a flourishing organisational culture (Tesla, 2018):

> At Tesla, we're solving the world's most important problems with talented individuals who share our passion to change the world. Our culture is fast-paced, energetic and innovative. Headquartered in the San Francisco Bay Area with office locations around the world, we work to build an inclusive environment in which everyone, regardless of gender, race, religion, age, or background, can do their best work.

Tesla's example provides an insight into features of an organisational culture underpinned by global talent, such as inclusivity and diversity, which value the contribution of talent that is not bound by gender, age or cultural stereotyping. There are other indicators or evidence to suggest that an organisation has shaped a culture that puts people first – these include the establishment of a level playing field and embedding a collaborative framework for talent to deliver value and impact for organisations.

Mike Hughes, President of Schneider Electric, UK and Ireland, highlights the importance of developing a level playing field for talent in the organisation that is an inseparable part of its people-led culture in the organisation (Schneider, 2018):

> As a company that puts diversity and inclusion at the centre of everything we do, we are committed to building a workplace that provides equal opportunities to everyone and to ensuring that all employees feel uniquely valued and safe to contribute at their very best.

Schneider Electric's approach has been particularly targeting the provision of an equitable field for female global talent in the workforce and workplace through collaborative and developmental initiatives that include women leaders' events, gender workshops for leaders, women in leadership development programmes, alongside taking action to reduce the gender pay gap (Schneider, 2018).

Another insight from practice into organisational drivers that promote a talent centric culture involves British Petroleum (BP), a multinational oil and gas company that has established specific lesbian, gay, bisexual and transgender (LGBT) policies and practices in the organisation. They enable global talent with diverse sexual identities and orientations to thrive in the organisation, strengthen their contribution and realise their full potential (BP, 2018):

> At BP, we believe progression should always be based on ability. Which is why we promote a positive environment where everyone can deliver their best regardless of their sexual orientation. We're very proud to be a business where you can be yourself.

In supporting the success of LGBT talent, BP has an established network of LGBT partnerships which support employees with diverse sexual identities and orientations. BP Pride and the appointment of a Pride Chair at BP are some of the initiatives run by the organisation in its efforts to establish an inclusive and valuing corporate culture for its talent (BP, 2018).

We can see that organisations are adapting their culture to reflect the diversity of the global talent pipeline, irrespective of or notwithstanding gender, race and sexual orientation. Organisational culture which is talent-driven also aims to align with the variety of demographic talent groups, such as millennials and over-65s.

In Part 1 of this text, we discussed the millennial generation, the new age individuals. In this second part of the text, we discuss the new age organisation or the people organisation that would need to adapt to millennials. The increasing proportion of the millennial workforce, together with technological developments in the world of work, has neccessitated the activation of new cultural enablers for embracing all talent in millenials.

Enablers of a talent-driven organisational culture

These enablers include features of the gig economy such as flexi work, as we discussed in Chapter 2, alongside the introduction of shorter working weeks. For example, these interventions support talent wellbeing, provide non-full-time employees with access to the job market and improve the productivity and value of this talent to organisations.

An example of an organisational culture that has been shaped by global talent and aligned with the millennial mindset to offer opportunities such as flexi work and fewer hours spent at work, is British Telecom's (BT) BT Workstyle project. At the time of the launch of this project, back in 2007, BT had over 70,000 flexible workers, from senior managers to contact centre staff. Sir Christopher Bland, the former chairman of BT Group, highlighted the growth of flexible working practices in the organisation and the benefits of these practices (BT, 2007):

> At BT, flexible working is business as usual. Already seven out of 10 people work flexibly and nearly 10% are home-based. It has saved the company millions in terms of increased productivity and cut costs. It has also motivated our people and released more potential.

In 2018, the company is still committed to its flexi-work policy and practice in supporting a more enabling talent culture. BT's case demonstrates how the flexi-work enabler helps improve the productivity and wellbeing of its predominantly millennial workforce.

Evidence from practice also exists to highlight the inclusion of another demographic in people organisations and their culture shaped by global talent – that of the rising proportion of over-65s in the workforce, and organisations in Japan serve as an apt example of this. Japanese manufacturing company, Isoda, has championed the inclusion of talent over the age of 65 in the workforce. The company has created a culture that values the contribution, expertise and knowledge that the senior workforce can bring to the workplace (*Financial Times*, 2016), which we discuss in detail in an industry insight.

INDUSTRY INSIGHT

Isoda's approach to developing an inclusive organisational culture for talent aged over 65

Isoda Metal, which was founded in 1905, is adapting its organisational culture to Japan's ageing society. A decade ago, the Tokyo-based company established practices to enable skilled workers to stay in employment past the retirement age of 65.

Isoda supplies parts for ships and other watercraft, including Self Defence Force submarines and Japanese coastguard patrol vessels. Maintaining the quality of production

(Continued)

(Continued)

is a top priority for the company. Isoda's president, Daisuke Hattori, highlighted that his company began offering post-retirement employment opportunities as he felt its skilled mechanics and other workers over the age of 65 are a valuable asset for the company who also play a vital role in training millennials and other, younger members of the company's workforce (FT, 2016): 'Many experienced mechanics in the past thought younger workers should learn by watching their seniors, rather than being taught. Now we are asking veteran workers to share their techniques.'

The company provides one-year contracts for workers who are aged 65 or older. As a result of this positive company culture change towards recognising talent from different generations, employees in their 60s to 80s now make up a quarter of the workforce.

These examples highlight the contribution of different generations in the workforce and show how some forward-looking organisations have adapted their culture to diversify their pool of global talent.

These examples illustrate that organisations must recognise the importance of establishing a range of enablers to support their transition from a product- to a talent-centred organisation.

Central to this is the notion of purpose. People organisations are driven by a purpose, not simply a product or a service; they are purpose-driven or value-led organisations. Purpose, according to the global consultancy firm Ernst & Young, is becoming increasingly important in defining business success and there is a growing expectation for organisations to measure their success beyond conventional outputs such as profits and products (Ernst & Young, 2016). Purpose puts an emphasis on the 'why' of organisations (Sinek, 2018), which often know 'what' they are doing in terms of the development of a product or service and 'how' they are doing it, yet very few of them define *why* they do what they do (Figure 5.2).

As Amanda Chua, Talent Accelerator Programme Manager at Leaderonomics, notes (2017), 'by linking purpose-driven organisations with talent in these organisations, questions that often come to employees' minds include: Why is my work important? What impact am I making? Am I making a difference in the world, to the environment, or to people? Do I believe in the company mission and values? How is my company living out its organisational mission and values?'

A clearly defined purpose allows people-orientated organisations to support the development and fulfilment of its people, to help them realise their potential, to make a fuller

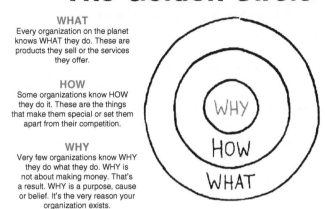

WHAT
Every organization on the planet knows WHAT they do. These are products they sell or the services they offer.

HOW
Some organizations know HOW they do it. These are the things that make them special or set them apart from their competition.

WHY
Very few organizations know WHY they do what they do. WHY is not about making money. That's a result. WHY is a purpose, cause or belief. It's the very reason your organization exists.

Figure 5.2   Purpose-driven organisations start with 'why'

(Source: Sinek, 2018)

impact on society through the work they do, to help grow and reinvent the organisation, and to amplify its impact on the wider economy, environment and society.

This discussion leads us to conclude that modern-day organisations need to strike a balance between people, purpose and profit in the process of shaping their vision, mission, strategy and culture if they are to be successful in luring global talent which are increasingly being seen as a competitive advantage for organisations.

GLOBAL TALENT AS A COMPETITIVE ADVANTAGE IN ORGANISATIONS

The role of talent in shaping competitive organisations

In most cases, the shift from a functional to a people organisation and the development of a vision, mission, strategy and culture that are informed by global talent serve a key purpose for organisations – to provide a competitive advantage. This competitive advantage can materialise through the development of a new product or service, increased productivity and revenue or an expanded global footprint that enables the organisation to better position itself in a competitive global market for products and services.

Rebecca O. Bagley, president and CEO of NorTech, highlights global talent as a source of competitive advantage in organisations as follows (Bagley, 2013):

There's nothing more crucial to the success of an organization than bringing the right people on board ... Recruiting and developing talent contributes to an organization's productivity and growth. Without talent, an organization can't transform. Without transformation, an organization can't grow.

Through their ability to innovate, advance and develop new products, services and experiences, global talent provide a competitive advantage for organisations amid a highly saturated global market and intense competition for talent globally.

In a similar vein, it has been argued that talent is the factor that strengthens an organisation's capacity to compete. Phil Cooper, Vice President, International Operations – EMEA and APAC Regions at Allegis Global Solutions, notes that the phrase 'people are a company's greatest asset', while being something of a cliché, now holds true more than ever (Cooper, 2016):

The workforce always has and always will be the deciding factor in whether a business fails or succeeds. From the boardroom down to the bottom level, it's the actions of people that determine profits and allow companies to establish a competitive advantage over their rivals.

In an influential study, Christopher A. Bartlett, Professor of Business Administration at Harvard Business School, and Sumantra Ghoshal, Professor of Strategic Leadership at London Business School, challenge the assumption that organisations are ready to embrace talent for a competitive advantage, despite many organisations claiming that people are their greatest asset (*MIT Sloan Management Review*, 2002). They conclude that the evolving focus of organisational strategy leans towards talent, where human and intellectual capital take over financial capital (Table 5.2).

Table 5.2   The evolving focus of strategy

	Competition for Products and Markets	Competition for Resources and Competencies	Competition for Talent and Dreams
Strategic Objective	**Defensible product–market positions**	**Sustainable competitive advantage**	**Continuous self-renewal**
Major Tools, Perspectives	• Industry analysis; competitor analysis • Market segmentation and positioning • Strategic planning	• Core competencies • Resource-based strategy • Networked organisation	• Vision and values • Flexibility and innovation • Frontline entrepreneurship and experimentation
Key Strategic Resource	Financial capital	Organisational capability	Human and intellectual capital

(Source: *MIT Sloan Management Review*, 2012)

Some 13 years later, Thomas H. Davenport and Julia Kirby concluded in a *Harvard Business Review* article that even technological developments, such as automation and robots, will not replace people as a source of competitive advantage in organisations (*Harvard Business Review*, 2015). Talent is in possession of some unique human capabilities such as emotional intelligence. Such capabilities are expected to keep the demand for global talent high, for the foreseeable future.

A new study by Sage highlights the role of talent in building people organisations to drive growth in the functions and operations of organisations. The study concluded that high-growth companies are people companies that enable and harness the power of their global talent (Sage, 2017):

> Our survey shows that these [fast growth] companies are highly likely to be evolving 'people companies', organizations that recognise the value of their people and see them as more than just a replaceable resource or human capital.

This research affirms that there is a correlation between global talent and organisational success. It is clear that global talent are seen as a source of competitive advantage, but what is meant by competitive advantage in an organisational context? The role of talent in the creation of value, innovation, growth and impact within organisations is an embodiment of that competitive advantage.

Talent is increasingly the only source of competitive advantage because other sources and approaches adopted by organisations such as technology, infrastructure, architecture and strategy can be replicated, unlike the unique human capabilities, qualities and traits that contribute to the ultimate growth and success of organisations.

Talent as a 'currency' for organisational competitiveness

Talent is, therefore, becoming more than just an overrated and overused buzzword in the world of work; it is rapidly turning into a currency for organisations and it is a source of competitive advantage through the value, innovation, growth and impact that people with a global mindset, heartset and skillset deliver in organisations.

Lauren Dixon, an associate editor at Human Capital Media, argues:

> Talent, in fact, is the world's most valuable resource, one no enterprise can move forward without. And for organizations to continue creating new value for their customers, business leaders need to fully embrace this credo and take charge of it as the key to building a better future. (2016)

Hence, there is a need for the development and implementation of a vision and mission that are informed by global talent from an organisational perspective. We later discuss this from a policy perspective, too, in Part 3 of this text, where global talent are seen as a source of competitive advantage to cities, regions and countries through their economic, socio-cultural and demographic contribution.

Amid this context of the rising importance of people organisations, PwC predicted in their study 'Workforce of the Future: The Competing Forces Shaping 2030' that new roles related to people and talent will emerge to capitalise on this powerful, people-centric shift in organisational planning and strategising (PwC, 2017). Roles, as projected by PwC, will include the Chief People Officer (CPO) – a powerful and influential figure, sometimes known as the 'Head of People and Productivity' appointed to oversee this organisational transition from products to people.

Emerging roles in people organisations remind us that leadership and management of this talent are crucial for delivering a sustained competitive advantage to these organisations and to the individuals themselves. Factors at play here are the attraction, development and retention of global talent – themes that we will discuss in detail in the next chapter of this text, but before that we offer you an in-depth insight into Sony's approach to establishing an enabling culture for the development of global talent.

CASE STUDY 5.1

Sony Japan – establishing a company culture that enables the development of global talent

Introduction to the Sony Group

Sony Group is one of the largest producers of consumer electronics in the world. The Japan-based brand has products under the following segments: Mobile Communications, Game & Network Services, Imaging Products & Solutions, Home Entertainment & Sound, Semiconductors, Components, Pictures, Music, Financial Services, and All Other businesses.

The success of the company relies on its highly skilled talent. The total number of employees in the Sony Group as of 31 March 2017 was 128,400. The value of global talent has been recognised and promoted on a corporate level at the organisation, as nearly one-fifth of Sony Group's directors and business executives are non-Japanese nationals (Sony, 2017a).

The company promotes a culture that has been shaped by global talent through its approach to recruitment, fostering international talent mobility and the provision of global talent training and development opportunities. Through such initiatives, Sony Group provides a stimulating and enabling environment for its increasingly global workforce.

Sony's approach to the recruitment of global talent

The company has developed and adopted a global talent strategy to enable the recruitment of diverse employees worldwide, which is crucial to its international operations. As a company with sales, manufacturing and R&D based in a number of different countries, Sony has its focus on the attraction of talent that can meet national, regional and local needs.

The key focus in its global recruitment strategy is on the development and attraction of international students and global graduate talent from key source countries and through innovative programmes. Unique to Sony is its international approach to the recruitment of university graduates. Sony attracts graduate talent from other countries to work in Japan, aiming to secure talent to drive its global business.

Sony has been hiring global graduate talent for nearly two decades, for example using targeted recruitment initiatives aimed at undergraduate and postgraduate students from China and India. Recruitment in China began in 2000 and in India in 2007. In both of these countries, Sony continues to secure top-level talent with the cooperation of local group companies.

The Global Internship Program, established by Sony, enables university students to join the company's headquarters worldwide. Going forward, Sony's intention is to continue to hire new graduates and create an enabling environment with diverse developmental opportunities, which may well be seen as a response to the country's ageing population challenge.

The World Economic Forum's Agenda series suggests that Japan's population has shrunk by nearly 1 million in the past five years, noting the first ever decline since the country's census began in 1920. In order to thrive, the country's shrinking economy now has a higher dependency on global talent from other countries to drive growth.

Hence, going forward, the company is planning to conduct global recruitment and branding activities, seeking to attract a wide variety of top talent internationally.

(Continued)

(Continued)

Enabling global talent mobility within Sony Group companies worldwide

Employees at Sony Group have the opportunity to work and undertake assignments in companies of the Group across the world and, as such, to develop global careers and gain global understanding of business practices in countries other than their own (Sony, 2017b):

> Employees have the opportunity to be transferred between Sony Group companies outside Japan. The purpose of this arrangement is to leverage personnel on a global scale, accomplish the transfer of technology and knowledge, and initiate new businesses.

Sony has an established inclusive and collaborative workforce environment through having processes and practices in place that recognise workforce diversity and its strength, and that enable productive global talent mobility within Sony Group's companies established worldwide. Some examples of these processes and practices are as follows (Sony, 2017b):

1. To enhance the ease and efficiency of moving human resources around the world, the organisation appointed experts on global personnel policies and standards and formulated common Sony Group policies that respond to specific in-country needs and to a wide variety of overseas assignments.
2. Sony Group has also developed internal websites, HR and accounting-related systems and other bilingual applications to enable non-native Japanese speakers to work effectively within the company using English as the second official language in the workplace.
3. To facilitate the smooth transition of non-Japanese employees into the organisation, Sony Group established initiatives to enable its workforce to develop interpersonal networks. Sony initiated the Buddy Program in 2013, in which non-Japanese company talent are paired with their Japanese counterparts to teach each other their respective languages. This workforce learning and acculturation approach also enables international Sony Group employees to develop a deeper understanding of one another's culture and personal and business practice.

Providing global talent training and development opportunities

In Japan, Sony Group offers more than 300 employee training programmes, some of which offer an international focus and the opportunity for its talent to develop a global perspective on business, culture, the environment and other themes of global relevance. Sony

Group recognises its talent as its most important management asset and the growth of its workforce as a crucial aspect of its management foundation. This is an aspiration captured in its statement on talent training and development opportunities (Sony, 2018):

> As a company that does business in a variety of countries and regions, Sony recognizes the importance of cultivating future business leaders with a global perspective and diverse cultures. Accordingly, Sony is implementing initiatives aimed at fostering such employees and bringing their capabilities into full play.

In line with this statement, Sony Group undertakes a broad range of global talent development and recruitment programmes to enable its workforce to grow and gain an international exposure and perspective. The organisation's core efforts are channelled into the development and deployment of core global talent that are capable of excelling globally through pioneering initiatives such as Sony University.

Established in 2000 to promote the cross-border and cross-business cultivation of global business leaders, Sony University, which is located in Tokyo's Shinagawa district, offers short- and long-term talent development courses to provide developmental opportunities encapsulating the Sony spirit, business vision, management decision-making capabilities and networking.

Adopting the principles of an interactive and cross-cultural learning environment, Sony University features a variety of programmes for both senior leadership and junior employees. Examples include a seven-month module for prospective core leaders and a future junior management programme. Other developmental opportunities for Sony's global workforce include the company's Global Leadership programmes around the world. One such programme is the Global Challenge programme established by Sony Global Manufacturing and Operations Corporation (SGMO) (Sony, 2018).

SGMO has established its Global Challenge programme to enable its employees who have worked abroad to apply what they have learned after returning to Japan and, as such, contribute to the success and future growth of SGMO. Under the programme, SGMO sends employees to work at offices in another country to allow them to experience a different culture and become directly familiar with the dynamics of a workplace outside Japan.

Further case study resources

Sony (2017a). *Employee data*. Available at: www.sony.net/SonyInfo/csr_report/employees/info [Accessed 5 April 2018].

Sony (2017b). *Fostering an environment conducive to global career development*. Available at: www.sony.net/SonyInfo/csr_report/employees/diversity/index5.html [Accessed 5 April 2018].

Sony (2018). *Training and talent development*. Available at: www.sony.net/SonyInfo/csr_report/employees/training [Accessed 5 April 2018].

REFLECTIVE EXERCISE

Organisational vision, mission and culture shaped by a global talent quiz

The 'Tomorrow's Global Talent: How Will Leading Global Companies Create Value through People?' report explores the changing landscape of global talent and how business organisations can discover, engage and lead talent through creating an enabling and talent-driven vision, mission and culture to enable this talent to thrive. The report provides diverse examples from organisational practice and company approaches to visioning, strategising and the development of a culture that has been informed by global talent.

You can access the report at the following link: http://tomorrowscompany.com/publication/tomorrows-global-talent-how-will-leading-global-companies-create-value-through-people

Reflective exercise: Having read this chapter and the 'Tomorrow's Global Talent: How Will Leading Global Companies Create Value through People?' report, take the following quiz, which will help you test your knowledge of key organisational global talent enablers from practice, including a global talent-driven vision, mission and organisational culture.

Question	Response
1: The 'Engaging through culture and values' section of the report on pp. 34–5 highlights that successful business organisations recognise that within a company culture there will usually exist a series of subcultures with distinct characteristics. With this in mind, it is important for organisations to maintain core values while letting different styles develop.	True/False
2: Being a successful company over the long term, in a world of unprecedented challenges, requires a breadth of diversity of thinking that can see and make connections and is able to respond in innovative ways. Diverse and global talent play a key role in this long-term vision for success. Which of the following talent characteristics which organisations should look for, does not belong to the characteristics discussed in the 'New kinds of talent' section of the report on p. 18? (A) Talent from different social and educational backgrounds (B) Individuals with different social networks (C) Highly skilled individuals with specialist knowledge	A B C

3:	Successful CEOs leading successful organisations will be 'chief talent officers'. They care about people, are interested in people and put talent at the top of the strategic agenda.	True/False
4:	The 'New kinds of talent' section of the report on p. 18 suggests that building a sustainable business in turbulent times requires talent agility. Which of the following characteristics of an agile workforce does not belong to the three characteristics discussed in the section? (A) Talent which share the company's vision (B) A workforce that understands the company's vision (C) Talent which deliver the company's objectives guided by senior leadership	A B C
5:	One of the most important ways of building global talent loyalty and engagement is for companies to have a strong set of values.	True/False
6:	Many organisations now adopt a talent vision and mission that seek to create value from people by matching personal qualities to the context, rather than the CV to the job description or person specification. Which company highlighted in the 'Talent, not credentials' section on pp. 24–5 seeks out people with multiple perspectives gained through a wide variety of experiences, not necessarily work-related. It looks for people who have experience of a range of different responsibilities and cultures. (A) Google (B) ARM (C) Microsoft	A B C
7:	Caroline Waters, Director of People and Policy at British Telecom, argued that engaging talent starts with an organisation's culture, values and leadership; it does not depend on an individual's educational or professional background.	True/False
8:	Organisations that pay only lip service to the statement that talent is their most valuable asset, provide little or no training and development opportunities or prevent discrimination on the grounds of race, disability, gender, age or any other irrelevant factor.	True/False

(Continued)

(Continued)

9: By taking a more inclusive route, many progressive companies have demonstrated the wide variety of ways in which talent can be successfully engaged by giving them space to innovate and creating cultures guided by values. Which company highlighted in the 'Engaging through inclusion' section on pp. 32–3 has no conventional chain of command and no organisation chart to enable a more inclusive working environment? (A) Google (B) WL Gore (C) Gore	A B C
10: IBM expects to more than double its Indian operations by 2010, adding more than 50,000 employees, while Infosys Technology, an Indian outsourcing and consulting firm, wants to hire 6,000 Chinese employees over the next five years. This makes a case for the importance of organisations with a vision and mission that are informed by global talent.	True/False

Answers to questions

Q1: True

Q2: Option C – while highly skilled individuals with specialist knowledge are always in demand in organisations, it is individuals with different personal interests that are required to ensure a breadth of diversity of thinking to see and make connections and be able to respond in innovative ways.

Q3: True

Q4: Option C – talent, which delivers the company's objectives without needing to be told what and how to deliver them.

Q5: True

Q6: Option C – Microsoft has a distinctive vision of the type of people it is looking for. It seeks out people with multiple perspectives gained through a wide variety of experiences, not necessarily work-related. It looks for people who have experience of a range of different responsibilities and cultures.

Q7:   True

Q8:   True

Q9:   Option B – WL Gore – creator of Gore-Tex fabric and other products from heart drugs to guitar strings – has no conventional chain of command and no organisation chart. Everyone at Gore, except for the president and treasurer, is called an 'associate'. Associates choose to accept projects on which they want to work. Teams organise to carry out specific projects and leaders emerge.

Q10:   True

Further reading and resources

Business Insider (2012). *This is how the best companies recruit and develop talent.* Available at: www.businessinsider.com/heres-how-the-best-companies-recruit-and-develop-talent-2012-4?IR=T [Accessed 9 August 2018].

PwC (2009). *Global talent innovation: Strategies for breakthrough performance.* Available at: www.strategyand.pwc.com/reports/global-talent-innovation-strategies-breakthrough [Accessed 9 August 2018].

Tomorrows Company (2009). *Tomorrow's global talent: How will leading global companies create value through people?* Available at: www.goodtalent.co.uk/_literature_107568/Tomorrows_Global_Talent [Accessed 9 August 2018].

REFERENCES

Astra Zeneca (2015). *Great place to work.* Available at: www.astrazeneca.com/content/dam/az/PDF/Great-Place-to-Work.pdf [Accessed 17 March 2018].

Bagley, R. O. (2013). *How to hire successfully: Focus on mission, values, talent.* Available at: www.forbes.com/sites/rebeccabagley/2013/03/01/how-to-hire-successfully [Accessed 17 March 2018].

British Petroleum (BP) (2018). *Diversity and inclusion – LGBT*. Available at: www.bp.com/en/global/bp-careers/working-at-bp/diversity-inclusion.html#lgbt [Accessed 18 March 2018].

British Telecom (BT) (2007). *Flexible working: Can your company compete without it?* Available at: www2.bt.com/static/i/media/pdf/flex_working_wp_07.pdf [Accessed 18 March 2018].

Chua, A. (2017). *Are you working for a purpose-driven organisation?* Available at: https://leaderonomics.com/business/purpose-driven-organisation [Accessed 19 March 2018].

Cooper, P. (2016). *How talent acquisition can establish a competitive advantage*. Available at: www.linkedin.com/pulse/how-talent-acquisition-can-establish-competitive-advantage-cooper [Accessed 18 March 2018].

County of San Mateo (2018). *HR mission statement, goals and values*. Available at: https://hr.smcgov.org/hr-mission-statement-goals-and-values [Accessed 17 March 2018].

Dixon, L. (2016). *Talent is the world's most valuable resource: It's time for leaders to elevate its strategic importance*. Available at: www.talenteconomy.io/2016/12/02/talent-valuable-resource [Accessed 21 March 2018].

Ernst & Young (2016). *Winning with purpose: EY entrepreneurial winning women conference, May 2016*. Available at: www.ey.com/Publication/vwLUAssets/EY-purpose-led-organizations/$FILE/EY-purpose-led-organizations.pdf [Accessed 18 March 2018].

Facebook (2018). *People and recruiting*. Available at: www.facebook.com/careers/teams/people [Accessed 17 March 2018].

Financial Times (2016). *Japan puts its seniors to work*. Available at: www.ft.com/content/7a879e66-6b78-11e6-a0b1-d87a9fea034f [Accessed 18 March 2018].

GISDA (2018). *About us*. Available at: www.gisda.org/eng/amdanom-ni.html [Accessed 17 March 2018].

Harvard Business Review (2014). *Building a game-changing talent strategy*. Available at: https://hbr.org/2014/01/building-a-game-changing-talent-strategy [Accessed 19 March 2018].

Harvard Business Review (2015). *Automation won't replace people as your competitive advantage*. Available at: https://hbr.org/2015/08/automation-wont-replace-people-as-your-competitive-advantage [Accessed 18 March 2018].

Indeed (2017). *'Culture is the DNA of the company': An interview with JetBlue's SVP of Talent, Rachel McCarthy*. Available at: http://blog.indeed.com/2017/08/08/culture-is-dna-company-interview-jetblue [Accessed 18 March 2018].

Korn Ferry Institute (2014). *Talent strategy that drives business strategy.* Available at: http://static.kornferry.com/media/sidebar_downloads/KFTalentStrategyWhitepaper.pdf [Accessed 21 March 2018].

Mayo, A. (2009). *Building a business-driven people strategy.* Available at: http://hrsociety.co.uk/resources/knowledge_resources/Developing_a_business-driven_people_strategy.pdf [Accessed 17 March 2018].

Mercer (2017). *The people strategy is the business strategy.* Available at: www.uk.mercer.com/our-thinking/peopleshaped/the-people-strategy-is-the-business-strategy.html# [Accessed 17 March 2018].

Miller, B. (2014). *Strategy, mission, and vision: How do they all fit together?* Available at: https://hrdailyadvisor.blr.com/2014/09/09/strategy-mission-and-vision-how-do-they-all-fit-together [Accessed 17 March 2018].

Ministry of Trade and Industry, Singapore (2018). *About MTI: Vision, mission and values.* Available at: www.mti.gov.sg/AboutMTI/Pages/Vision,%20Mission%20and%20values.aspx [Accessed 17 March 2018].

MIT Sloan Management Review (2002). *Building competitive advantage through people.* Available at: https://sloanreview.mit.edu/article/building-competitive-advantage-through-people [Accessed 18 March 2018].

Ohmer, W. (2017). *What vision and mission statements mean for your organization.* Available at: www.corporatetalentinstitute.com/single-post/2017/03/19/What-Vision-and-Mission-Statements-Mean-for-Your-Organization [Accessed 17 March 2018].

PricewaterhouseCoopers (PwC) (2017). *Workforce of the future: The competing forces shaping 2030.* Available at: www.pwc.com/gx/en/services/people-organisation/workforce-of-the-future/workforce-of-the-future-the-competing-forces-shaping-2030-pwc.pdf [Accessed 18 March 2018].

Sage (2017). *Fighting for talent: Building people companies to drive business growth.* Available at: www.sagepeople.com/resources/press-releases/companies-recognize-need-to-focus-on-people [Accessed 18 March 2018].

Schneider (2018). *Diversity and inclusion: Initiatives.* Available at: www.schneider-elecctric.co.uk/en/about-us/diversity-and-inclusion/initiatives.jsp [Accessed 18 March 2018].

Sinek, S. (2018). *My why.* Available at: https://startwithwhy.com/simonsinek?ref=topnav [Accessed 29 March 2018].

Society for Human Resource Management (SHRM) (2018). *Mission and vision statements: What is the difference between mission, vision and values statements?* Available at: www.shrm.org/resourcesandtools/tools-and-samples/hr-qa/pages/istherea

differencebetweenacompany'smission,visionandvaluestatements.aspx [Accessed 17 March 2018].

Tesla (2018). *Careers*. Available at: www.tesla.com/en_GB/careers [Accessed 17 March 2018].

Turner, P. and Kalman, D. (2014). *Make your people before you make your products: Using talent management to achieve competitive advantage in global organizations*. Chichester: John Wiley & Sons.

University of Nottingham (2018). *HR vision and values*. Available at: www.nottingham. ac.uk/hr/aboutus/hr-vision-and-values.aspx [Accessed 17 March 2018].

WPP (2018). *Our mission*. Available at: www.wpp.com/wpp/about/whoweare/mission [Accessed 17 March 2018].

6

ATTRACTION, DEVELOPMENT AND RETENTION OF GLOBAL TALENT

Chapter contents

Attracting talent globally

- Global talent attraction
- Establishing an organisational strategy for the attraction of global talent
- Reflecting on the war for global talent
- Organisational approaches to the attraction of global talent

Developing talent

- Global talent development
- Establishing an organisational strategy for the development of global talent
- The role of coaching and mentoring in the development of talent
- The interplay between talent development and organisational learning

Approaches to talent retention

- Global talent retention
- Organisational strategies for the retention of global talent
- Rewards and promotion strategies
- Employer loyalty and the millennial generation

Interview with a senior representative from a global recruiting firm – Martin Pardey, Hays

Reflective exercise: Global talent attraction, development and retention in practice quiz

---

Learning objectives

After reading this chapter, you will be able to:

- understand current developments in the attraction, development and retention of global talent
- gain insights into a diverse set of organisational approaches to attract, develop and retain talent
- appreciate the millennial mindset and the implications for organisations.

ATTRACTING TALENT GLOBALLY

This chapter explores the myriad of approaches available to leaders and managers to attract, develop and retain organisational global talent. As such, the chapter is not intended to provide a comprehensive perspective on strategic Human Resource Management (HRM) or an account of the HR function in organisations. Instead, the chapter provides an overarching framework for proactive and effective global talent management.

Global talent attraction

The ability to attract talent is of prime importance to any organisation. Having a vision, mission, strategy and culture that are talent centric sets the foundations to attract the best.

Why do organisations focus on the attraction of global talent? McKinsey senior partners Scott Keller and Mary Meaney contend that the attraction of high-performing global talent is central to the growth and productivity of business organisations and to improving organisational performance (McKinsey, 2017).

To support their argument, Keller and Meaney undertook a study of over 600,000 researchers, entertainers, politicians and athletes, which found that high-performing talent are 400% more productive than talent with average performance. In most highly complex occupations, people who are high performers can be up to 800% more productive than the average employee in an organisation (Figure 6.1).

As a key organisational resource, companies will go to great lengths to attract and recruit the most productive and highly skilled global talent. Global talent

The relationship between quality of talent and business
performance is dramatic.

Productivity gap between average performers and high performers, by job complexity, %

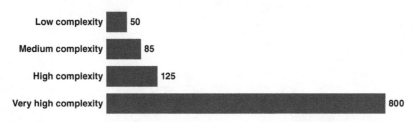

Figure 6.1   The relationship between quality of talent and organisational performance
(Source: McKinsey, 2017)

attraction is also important amid global technological, demographic, economic and
environmental trends and developments that influence the supply of the skilled workforce in organisations. The limited supply of talent can also pressure organisational
recruitment efforts.

The Boston Consulting Group identified six forces that will transform the future supply of talent (Figure 6.2). Collectively, these forces could have profound implications for
the ability of organisations to attract talent. These forces are divided into two groups:

- *shifts in resource distribution*: a new demographic mix, skill imbalances and shifting geopo-
litical and economic power
- *changing workforce cultures and values*: diversity and inclusion, individualism and entrepreneurship, and wellbeing and purpose. (Boston Consulting Group, 2017)

Take skills imbalances, for instance. It is predicted that 20% of all new jobs in technology
will remain unfilled by 2020 due to the shortage of talent with the right skills, knowledge
and abilities. Individualism and entrepreneurship are yet another force that will reshape
the supply of global talent to organisations – it is projected that by 2020, 50% of the
global workforce will be engaged in freelance and entrepreneurial modes of employment
(Boston Consulting Group, 2017). What do these two observations mean for the attraction of global talent? The straight answer is: organisations will simply have access to an
even smaller pool of global talent.

With the uncertainty and volatility in the world of work and the world in general, the
attraction of global talent is a key priority for organisations. Companies that want to stay
abreast of their market competition need to reinvent their current talent pipelines and
adopt fluid and agile approaches to the way they attract talent.

Figure 6.2   Six forces transforming the supply of talent

(Source: Boston Consulting Group, 2017)

Establishing an organisational strategy for the attraction of global talent

Amid the fierce competition for global talent among organisations, it would be imperative to establish effective forward-looking organisational strategies and competitive talent propositions for the attraction of global talent. Some key features of such strategies include the provision of a compelling employee value proposition, its alignment with practice on the ground, alongside an integrative cultural framework in operation. We discuss these in detail through the provision of illustrative examples from practice.

The development of a compelling employee value proposition plays an important role in the attraction of global talent. An employee value proposition, according to global recruiting firm Michael Page, implies defining the essence of an organisation, its differentiating factors and what it represents (Michael Page, 2016). Such a value proposition, boasts an inspiring vision or a distinctive culture and is central to the attraction of talent. An employee value proposition has to be clear and consistent across the full spectrum of an organisation's recruitment strategy. This includes adverts, job descriptions, websites and collateral to external recruitment agencies and headhunters. If this proposition is unclear, inconsistent or poorly communicated, prospective employees may question the very essence of what the organisation stands for and may be deterred from applying. Word of mouth focused on the employee proposition or the 'inside culture' may also have important implications for organisations' ability to attract talent.

Another key feature that organisational strategies aimed at the attraction of talent need to consider is the alignment between organisational vision and mission employee value proposition and the reality of the recruitment practice on the ground. One example is the British Broadcasting Corporation (BBC) in the UK, an employer that claims to have cemented its commitment to equality, diversity and inclusion through the launch of its Diversity and Inclusion Strategy 2016–20 (BBC, 2016): 'We support diversity at every level – not just for our entrants but for individuals in mid-career and at leadership level too. We have set new, ambitious diversity objectives for the leadership and team manager populations.'

Yet the organisation's commitment to this agenda has come into question in recent months. Against a strategic target of 15% of its workforce being black, Asian and minority ethnic (BAME), the BBC reported an achievement of reaching 13.4% in 2016, which was later revealed as an over-inflation of the actual figure of 9.2%. The inflated figure included BBC staff employed outside the UK (Albury, 2016). Another example of the BBC's misalignment of organisational vision/mission and actual practice is its lack of gender diversity and the gender pay gap across its top media talent, which has been exposed on a number of occasions (BBC, 2017) and most recently in January 2018. Such misalignments of organisational vision and actual practice as regards gender equality and racial diversity impact the ability of organisations to recruit talent.

Talent's fit and integration with the organisational culture is another feature of a global talent attraction strategy that has to be taken into account. The alignment of the future aspirations, motivations and expectations of prospective recruitees with those of the organisation's culture and values therefore becomes essential.

Katie Bouton, founder and president of Koya Leadership Partners, writes in the *Harvard Business Review* that talent's culture fit is a key trait that organisations need to look for when recruiting. Poor culture fit can cost an organisation between 50% and 60% of that person's annual salary (Bouton, 2015). Organisations need, nevertheless, to be able to define and articulate their culture, vision and practices, and to communicate them to prospective employees and during the recruitment process before they attempt to measure the cultural fit of talent.

The importance of diversity and recruiting talent with a global mindset has also been recognised by Alibaba. We now go on to provide an insight into how Alibaba, the Chinese and global e-commerce giant, has led a strategy for the attraction of global talent to internationalise its predominantly Chinese workforce and scale up its international presence and operations through talent (Wang, 2016).

INDUSTRY INSIGHT

Alibaba Global Leadership Academy

In 2016, Alibaba launched an innovative employee recruitment and training programme called the Alibaba Global Leadership Academy (AGLA), which seeks to attract talent from major potential markets for the company outside of China for an initial on-the-job training and cultural immersion period of 16 months at Alibaba headquarters in Hangzhou, China.

With over 46,000 employees and recently opened offices in Italy, France, Germany, India, the UK and the Netherlands, Alibaba is looking at opportunities to expand its global business footprint, and the development of an innovative and proactive talent strategy is set to be key to this (Wang, 2016).

The AGLA programme is an expression of Alibaba's ambitious plans to expand its operations internationally, which, according to leaders in the company, cannot be accomplished without a significant re-profiling of its overwhelmingly Chinese workforce.

'Our new AGLA program will help us build a strong foundation for our future international footprint', concludes Brian Wong, Alibaba vice president and executive director of the AGLA. This emphasis on global talent recruitment also resonates with Jack Ma, Alibaba's founder and executive chairman (Wang, 2016):

> We know that for Alibaba to have a meaningful global impact, we have to be able to understand other cultures, respect other cultures and appreciate other cultures. The AGLA is one way we are building that trust and mutual understanding.

Alibaba uses this innovative recruitment strategy as a platform to attract and develop its future leaders that will take up employment in the company's offices across the world. AGLA graduates, who are also full-time Alibaba employees, will be placed in one of the company's international offices once their initial training and immersion have been completed.

It is critical that organisational strategies for the attraction of global talent not only focus on the recruitment of talent from abroad but that they also enable the recruitment of home-grown talent. For example, many companies in the UK are expected to reshape their talent-attraction strategies and concentrate their efforts on the recruitment of home-grown talent post-Brexit, particularly if the country's labour market is tightened and barriers are introduced to impede talent coming in from the European Union (EU). Findings from the 2017 Albion Growth report reveal that 12% of organisations are already changing their recruitment strategies post-Brexit (Albion Capital, 2017).

Amid this uncertainty, where Brexit is just one example, we expect to see more organisations cultivating a home-grown talent strategy together with a balanced recruitment of talent from abroad, should the policy and politics landscape permit it.

Reflecting on the war for global talent

In Part 1 of this text, we discussed the global 'war' for talent, i.e. an intense competition for talent is a global trend with talent increasingly seen as a source of competitive advantage. However, because this talent is finite, it may not be able to respond to the demands and needs of all and thus creates the conditions for a talent war where individual organisations in these countries compete for this global talent.

Fierce competition now exists in the world of business where the war for global talent takes shape as organisations compete to attract the brightest and the best. A leading example of this is the long-term talent war in Silicon Valley, between technology-enabled businesses. Innovative approaches to luring global talent include improved company perks and remuneration packages. Google and Facebook, in particular, have adopted approaches, in order to recruit the top-performing technology talent, which include tailoring offers and producing counter-offers.

Which are the successful organisations in this new war for talent? Top Prospect, a large-scale recruiter in Silicon Valley's technology sector, gathered employment data from over 2.5 million profiles in their database to track the number of users that have changed jobs in the last two years (Empson, 2011). Findings from the research suggest that Facebook, LinkedIn and Google have been the companies to gain the most new talent (Figure 6.3).

Figure 6.3 provides a helicopter view of the war for talent among Silicon Valley companies. Facebook, for example, has won 15 employees from Google for every employee that has left the company to join the largest search engine in the world. Amid this rising war for global talent on an organisational level, there is the importance of establishing organisational approaches for the attraction of global talent that support an organisation's vision, mission and culture for putting people first.

Talent Traffic

Ratio is number of employees moving from Company A to Company B for every one employee
going in the other direction. Arrows point to the company winning the talent battle.

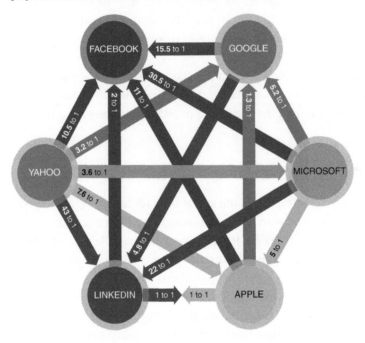

Figure 6.3   The competition for talent among Silicon Valley companies

(Source: Empson, 2011)

Organisational approaches to the attraction of global talent

As the competition for talent intensifies, organisations have been innovative in the way
they attract global talent and in their communication strategies.

Crafting a compelling global talent proposition is an important organisational
approach that influences the success of attracting global talent. If an organisation advocates through its policy that it embraces diversity, equality and openness in its vision and
mission, but in the way its job opportunities are written it is discriminatory or does very
little to communicate that it is a talent-driven organisation and supports equality and
diversity, then the recruitment efforts of this organisation may be jeopardised. Therefore,
what is important is that the employee proposition is aligned to the organisational mission and values.

Alongside talent-centric strategies for the recruitment of a highly skilled workforce with a global mindset, as we have seen from Alibaba's example, other examples of approaches from practice include the profiling of global talent and the tailoring of offers and counter-offers, as in the case of Facebook luring talent from its competitor, Google. Talent-driven organisations often go the extra mile in order to attract the brightest and the best. The latter cohort are often seen as a source of competitive advantage that will help them innovate in the products, services and experiences they develop and elevate their global profile and reputation.

Another organisational approach is the deployment of talent recruitment champions, who have a specific set of skills to attract and recruit the best talent. What we have seen as a result, particularly in the past decade, is the emergence of new roles in the world of recruitment, such as talent acquisition directors and heads of talent highlighting the rising importance of talent to organisations. For example, Nike's recruitment adverts for a talent acquisition director evidence how important and valuable talent recruitment champions are to organisations and have the ability 'to bring the most inspired, innovative people to Nike and unleash their potential' (Velvet Jobs, 2017). For Nike, a talent acquisition director creates and champions the future of its talent strategy around the world. There are other examples, such as chief people officer, as we discussed in Chapter 5. In essence, this role is turning into an important approach to support people organisations in their efforts to attract global talent.

One conclusion is that recruitment practices need to evolve as the war for talent is at every level – it is global, it occurs between organisations, it is intense and extremely differentiated. In some areas, this shift in the way talent is attracted and recruited requires a balance of organisational culture 'offer and asks', while in other areas it requires tailoring and personalisation. Talent is unique; approaches to its recruitment need to reflect this for future success.

DEVELOPING TALENT

Global talent development

Developing global talent has been at the forefront of organisational workforce policy and practice for a long time. HR officers within organisations have been primarily tasked with talent development initiatives. Yet, as Drew Hansen, founder of an online marketplace for on-demand skills development, Gilded Network, concluded, leaders in organisations may well acknowledge the importance of developing talent but few of them deliver the coaching and training that provide the appropriate development opportunities for their staff (Hansen, 2011).

Talent development has recently gained greater traction in organisations and in their profile and growth strategies, amid a plethora of global trends and developments that introduce both opportunities and challenges to those of them that aspire to put people first. The Boston Consulting Group (BCG) identified some key developments in future organisational behaviour over the next few years, driven by major technological and demographic disruptions in the world of work, as depicted in Figure 6.2 earlier in this chapter. The Group suggested that the continuous development of people and the focus on a diverse pool of talent are projected to take centre stage in the near future and provide a response to these disruptions (BCG, 2017): 'Companies will continually develop (and redevelop) their people, so that they are equipped to deal with the tidal wave of change. They will also inculcate diversity, inclusion, and flexibility in their corporate DNA.'

Michael Mankins, Organisation and Strategy Partner at Bain & Company, however, concludes that most organisations have been slow to react to disruptions identified by the Boston Consulting Group. Given the time it takes to develop global talent, Mankins argues that it is critical that companies start building the workforce they will need in the fast-paced world of work.

The impact of technology and 4IR developments on the world of work, as discussed in Chapter 4, is what Mankins believes should serve as a call for organisations to start developing the workforce they need to stay ahead, though the scale of growth of 4IR developments and their uncertain influence on the world of work bring a significant degree of complexity when organisations aspire to develop future-proof strategies and interventions to develop talent (*Harvard Business Review*, 2017a): 'with technological innovation, there will always be a high degree of uncertainty regarding the kind of talent your company will need in the future. This makes it challenging for leaders to plan ahead and place bets early.'

Amid these challenges, the ability of organisations to develop their existing talent then becomes just as important as their ability to attract and recruit outside talent. The insights provided by Bain & Company and the Boston Consulting Group provide evidence that organisations will need to focus on developing agile and adaptable workforce development strategies and interventions to allow for a change in direction in the way talent are developed over time.

Establishing an organisational strategy for the development of global talent

Amid the rising importance of the provision of developmental opportunities for talent, organisations need to establish strategies, policies and good practice to enable this development. The policy aspect is important, ranging from frameworks that empower people managers in the organisation to developing talent at all levels. Examples of organisational policy interventions include progression and succession planning, alongside investing in the development of talent in areas that are considered a priority for the organisation, such as talent capabilities to support technology adoption. Other interventions include mentoring, coaching and other supportive employee learning and development, which we discuss later in this chapter.

Given that talent has many avenues for alternative employment, offering them the opportunity to develop and grow their knowledge, skills and capabilities is an essential incentive for them to remain within the organisation.

In supporting their talent development strategy, policy and good practice, organisations need to acknowledge and learn from industries such as sports clubs where talent development is at the very heart of organisational success. Football clubs are often seen as role-model organisations that showcase best practice in developing talent. They put developing talent at the heart of their organisational vision and mission and strategy, as that talent defines the performance and success of the club.

We explore the case of Manchester United Football Club (MUFC) – a well-known English club that competes in the Premier League. Stefan Szymanski, a co-director at the Michigan Centre for Sport Management at the University of Michigan, highlights that talent management has been key to the success and organisational performance of MUFC. This has been attributed to developing policies and practices to grow talent in-house (London Business School, 2012).

What talent development policies and practices have contributed to the success of MUFC? For David Horrocks and his team at the International Centre for Football Research, MUFC's success in developing serial football talent is the organisation's culture, behavioural characteristics, practice engagement and the managing and guiding of performance 'potential' (Horrocks et al., 2016).

Through a prolonged engagement with the high-performing club, which included a comparative element of MUFC's policies and practices with existing sport talent development models, Horrocks and his team came up with an evidence-based, football-specific model for talent development.

This model for talent development adopted by Manchester United is focused on the development of youth as future talent. It reflects a systematic developmental process comprising of four main stages of development and a fifth stage of excellence:

- *Stage 1*: Romance – deliberate play and curiosity
- *Stage 2*: Elementary educational – early education phase within the academy structure
- *Stage 3*: Advanced educational – youth team, aged 16–18, reserve and underage international player

- *Stage 4*: Graduation – developing first-team player
- *Stage 5*: Evolutionary excellence – serial club-level winner and regular full international player. (Horrocks et al., 2016)

Alongside these five main stages, the model, as the authors highlight, comprises of '50 micro components' or enablers across the lifespan, which have been depicted in Figure 6.4. These components continuously evolve through the five stages in terms of detail, quality, execution and purpose.

What can be learnt from the talent development approach developed by one of the most iconic football clubs in the world? A cultural content that recognises the importance of top talent and the provision of opportunities for this talent to develop and excel. As Horrocks concluded, the organisational culture at Manchester United is facilitative and encouraging, one that nurtures individual and team talent behaviour. This organisational culture includes features that support developmental behaviours in a systematic, phased fashion – features such as goal setting, self-reflection, a winning mentality, deliberate practice, transition and adaptability, among other features. We would encourage you to explore the full study conducted by Horrocks and colleagues, which can be found in the further reading and resources section at the end of this chapter.

Another exmple is provided by the global consultancy firm Ernst & Young through its 'Vision 2020' for the development of global consulting talent. For Nancy Altobello, Global Vice Chair for Talent at Ernst & Young, investing in EY's people, the organisation's 250,000-strong global workforce, is central to embracing change in the way its business and services are being conducted internationally. Equally, for Mark Wenberger, EY global chairman and CEO, the organisation's focus on talent development aims to future-proof Ernst & Young (2017):

> Our people are the lifeblood of our organization. They have the power to build, grow, innovate, create and add value to our clients, people and communities. And we have a responsibility to equip them with the right tools and skills, and anticipate the skills they will need in the future.

The organisation has introduced a range of talent development initiatives to support its employees in order to stay abreast of disruptions in the world of work. They have developed team-based simulation training with a view to providing learning and skills development opportunities that are interactive, engaging and meaningful. In developing its talent, Ernst & Young is also introducing a new programme that will enable the company to acquire digital credentials in skills that provide a competitive advantage, such as data visualisation, artificial intelligence, data transformation and information strategy.

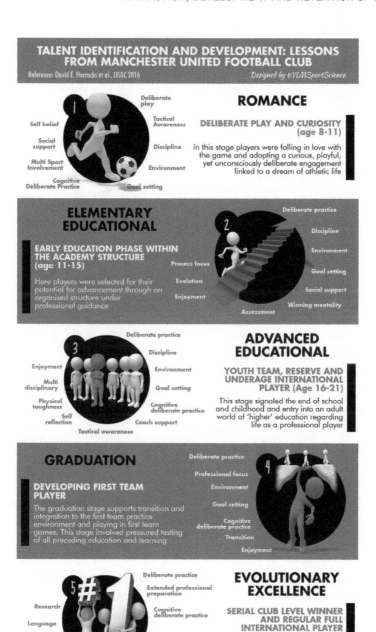

Figure 6.4   Manchester United's talent development model

(Source: YLM Sport Science, 2016)

What is common across both examples is that both organisations have shifted their focus to global talent development through team-based skills development and practice, alongside providing opportunities for mentoring and coaching, which we discuss next.

The role of coaching and mentoring in the development of talent

Coaching and mentoring are of key importance to the development of global talent. Millennials, as the largest generation in the global workforce, are perhaps prime candidates for this.

Mentoring opportunities prove to be extremely important for the attraction, development and retention of global talent, particularly with the steady increase in the proportion of millennials joining the workforce. Millennials are estimated to form over 50% of the global workforce by 2020 and mentoring forms an important part of the needs and expectations of the millennial workforce from the world of work.

Deloitte's Millennial Survey 2016 identified opportunities for coaching and mentoring as a key differentiator for millennials to stay with an employer. The study, conducted by global consultancy firm Deloitte, suggests that mentorship and coaching continue to provide a competitive advantage for companies and a source of talent development (Deloitte, 2016a). Millennials with mentors have the opportunity to develop their leadership skills and abilities, while 81% of them report higher job satisfaction.

Sun Microsystems, the company that created the Java programming language, has been pioneering the provision of workplace mentoring prior to its acquisition by Oracle, a multinational computer technology corporation. The organisation estimated that the Return on Investment (ROI) on their mentoring programmes in the period between 1996 and 2009 has been as much as 1,000%.

According to Sherman Morrison from Talent Management 360, the success of mentoring programmes deployed at Sun Microsystems lie in the in-house, formal approach that the organisation has taken. Unlike the majority of organisations that focus on informal mentoring, Sun Microsystems has established formal mentoring programmes that are able to demonstrate real business impact and, as a result, enable the sustainable funding and expansion of these programmes. One such example is the Sun Engineering Enrichment & Development (SEED) programme, which has built-in success metrics including satisfaction, participation, diversity, promotion rate, annual performance evaluation and attrition (Morrison, 2015).

The largest internet search engine, with a market capitalisation of $565 billion, has also adopted an innovative approach to mentoring. Google has over 57,000 full-time employees and personal and professional development is at the core of the company's talent strategy. In addition to the extensive catalogue of company benefits on offer, Google pays some of the industry's highest average salaries in order to attract and retain talent. However, its mentoring opportunities are another differentiator, which also proves to be a pull factor for the best and the brightest talent, who are keen to join the company.

The industry insight highlights Google's approach to mentoring and offers a glimpse into how the company's mentoring programme extends beyond addressing corporate needs to capturing diverse groups of talented students and impacting the lives of communities internationally.

INDUSTRY INSIGHT

Google's global approach to mentoring

Google's corporate mentoring approach

Newly recruited Google employees or Nooglers, a term derived by merging the words 'new' and 'Google', have access to a variety of mentoring opportunities to help them with induction, immersion, personal development and on-the-job training once they join the company.

Every Noogler is assigned a mentor who is successful within the company and who has taken a course on typical Nooglers' needs. At first, the mentor is just a friendly face to meet them at the end of their first day and show them the facilities, but the formal relationship between a Noogler and their mentor spans an average of three months. Google's approach to mentorship is of a more informal nature, which means some mentors are better than others–and some veteran Googlers may take responsibility for mentoring whole groups of Nooglers.

Google adopts a slightly different mentorship approach to its engineer Nooglers. Unlike its widely used peer-to-peer mentorship approach, Google organises its Noogler engineers in small teams to minimise the complexity of the environment. This arrangement allows for building close-knit collaborative professional relationships, or cognitive

(Continued)

(Continued)

apprenticeships, between Nooglers and experienced Google engineers, who provide mentoring opportunities to them.

To overcome the barriers that Nooglers face, particularly when they are afraid of asking questions they may deem as silly, Google has created NEHEN or 'Noogler Engineers Helping Engineering Nooglers', a dedicated mailing list, which is highly used by its employees, particularly at the beginning of their career journey with Google.

Google's mentoring programmes for students and future employees

Not only does Google offer extensive mentorship opportunities to its current employees, but it also covers students and graduates, who may join the company as future talent. Google's Summer of Code (GSoC) is a pioneering mentoring initiative for students established back in 2005, which has engaged over 12,000 students from 104 countries over the past 12 years. Students who have taken part in GSoC have developed 568 open-source projects and written over 30 million lines of code.

GSoC enables students to spend their summer break writing code and immersing themselves in open-source development. Participants work with a mentor and are part of the open-source community. Mentors help students build their chosen project's code and identify bugs and patches for bugs. Resources are targeted and channelled at their future development as open-source developers.

While some of Google's mentoring programmes are particularly aimed at fostering tech talent and developing individuals with entrepreneurial mindsets, other initiatives place emphasis on the importance of diversity and inclusion in providing mentoring opportunities. This includes the provision of mentoring opportunities for people from ethnic minorities or lower socio-economic backgrounds, and one such example is Google's 'Top Black Talent Program' aimed at student and graduate talent.

This initiative by Google is an exclusive career event and mentoring programme for the UK's black and minority ethnic students, who are passionate about Google and aspire to join its increasingly diverse workforce. Selected students are invited to take part in a carefully tailored mentoring programme which lasts 12 weeks.

The mentoring programme consists of eight mentoring meetings held virtually and in Google's London office. Students participating in the programme are assigned individual Google mentors, who offer guidance on improving technical skills, solving tasks related to studies, confidence building, career planning, developing personal and professional skills, acquiring knowledge of Google products and services, and personal technical project coaching.

Google's mentoring programmes for delivering global impact

Google has a range of international programmes, dedicated resources and mentoring initiatives to help entrepreneurs and start-ups make an impact in organisations and communities. A 2017 international mentoring initiative that is gaining traction is the Google developers' Solve for India programme. Solve for India aspires to provide a platform for developers and entrepreneurs in smaller cities to hear from experts and gain access to direct mentoring and support from Google. The initiative aims to reach, support and mentor change makers across India through access to open technologies, training and recommendations at networking conferences reaching the grassroots in 13 cities in India. Through this initiative, Google wants to encourage Indian entrepreneurs and innovators on the tech scene to come up with solutions that address real-life problems faced in India, with a particular focus on underprivileged communities and individuals.

Our discussions of good practice approaches to mentoring highlight the importance of establishing in-house knowledge, skills and ability development opportunities for talent and evolving practice to suit an increasingly millennial workforce.

The interplay between talent development and organisational learning

Organisational policies and practice channelled toward talent development also support organisational learning at large. The interplay between talent development and organisational learning is a two-way process that enables talent-driven organisations to learn from global talent as they develop as employees. How do we create learning organisations that are powered by their talent?

Deloitte notes that many firms are struggling to turn into learning organisations but the successful ones are those that place talent at the centre of a new company architecture that treats learning as a continuous process and a company-wide responsibility (Figure 6.5). This is a transition from niche talent development initiatives and interventions to a learning and development model that runs across the organisation, both horizontally and vertically (Deloitte, 2016b). This, according to Deloitte, is a model that embraces digital innovations and resources to provide talent with the opportunity to develop new knowledge, skills and abilities at any time and at their own pace.

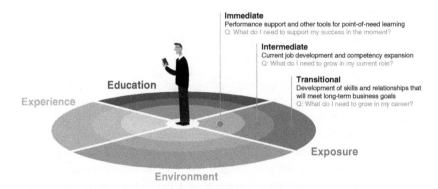

Figure 6.5 A continuous organisational learning model

(Source: Deloitte, 2016b)

What is organisational learning and can organisations learn from their employees? Organisational learning can help a company stay competitive in a disruptive global context. Organisations can learn when employees learn, according to Richard Boateng, an Associate Professor at the University of Ghana Business School; this, however, depends on the development of an open and collaborative culture to enable this learning to reach the organisation in its entirety (Boateng, 2011).

Providing opportunities for the development of talent through mentoring, coaching and other organisational approaches also leads to a better retention of talent, and in the next section of this chapter we provide an insight into how organisations redefine their culture for global talent and establish policies and practices to enable them to retain this talent.

APPROACHES TO TALENT RETENTION

Global talent retention

The importance of global talent retention in the world of work has been discussed widely. Companies that are able to retain their talent are more productive, grow faster and are able to reduce their recruitment and training costs. Employees who leave are generally considered to be an expensive investment for organisations. In fact, replacing an employee who quits the organisation, costs on average, 21% of their annual pay (*Harvard Business Review*, 2017b). There are, of course, other factors at play, particularly if high-performing and highly skilled employees leave – this can drive recruitment costs up even further, and ultimately impact organisational productivity and performance.

There are some key factors that drive employees to leave a company, according to Andrew Chamberlain, Chief Economist at jobs site Glassdoor and Director of Research at Glassdoor Economic Research, who studied over 5,000 job transitions of talent. These factors include, but are not limited to, the lack of:

- opportunities for personal development, growth and promotion in the organisation
- competitive remuneration packages and employee rewards
- positive and enabling company culture and values. (*Harvard Business Review*, 2017b)

This reinforces the importance of establishing organisational strategies focused on the retention of global talent.

Organisational strategies for the retention of global talent

As in the case of attraction and development, organisations that are talent-driven also need to finesse their ability to retain this global talent. For this reason, organisations go on to establish a range of talent-retention strategies, policies and practice that are largely based on the core organisational culture. Organisational culture is seen as the biggest determinant in every company's efforts to retain its global talent.

One of the key elements of this culture is the crafting of a compelling employee value proposition – or, in other words, what prospective employees get as an environment for what they provide in terms of skills, knowledge and abilities that are in demand by the organisation.

Tata, the Indian multinational conglomerate, which operates across a diverse range of sectors such as the automotive, energy, chemicals, retail and consultancy services, provides an interesting example. Tata is one of the world's largest private-sector employers employing over 695,000 people internationally. The company elevates the role of talent in contributing to its success. It has redefined its organisational culture and developed new approaches to help the organisation retain its large talent pool.

Nupur Singh Mallick, HR Director at Tata Consultancy Services (TCS), highlights:

We have over 350,000 of the world's best trained IT consultants in 46 countries worldwide. Like many organisations, the long-term success of our business depends on our ability to not only attract but also to retain the best talent across all age groups. (2017)

Talent retention at TCS is achieved through a significant programme of investment in employee-engagement activities, which promote meaningful career paths and create a supportive working environment. TCS's successful talent-retention strategy is rooted in its employee value proposition. This value proposition has three core pillars:

- *Pillar 1*: Global exposure – a key part of the TCS employee value proposition offered to all of its employees. Through global exposure, talent at Tata have the opportunity to work in multiple sectors, with different technologies and across diverse teams to help them gain exposure to all aspects of the organisation and the sectors it operates in.
- *Pillar 2*: Attitude is more important than skill – an approach where priority is given to talent attitude rather than talent skills and knowledge. TCS unlocks and nurtures curiosity and determination as important characteristics for talent in the company.
- *Pillar 3*: Maitree – taken from a traditional Hindi word which translates as camaraderie. This pillar implies that a fundamental part of employee engagement is making the workplace a positive and enjoyable place to work that is supported by a diverse and vibrant culture. (Mallick, 2017)

Alongside the three pillars, which have been instrumental to employee engagement, Mallick notes that TCS's approach to being a people organisation and its shift from human resources to human relationships, have been key to delivering its talent-retention success:

> Ultimately, it's about human relationships, not human resources. Whether it's a team of ten, a hundred or a thousand, nurturing those relationships and treating employees like people rather than just workers is the key to success.

Rewards and promotion strategies

Initiatives that reward talent provide a critical pathway back to a consistent employee value proposition in support of an organisation's talent-retention efforts. Emergent trends in the approaches organisations have adopted to respond to challenges related to the retention of global talent increasingly include the use of third-party organisations and services specialising in the provision of employee rewards in the form of perks. Let us consider an example of this in our industry insight next.

INDUSTRY INSIGHT

Perks at Work – employee perks to reward and retain talent

Perks at Work provides a free perks platform that offers over 30,000 unique discounts, and the ability to integrate a suite of tools designed to improve the workplace culture of talent who have access to this platform. Over 70% of the Fortune 1000 companies, alongside over 100,000 small businesses, provide their employees with access to Perks at Work. Large-scale organisations with a membership in the third-party perks provider include AT&T, Tesla and JP Morgan & Chase.

The platform offers a free suite of culture applications. These are essentially software applications that are designed to increase employee engagement and improve the workplace culture for talent employed by member organisations. The suite features applications that provide employee feedback, recognition, and development opportunities alongside a savings platform, access to health and sport facilities, giving back and hiring services and perks.

Perks at Work provides an enhanced employee engagement through personalised accounts based on what matters most to talent using their service. A perk management technology allows participating organisations to organise, manage and analyse their tailored perks and employee programmes from one platform (Perks at Work, 2018).

Alongside reward, promotion and progression is another big influencer in talent-retention efforts of organisations. Inditex, a Spanish multinational clothing company that owns brands such as Zara and Bershka, has redefined its culture for global talent through its new internal-promotion programme with a focus on women. Some 17.4% of Inditex's 45,000-strong workforce were promoted in 2016 alone; of that number, 75.6% were women. The organisation has also launched the Go! and InTalent projects to identify and promote internal talent across its retail and logistics businesses (Inditex, 2018).

JP Morgan, a global investment and consultancy firm, has followed suit by expanding its accelerated-promotions programme for excellent performers and introducing a new mentorship programme to help junior bankers progress with their careers by spending more face-to-face time with senior bankers in the organisation (Business Insider, 2016).

Rewards and promotion are established strategies for talent retention, yet they will need to evolve to accommodate the millennial mindset as this generation enters the workforce.

Employer loyalty and the millennial generation

Millennials, as we discussed in Chapter 3 of this book, are poised to take over the global workforce. They are the generation born between 1981 and 1995 and for them the frequent change in employment, or sometimes having multiple jobs and assignments at any one time, is turning into the new normal. This suggests that employer loyalty is of diminished value to the millennial generation thus impacting the retention of this talent in organisations.

A study by Red Brick Research on millennials provides insights into the challenges involved in retaining this generation of talent within organisations. The research found that 58% of millennials reported that they intended to stay in their current role for fewer than three years, while 52% of them viewed the concept of employee loyalty as being overrated (Red Brick Research, 2015).

Equally, findings from Gallup's 'How Millennials Want to Work and Live' found that only 40% of millennial employees surveyed felt strongly connected to their company's mission. Labelling millennials as the 'job-hopping generation', Gallup found that they are prone to change jobs more frequently than previous generations in the workforce – 21% of millennials had changed jobs within the past year; this is more than three times the number of non-millennials (Gallup, 2016).

The results of Deloitte's Millennial Survey also confirm these behavioural characteristics of millennials in the workplace (Figure 6.6). Deloitte concluded that 25% of millennials expected to leave their current employer in 2017, while two thirds of respondents, or 66%, expect to have left the organisation they work for by the end of 2020 (WEF, 2016).

These findings show that millennials are not loyal and that organisations need to reinvent the way they approach talent retention should they want to keep their

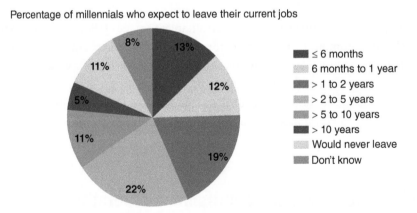

Percentage of millennials who expect to leave their current jobs

■ ≤ 6 months
6 months to 1 year
■ > 1 to 2 years
> 2 to 5 years
> 5 to 10 years
■ > 10 years
Would never leave
■ Don't know

Figure 6.6   Proportion of millennials who expect to leave their jobs

(Source: WEF, 2016)

millennial workforce. The rich evidence from organisational practice, global recruiters and consultancy firms that we have discussed thus far in this chapter highlights the importance of understanding the millennial mindset.

Millennials have greater loyalty to societal and social values than to organisational and employer concerns and they express this loyalty through a set of millennial values that shape the mindset of this generation and ultimately their behaviour in the world of work.

Therefore, it is critical for organisations to understand the values that define the millennial mindset. The millennial employee mindset is technology-driven, values collaboration and is socially conscious (Figure 6.7). They value features in the workplace that promote coaching and mentoring opportunities, alongside approaches that empower and engage. The Millennial Mindset, a consultancy firm, argues that technology has been instrumental in the shift in millennial thinking – technology has changed the way this generation communicates, learns and engages with others. Technology has also enabled millennials to have access to rich information, which has broadened their perspectives (Millennial Mindset, 2018).

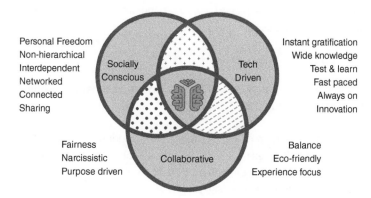

Figure 6.7   The millennial mindset

(Source: Millennial Mindset, 2018)

So, how are organisations making sure that this millennial mindset is reflected in their talent strategies? By 2025, 75% of the global workforce will comprise of millennials and organisations will need to adapt to the millennial mindset if they want to be able to attract, develop and retain this generation and make the most of their potential to deliver impact and bring change. We anticipate a shift in organisational culture, one that is led by millennial values; and a change of direction in organisational vision and mission that is aligned with millennial values.

Interview with a senior representative from a global recruiting firm – Martin Pardey, Business Director – Digital Technology, IT and Finance, Hays Plc

Q: Please tell me more about yourself and Hays Plc, the organisation you represent, which is in fact one of the largest recruiting firms in the world.

I have worked for Hays for over 10 years, and am currently responsible for digital technology and IT recruitment for a range of organisations across the South of England. I focus on placing candidates with Business Intelligence, Analytics and Data Science skills. Hays is the leading global expert in qualified, professional and skilled recruitment, and employs 10,000 people around the world. We operate in 33 countries with 250 offices, and have over 6,800 consultants globally recruiting for roles in 20 specialisms, from IT to construction, education to engineering, giving us a global perspective on recruitment.

In our 2017 financial year we placed 70,000 candidates into permanent roles, and 240,000 into temporary and contractor roles.

Attraction of global talent

Q: What are the latest trends in the attraction and recruitment of global talent and what should we watch for in 2018?

Skill shortages remain widespread in the markets we operate in, and in the UK this is particularly evident in industries such as IT and construction. At the same time, the rapid advancement of technology is creating new jobs and new skills requirements, and there is a global competition for these new skills.

In markets such as the UK, where there are candidate shortages across many industries, employers are having to work hard to attract the talent they need. This means investing in employer brand, the application process, and ensuring an attractive pay and benefits package.

Our Hays Global Skills Index report in 2017 (www.hays-index.com), which measures how easy or difficult it is for firms to attract and retain the most talented workers in 33 countries, showed a small decrease in labour market pressures overall, suggesting that, on a country-by-country basis, governments, educational establishments and organisations are becoming more focused on the levers and dynamics driving the supply and demand of skills.

Political and economic changes, including the UK's exit from the EU, may be a driving force behind trends in global talent management in 2019, but whatever the outcome of the negotiations it is those employers who are best able to adapt their recruitment and retention plans to changing skills requirements who will be best placed to succeed.

Q: How far do you think the global war for talent will go? Which countries do you predict to be the key gainers and losers in this war for global talent?

Labour markets are evolving at a rapid rate, from how workers connect with employers to automation of the workforce. The labour market must now adapt to the sweeping changes affecting labour markets globally and navigate the complexities of supply and demand of skills.

Our Hays Global Skills Index examines in detail the labour market conditions of 33 countries – at www.hays-index.com.

Looking into the future

Q: By 2020, 50% of the global workforce will consist of millennials. How do you think that the dominance of the millennial workforce will shape the talent attraction, development and retention strategies of business organisations?

It's important that employers recognise the changing demographics and expectations of the workforce. We are witnessing a shift in employees' expectations for their working lives, driven by the millennial generation, and the movement towards temporary, part-time, freelance and self-employment options is an increasing trend in labour markets around the world. Technology is facilitating these changes, making remote and flexible working more possible, and we are also seeing a change in the expectations of employees as to how they use technology both to apply for jobs and in work itself.

What could be perceived as declining loyalty among millennials equally creates opportunities for employers to access talent in different, more flexible, ways. With rapidly changing skills requirements, employees are realising that they may need to change career paths more frequently throughout their careers, contributing to a more flexible talent pool.

That said, not all millennials are alike, and recognising the motivations and influences on different groups within the workforce will become increasingly important to employers.

(Continued)

(Continued)

Equally, with people living and working for longer, the potential of the older members of the workforce should not be neglected. Coaching and mentoring remain relevant approaches, and some organisations are now adopting reverse mentoring for senior-level executives by millennials to foster diversity, skills development, the idea of lifelong learning and an inclusive culture.

Overall, we are seeing high expectations of technology having an influence on employee expectations – workers are used to instant access to technology and expect the technology they use at work to be as effective as in their personal lives. Employers should also look to the future, beyond the millennials, to the changes that Generation Z will bring to the workforce.

REFLECTIVE EXERCISE

Global Talent attraction, development and retention in practice quiz

Chapter 6 discussed recent trends in the attraction, development and retention of global talent. The attraction of highly skilled global talent was seen as a competitive advantage in the 'war for global talent'. The chapter also covered recent trends in the development of global talent through the lens of coaching and mentoring adopted by organisations. In terms of the retention of global talent, the chapter had a particular focus on understanding the millennial generation, one that is expected to make up over 75% of the global workforce by 2025. The chapter also provided an interview with a senior representative from a global recruiting firm and their perspective on the attraction, development and retention of global talent in practice.

The 2016 Global Talent Management and Rewards Study conducted by Willis Towers Watson, discussed in this chapter, included insights from over 2,000 organisations – who collectively employ almost 21 million people worldwide – into the key attraction, retention and engagement challenges. The study is available at the following link: www.willistowerswatson.com/en/insights/2016/09/employers-look-to-modernize-the-employee-value-proposition

Reflective exercise: Having read this chapter and the Global Talent Management and Rewards Study conducted by Willis Towers Watson, take the following quiz, which will help you test your knowledge of key concepts, developments and trends in the attraction, development and retention of global talent.

	Question	Response
1:	LinkedIn's 2017 Global Recruiting Trends report highlighted that the single biggest challenge faced by teams and organisations (according to 57% of them) across the world is the competition for talent.	True/False
2:	The Global Talent Management and Rewards Study by Willis Towers Watson identified seven global drivers of talent attraction from the perspective of employers. Which of the following global drivers of talent attraction does not belong to the top five global drivers provided in the study report? (A) Reputation of the organisation as a great place to work (B) Career advancement opportunities (C) Organisation's vision, mission and values (D) Challenging work (E) Base pay or salary	A B C D E
3:	The Global Talent Management and Rewards Study by Willis Towers Watson highlighted that base pay continues to be the top driver of attraction and retention for employees in both developed and emerging economies.	True/False
4:	The 2017 Deloitte Millennial Survey discussed in the chapter provided insights into the attitudes of the millennial workforce towards loyalty, which is key for talent retention. The survey suggests that, in 2017, 38% of millennials expected to leave their current employer within the next two years – a figure that has increased since 2016.	True/False
5:	The Global Talent Management and Rewards Study suggests that global talent retention remains a challenge in emerging economies, with 41% of organisations reporting difficulties in keeping employees.	True/False
6:	The Global Talent Management and Rewards Study suggests that developing jobs that not only capture the changing nature of work but also facilitate skill growth and career development for employees, is an important consideration for the employer–employee relationship in organisations.	True/False

(Continued)

(Continued)

7:	The 2017 Deloitte Millennial Survey discussed in the chapter provided insights into the attitudes of the millennial workforce towards job loyalty, which is key for talent retention. Millennial employees who feel their jobs have meaning, or that they are able to make a difference, exhibit greater levels of loyalty.	True/False
8:	The Global Talent Management and Rewards Study suggested that organisations which prioritise key elements of the employer–employee relationship will be able to develop more relevant employee experiences, and companies will be able to connect with employees on a deeper level. Which of the following elements of the employer–employee relationship does not belong to the five priority elements identified in the study report? (A) Senior leaders and managers who develop trust-based relationships with employees (B) Transparency in all aspects of the work experience from base-pay policies to performance reviews to career advancement opportunities (C) Personalised performance management of employees (D) Development of an alternative to pay-for-performance pay strategies (E) Employer flexibility, which offers alternative career paths and non-traditional opportunities for skill development	A B C D E
9:	The Global Talent Management and Rewards Study suggests that employees are looking for more than a job – they expect a personalised work experience aligned with their values and preferences.	True/False
10:	The 2017 Deloitte Millennial Survey discussed in the chapter provided insights into the attitudes of the millennial workforce towards the relationship between automation and personal development. Millennials see automation as providing opportunities for value-added or creative activities, or the learning of new skills.	True/False

Further reading and resources

Horrocks, D. E., McKenna, J., Whitehead, A., Taylor, P. J. and Morley, A. M. (2016). *Qualitative perspectives on how Manchester United Football Club developed and sustained serial winning*. Available at: http://journals.sagepub.com/doi/abs/10.1177/1747954116655053 [Accessed 20 March 2018].

REFERENCES

Albion Capital (2017). *2017 growth report.* Available at: www.albion.capital/file/1431/ download?token=Krw57qnZ [Accessed 19 March 2018].

Albury, S. (2016). *The BBC's diversity strategy is not good enough.* Available at: www.the-guardian.com/media/2016/may/04/the-bbcs-diversity-strategy-is-not-good-enough [Accessed 21 March 2018].

Boateng, R. (2011). Do organizations learn when employees learn? The link between individual and organizational learning. *Development and Learning in Organizations: An International Journal,* 25(6), 6–9.

Boston Consulting Group (BCG) (2017). *Twelve forces that will radically change how organizations work.* Available at: www.bcg.com/publications/2017/people-organization-strategy-twelve-forces-radically-change-organizations-work.aspx [Accessed 17 March 2018].

Bouton, K. (2015). *Recruiting for cultural fit.* Available at: https://hbr.org/2015/07/recruiting-for-cultural-fit [Accessed 21 March 2018].

British Broadcasting Corporation (BBC) (2016). *Diversity and inclusion strategy 2016–20.* Available at: http://downloads.bbc.co.uk/diversity/pdf/diversity-and-inclusion-strategy-2016.pdf [Accessed 21 July 2018].

British Broadcasting Corporation (BBC) (2017). *Female stars call on BBC 'to sort gender pay gap now'.* Available at: www.bbc.co.uk/news/uk-40696402 [Accessed 21 March 2018].

Business Insider (2016). *JPMorgan is taking on one of the most notorious problems on Wall Street.* Available at: http://uk.businessinsider.com/bank-protected-weekend-policies-2016-1?r=US&IR=T [Accessed 20 March 2018].

Deloitte (2016a). *Deloitte millennial survey 2016.* Available at: www2.deloitte.com/al/en/ pages/about-deloitte/articles/2016-millennialsurvey.html [Accessed 20 March 2018].

Deloitte (2016b). *Learning: Employees take charge.* Available at: www2.deloitte.com/ insights/us/en/focus/human-capital-trends/2016/fostering-culture-of-learning-for-employees.html [Accessed 20 March 2018].

Empson, R. (2011). *A look at who's winning the talent wars in tech (Hint: it rhymes with Twitter).* Available at: https://techcrunch.com/2011/06/07/a-look-at-whos-winning-the-talent-wars-in-tech-hint-it-rhymes-with-twitter [Accessed 19 March 2018].

Ernst & Young (2017). *Global review 2017: Our performance this year.* Available at: https:// betterworkingworld.ey.com/sites/default/files/2017-09/EY%20Global%20review%20 2017.pdf [Accessed 20 March 2018].

Gallup (2016). *Millennials: The job-hopping generation.* Available at: http://news.gallup. com/businessjournal/191459/millennials-job-hopping-generation.aspx [Accessed 20 March 2018].

Hansen, D. (2011). *5 keys for developing talent in your organization*. Available at: www. forbes.com/sites/drewhansen/2011/12/02/5-keys-developing-talent-in-your-organization/#69fb083229a8 [Accessed 20 March 2018].

Harvard Business Review (2017a). *How leading companies build the workforces they need to stay ahead*. Available at: https://hbr.org/2017/09/how-leading-companies-build-the-workforces-they-need-to-stay-ahead [Accessed 20 March 2018].

Harvard Business Review (2017b). *Why do employees stay? A clear career path and good pay, for starters*. Available at: https://hbr.org/2017/03/why-do-employees-stay-a-clear-career-path-and-good-pay-for-starters [Accessed 20 March 2018].

Horrocks, D. E., McKenna, J., Whitehead, A., Taylor, P. J. and Morley, A. M. (2016). Qualitative perspectives on how Manchester United Football Club developed and sustained serial winning. *International Journal of Sports Science & Coaching*, 11(4), 467–77.

Inditex (2018). *Attracting, developing and promoting talent*. Available at: http://static. inditex.com/annual_report_2016/en/our-priorities/people/attracting-developing-and-promoting-talent.php [Accessed 20 March 2018].

London Business School (2012). *Why is Manchester United so successful?* Available at: www.london.edu/faculty-and-research/lbsr/why-is-manchester-united-so-successful#. WrDcTq2cZTZ [Accessed 20 March 2018].

McKinsey (2017). *Attracting and retaining the right talent*. Available at: www.mckinsey.com/ business-functions/organization/our-insights/attracting-and-retaining-the-right-talent [Accessed 19 March 2018].

Mallick, N. S. (2017). *Unlocking the secrets of employee engagement*. Available at: http:// engageforsuccess.org/unlocking-secrets-employee-engagement [Accessed 20 March 2018].

Michael Page (2016). *Create a great employee value proposition*. Available at: www. michaelpage.co.uk/advice/management-advice/attraction-and-recruitment/create-great-employee-value-proposition [Accessed 21 March 2018].

Millennial Mindset (2018). *Understanding the mindset of millennial employees*. Available at: https://millennialmindset.co.uk/millennial-employee-research [Accessed 20 March 2018].

Morrison, S. (2015). *Masterful mentoring at Sun Microsystems*. Available at: https://talent-management360.com/masterful-mentoring-at-sun-microsystems [Accessed 20 March 2018].

Perks at Work (2018). *Perks at work for employees*. Available at: www.perksatwork.com/ login/hr [Accessed 20 March 2018].

Red Brick Research (2015). *The 2015 millennial majority workforce: Study results*. Available at: www.slideshare.net/oDesk/2015-millennial-majority-workforce [Accessed 20 March 2018].

Tata Review (2013). *A rich resource*. Available at: www.tata.com/article/inside/A-rich-resource [Accessed 20 March 2018].

Velvet Jobs (2017). *Talent acquisition director, global brand marketing*. Available at: www.velvetjobs.com/job-posting/talent-acquisition-director-global-brand-marketing-508294 [Accessed 17 March 2018].

Wang, S. (2016). *Alibaba's global talent training program gets underway*. Available at: www.alizila.com/alibabas-global-talent-training-program-gets-underway [Accessed 19 March 2018].

World Economic Forum (WEF) (2016). *How loyal are millennial employees?* Available at: www.weforum.org/agenda/2016/02/how-loyal-are-millennial-employees [Accessed 20 March 2018].

YLM Sport Science (2016). *Talent identification and development: Lessons from Manchester United Football Club*. Available at: https://ylmsportscience.com/2016/01/04/talent-identification-and-development-lessons-from-manchester-united-football-club-by-ylmsportscience [Accessed 20 March 2018].

7

PERFORMANCE, PRODUCTIVITY AND ANALYTICS IN GLOBAL TALENT MANAGEMENT

Chapter contents

Managing performance in global talent

- Performance management
- Establishing an organisational strategy for identifying, measuring and improving performance
- New organisational approaches and developments in talent performance

Productivity in global talent management

- Global talent productivity
- Establishing an organisational strategy for identifying, measuring and improving productivity
- New organisational approaches and developments in productivity

Global talent analytics

- The case for the deployment of analytics
- Use of analytics to drive the performance and productivity of global talent
- New approaches and developments in global talent analytics

Case study 7.1: LinkedIn's approach to the deployment of people analytics

Global talent performance, productivity and analytics in practice quiz

Learning objectives

After reading this chapter, you will be able to:

- understand performance and productivity in global talent management
- critically reflect on approaches to identifying, measuring and improving performance and productivity
- gain practical insights into innovative organisational practice in these areas
- critique the role of global talent analytics in improving performance and productivity.

MANAGING PERFORMANCE IN GLOBAL TALENT
Performance management

Performance and productivity management has several approaches associated with it, ranging from the traditional to the more modern, including use of analytics in recent years, to assist global talent management practice. Our chapter is not propagating one approach over another but the central argument we posit is that effective global talent management deploys a diversity of approaches in performance and productivity management, rather than simply homogenising people and their performance against benchmarks.

Quantifiable benchmarks, while objective, are a myopic way of managing talent as they disadvantage those that do not perform well on certain metrics without taking into account a fuller or more holistic contribution being made elsewhere and which may be beyond metrification.

On the other hand, methodologies that are not quantifiable or measurable cannot be scaled up in large corporate settings for talent management. We will return to this when we discuss analytics but our central premise is that there is no single best approach, rather that effective global talent management would utilise a diverse set of mechanisms to identify, measure and improve human productivity and performance.

How do we define performance in managing global talent? According to Oriane Perrin, Customer Success and Growth Manager at EmployeeConnect, performance can be defined as 'the ability of an employee to accomplish his or her mission based on the expectations of an organisation' (Perrin, 2017). According to Elizabeth Houldsworth and Dilum Jirasinghe, authors of *Managing and Measuring Employee Performance* (2006), the concept of performance management, both on talent and organisational levels, has been discussed extensively in academic publications and has had many applications in practice since the 1950s.

Clive Fletcher, a professor at Goldsmiths, University of London, highlights that performance management from a global talent perspective can be traced back to the years after the First World War when personality-based appraisals were introduced in the world of work. In the 1960s, performance management and appraisal mechanisms involved the introduction of goal setting and assessment of the performance-related abilities of talent. In the late 1980s and throughout the 1990s, performance management became far more integrated in organisational policy and practice, in pursuit of a more holistic approach to managing people (Fletcher, 2002). With these developments, many organisations introduced performance management systems with a view to conducting talent performance management functions in a more consistent and integrated manner.

However, performance management and appraisal frameworks have changed significantly, especially after the turn of the millennium, to reflect wider organisational needs and priorities. They have become more strategic and accommodative of new functions and dimensions in talent management.

In its 2017 *Handbook for Measuring Employee Performance*, the US Office of Personnel Management (OPM) highlighted the transition to a broader definition and functions of employee performance management that go beyond following regulatory requirements to appraise and rate performance. Performance management, according to OPM, is a systematic and more comprehensive process that includes the following elements:

- planning work and setting expectations
- continually monitoring performance
- developing the capacity to perform
- periodically rating performance in a summary fashion
- rewarding good performance. (OPM, 2017)

Uncertainty, volatility and increased competition in the organisational environment, fuelled by globalisation and other 'local-to-global' factors, have led to an upward interest in the adoption of talent and organisational performance approaches as a source of competitive advantage. These developments in organisations have further strengthened the case for introducing effective and efficient strategies and frameworks that identify, measure and improve performance.

Establishing an organisational strategy for identifying, measuring and improving performance

The importance of establishing an organisational strategy for identifying, measuring and improving performance has never been more important. As organisations compete, they need talent who will be able to deliver against ambitious business objectives with optimal resources and investment.

We see three fundamental pillars that every performance management strategy, when applied to global talent management, should be founded on – the identification of benchmark performance, measuring against this benchmark and the support for improvements in performance.

Identifying performance

Before an individual's performance can be measured and improved, organisations need to define the terms of performance aligned to the business and organisational objectives. It is imperative to identify an organisation's perspective and definition of their 'benchmark' performance. From this, performance indicators can be set as benchmarks against which people can be evaluated. These indicators can be given a volume or value dimension and can be informed by a range of organisational-level priorities and measures, including:

- performance measures and indicators that are already in place
- specific performance goals and aspirations linked to the organisation or aspects of its business or operations
- meaures aligned to the organisation's mission on industry standards.

Examples of specific performance indicators for employees may be:

- the amount of partnership agreements secured in a set period of time (logistics firm)
- the number of vehicles sold (car manufacturer)
- the number of job assignments completed
- the value of business deals won
- the number of products developed by an employee.

A number of qualitative and subjective indicators can also be applied:

- teamwork
- self-initiative
- quality of communication
- technological efficiency
- creativity.

One performance indicator, for instance, may be the number or value of partnership agreements that an employee in a logistics firm has been able to secure within a set period of time. The number of vehicles sold by an employee of a car manufacturer can be seen as another example of a performance indicator that can be measured by organisations. There are a number of other performance indicators that vary across different organisations according to the nature of the business they conduct, and these can range from the number of job assignments completed to the value of business deals closed and the number of products developed by an employee. There is also a range of qualitative and rather subjective indicators that can be used to determine the performance of an employee at work – these include teamwork, self-initiative, quality of communication, technological efficiency and creativity, to name a few. A persistent challenge in modern-day organisations is the complexity of developing well-rounded, quantitative and qualitative performance indicators.

Measuring performance

Once a set of performance indicators is in place, organisations can measure the performance of their employees against these indicators and establish employee performance plans. These plans and frameworks can be underpinned by different approaches.

Traditionally, most organisations develop their performance plans by aligning the activities described in an employee's job description to the appraisal form. This approach to talent performance management, according to the Office of Personnel Management, has its focus on activities, rather than on the accomplishments of talent in the workplace. The latter should be better aligned with performance indicators to provide a more meaningful picture of the performance of global talent in organisations.

The majority of approaches to measuring the performance of talent in organisations have, consequentially, been quantitative in nature, typically a measure of the 'number of sales' and 'number of units produced' or the equivalent in service sectors. These approaches are largely objective and unbiased as they focus on a simplistic measurement of performance. One example is the financial software, data and media company

Bloomberg, which tracks the number of keys that the organisation's 2,400 journalists hit per minute when they develop content.

Nikoletta Bika, a researcher and writer at Workable, argues for the 'management by objectives' approach, already firmly established by authors such as Odiorne (1965) and Carroll and Tosi (1973), whereby performance indicators are more concerned with the quality of outputs. Management by objectives is an approach aimed at improving the performance of organisations by translating organisational-level objectives and goals into individual goals. This may involve asking questions, after Bika (2016), such as:

- What percentage of critical objectives did the employee meet?
- What percentage of main/secondary tasks did the employee complete?
- What percentage of goals did the employee put aside/find unattainable?

The 360-degree feedback approach, which provides a well-rounded picture of talent performance against organisational goals and objectives, follows the same vein. Erik van Vulpen, founder of Analytics in HR and trainer on people analytics, provides an insight into how this approach to talent performance evaluation works in practice (van Vulpen, 2016):

> To assess an employee's score, his peers, subordinates, customers, and manager are asked to provide feedback on specific topics. This feedback often represents an accurate and multi-perspective view of an employee's performance, skill level and points of improvement.

The most effective frameworks, as we have argued earlier, combine quantitative and qualitative performance indicators – frameworks that are holistic in nature. Table 7.1 illustrates some examples of quantitative and qualitative performance indicators that could be used together to provide a balanced approach to talent performance management.

Table 7.1 Examples of quantitative and qualitative performance indicators and metrics

Quantitative metrics	Qualitative metrics
Number of defects	Teamwork
Number of calls per hour	Dependability
Number of customer calls	Initiative
Percentage complete	Planning and Organisation
Percentage of projects completed on time	Enthusiasm

(Continued)

Table 7.1   (Continued)

Quantitative metrics	Qualitative metrics
Number of projects completed on time and within budget	Mentoring and coaching
Number of projects completed within budget	Communication
Percentage of performance appraisals (of direct reports) complete	Empathy
Profit contribution	Cross-training
Sales	Customer orientation
Win rate	Cooperation
OSHA recordables (injuries reported to OSHA)	Quest for learning
Shrinkage	Project management
Number of patient re-admissions	Technological efficiency
Number of infections	Resourcefulness
On-time delivery rate	Inquisitiveness
Returns per employee	Creativity
Sales per employee	

(Source: Dummies, 2017)

Improving performance

The outcomes of the measurement of performance, one would assume, lead to a focus on improving performance. However, in practice, this does not automatically follow.

Luc Hanna, Talent Management Practice Consultant at Willis Towers Watson, highlights that traditional approaches to talent performance management often focus on past performance, rather than on what employees can do to improve their performance in the future (Hanna, 2018). He concludes that organisations should concentrate their efforts on creating a performance management plan that is not solely focused on the assessment of performance, but also drives global talent performance upwards. Improving talent performance is, therefore, another important pillar that can be embedded in every talent performance management strategy.

What are the key factors that assist improvements in talent performance? According to Solomon Kompaso, Assistant Professor of Management at Addis Ababa University in Ethiopia, employee engagement is a key factor leading to improvements in talent performance. He sees employee engagement as a strong predictor of positive organisational performance that is facilitated by a two-way relationship between employer and employee (Kompaso and Sridevi, 2010).

Other factors include incentivisation employees, establishing development, and the need to enable performance management frameworks to match tasks to skills, among other approaches.

Having discussed some approaches to the identification, measurement and improvement in global talent performance, we proceed to discuss some innovative approaches adopted by organisations in this area of their practice.

New organisational approaches and developments in talent performance

General Electric, an American multinational telecommunications conglomerate with over 300,000 employees, has introduced an innovative approach to performance management by replacing its performance management system, which has been in place for 40 years, with one focused on performance development.

At the heart of General Electric's transformation in employee performance lies a new mobile application – PD@GE – which prompts employees to work on development areas and provides real-time feedback to assist performance improvement.

This all-inclusive, interactive web-based and mobile app is designed to manage and evaluate the performance of General Electric talent on a daily basis. It creates a single place where employees can set priorities, organise discussions with managers and share insights with fellow team members.

The organisation's real-time performance development innovation, according to Leonardo Baldassarre, engineering executive, and Brian Finken, operations executive at GE, places emphasis on the day-to-day development of company employees and, as a result, it is projected to drive better performance overall (*Harvard Business Review*, 2015):

> At its core, the approach depends on continuous dialogue and shared accountability. Rather than a formal, once-a-year review, managers and their direct reports hold regular, informal 'touchpoints' where they set or update priorities that are based on customer needs. Development is forward looking and ongoing; managers coach rather than critique; suggestions can come from anyone in an employee's network.

The talent performance management shift from 'command and control' to 'empower and inspire' has contributed to a fivefold increase in productivity in General Electric's Oil and Gas Turbomachinery Solutions department, according to Baldassarre and Finken.

Another example can be found in Accenture, one of the largest global consultancy firms. Accenture boasts a strong workforce of over 330,000 people in 120 countries, who provide strategy and consulting services and products to over 19 sectors of the economy.

In an interview for *The Washington Post*, Pierre Nanterme, CEO of Accenture, speaks of the large scale change (Accenture, 2015):

> Performance is an ongoing activity. It's every day, after any client interaction or business interaction or corporate interaction. It's much more fluid. People want to know on an ongoing basis, am I doing right? Am I moving in the right direction? Do you think I'm progressing? Nobody's going to wait for an annual cycle to get that feedback. Now it's all about instant performance management.

Whilst the previous approach to performance management was based on annual reviews the new strategy aligns with the rising proportion of millennials in the workforce who want to be recognised and measured in different ways and in real time.

Elsewhere, there is an ongoing debate in the corporate space as to whether current talent performance management approaches and performance indicators measure the right outputs, outcomes and achievements. Questions asked include – are the performance evaluation strategies comprehensive, forward looking and inclusive of the impact that global talent deliver in organisations.

We would argue the need for more hybrid approaches that combine quantitative and qualitative indicators and that have a focus on the employee rather than the product, service or experience that the company specialises in.

Such an approach implies the introduction of an employee-centric approach that would enable firms to assess their employees' current performance on a regular basis and provide a range of developmental opportunities for them to improve that performance. As annual reviews are predicted to fade away, Kris Duggan, CEO and co-founder of BetterWorks, argues that the future of performance management is projected to include more opportunities for the provision of feedback and critical reflection – activities that are carried out more frequently and place a greater emphasis on employee development (Duggan, 2015).

As production costs fall and adoption rates rise, performance-development applications will replace the process aligned to performance management (Figure 7.1). Boris Ewenstein, Bryan Hancock and Asmus Komm who are principals at the global consultancy firm McKinsey, conclude that applications that collect real-time performance data from a variety of sources with opportunities for instant feedback provide an efficient and effective alternative to traditional annual appraisals (McKinsey, 2016).

General Electric and Accenture provide examples from performance management practice that combine economic and social indicators with a focus on deve-lopmental aspects of talent to support employee engagement and improved performance.

Continually crowdsourcing performance data provides fresher and more timely insights.

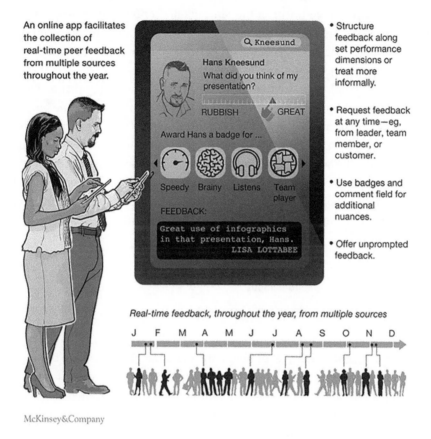

An online app facilitates the collection of real-time peer feedback from multiple sources throughout the year.

- Structure feedback along set performance dimensions or treat more informally.

- Request feedback at any time—eg, from leader, team member, or customer.

- Use badges and comment field for additional nuances.

- Offer unprompted feedback.

McKinsey&Company

Figure 7.1 Performance-development applications

(Source: McKinsey, 2016)

PRODUCTIVITY IN GLOBAL TALENT MANAGEMENT

Global talent productivity

As with performance, productivity also takes centre stage in the human capital and global talent literature. People and talent productivity is an important aspect of every organisation. Successful organisations appreciate the importance of productivity in the workplace as productive employees improve organisational capacity and expand growth and revenue options.

The ability of organisations to measure the productivity of this talent becomes mission critical then. Actions taken toward it would therefore: include, but are not limited to, the justification of investment in human capital, training and development; enable integration between organisational productivity objectives and individual productivity potential; and support talent with improving their productivity and alignment with strategic organisational objectives.

A simplistic approach to measuring talent productivity may imply that employee productivity is a derivative of the total employee output and input. While the output is the product or service generated by an employee, the input is the amount of time or resources used by the employee to generate this output (Figure 7.2). More contemporary approaches to measuring and improving the productivity of talent would see the deployment of a range of complex factors impacting both inputs and outputs. We discuss these approaches later in this chapter. Effective global talent management would look to the deployment of an inclusive framework for productivity management and measurement.

$$\frac{\text{Total output}}{\text{Total input}} = \text{Labour productivity}$$

Figure 7.2   Classic labour productivity equation

Organisational and employee productivity has unarguably always been high on the agenda for businesses and business leaders, but more so in recent times. Michael Mankins, Organisation Practice Leader at Bain & Company, concludes that the ability of business leaders to adopt a productivity mindset is projected to be paramount for the next decade (*Harvard Business Review*, 2017):

> At a time when so many companies are starved for growth, senior leaders must bring a productivity mindset to their business and remove organizational obstacles to workforce productivity. By systematically removing obstacles to productivity, deploying talent strategically, and inspiring a larger percentage of their workforce, leaders can dramatically improve productivity and reignite top-line growth.

Mankins further argues that productivity is directly tied to employee performance. Talent that is productive in their day-to-day tasks and activities also demonstrate high performance in the workplace. Increased talent productivity and performance then translate into organisational success and growth. Hence, it is important for organisations to establish a strategy that can identify and effectively measure employee productivity – a strategy that will help them harness the dividends accrued from increased talent productivity.

Establishing an organisational strategy for increased productivity

Developing an organisational strategy with a focus on identifying, measuring and improving productivity is a pre-requisite to an effective talent development pursuit in organisations.

Following the same structure as we did for performance we now discuss poductivity – its identification, measurement and improvement.

Identifying productivity

As with performance, organisations would normally establish a baseline against which productivity can be monitored, measured and improved. This process of establishing a baseline is achieved through the setting of a range of input and output measures, indicators or factors to enable talent productivity management strategies to work in practice.

Input measures, for instance, can be the amount of time being spent on a task such as the number of hours or days, while some output measures include the revenue being generated by an employee or the number of critical mission tasks that they have been able to resolve in a set period of time. Alongside these predominantly quantity-driven input and output measures, indicators or factors may also include those focused on quality over quantity, such as the way critical mission tasks have been handled and the outcomes of this approach. Organisations nevertheless often adopt hybrid approaches that bring together diverse quantitative and qualitative measures and indicators.

Measuring productivity

According to Dan Albright of Hubstaff, a firm that provides staff-monitoring solutions, in their attempt to measure productivity, organisations should not simply divide output by input. It is now more important than ever for organisations to establish approaches that measure employee productivity in an appropriate and adequate way (Albright, 2017):

> That starts with valuing the quality of the work as much as the quantity and resisting the urge to implement blanket policies that can alienate high-producing employees and cause overall morale to plummet ... the classic formula for productivity no longer applies.

Albright concludes that organisations would significantly benefit from having access to productivity-measuring tools that allow them to monitor, streamline and manage projects conducted by individual employees and across teams and entire firms. One example is Hubstaff's real-time solution that measures employee performance through the assignments they work on and the amount of time they spend on these projects, tasks and activities (Figure 7.3).

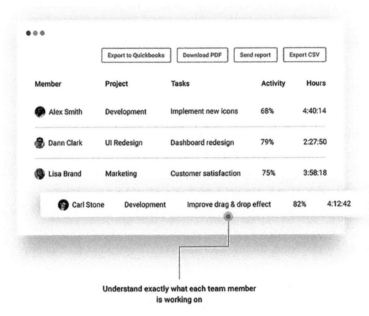

Figure 7.3   Real-time employee productivity solution

(Source: Hubstaff, 2018)

The solution also measures employee engagement levels and computer behaviours that may be affecting productivity (Hubstaff, 2018). Technology-enabled tools that focus on important aspects of employee performance can provide a competitive advantage and enable senior leaders to monitor and guide their employees, and help them focus on the right priorities.

Equally, in its report on measuring employee productivity, Public Health England (PHE), an executive agency of the Department of Health and Social Care in the UK, highlights that existing approaches to measuring labour productivity are often too narrow, as they do not always fit with the nature of many jobs. They also only provide a limited view of employee productivity due to the fact that they predominantly focus on quantity over quality when measuring employee productivity (PHE, 2015): 'quality is often as important, if not more important, than quantity in the workplace. Striking a balance between quantity and quality is a challenge for organisations, particularly given increasing globalisation and a consumer demand for value.'

Public Health England concludes that organisations should work towards integrating multiple input and output factors, including a focus on the quality of the work completed. They would also benefit from identifying the factors that may impact the productivity of their workforce and focus on developing measures that specifically target them (PHE, 2015).

Our discussion so far indicates that current approaches to measuring productivity are shifting towards a balance between the quantity and the quality of outputs produced and delivered by productive employees. It is thus important for organisations to take stock of how they measure the productivity of their employees and take steps to embed multiple input and output measures, indicators or factors. This shift would enable organisations to gain a fuller understanding of individual-level productivity, which feeds into organisational-level productivity.

Improving productivity

Alongside measuring productivity, allied management strategies could benefit from directing efforts at improving the productivity of employees. Within this context, it is particularly important for organisations to be able to identify key factors that may be contribute to lower productivity. Some examples include:

- a lack of organisational policies and practices to support employee wellbeing, such as an unsupportive working environment and employee contracts that do not consider employee wellbeing, among other policies and practices
- organisational approaches that are not specifically targeted at employee productivity through the inclusion of a variety of incentives such as pay rises, bonuses, medical insurance or a variety of perks
- the limited adoption of technology and specific tools to aid the productivity of employees, including a lack of investment or resources to support an employee in conducting their primary job in a more efficient and effective manner
- fewer opportunities for personal and professional development, including limited investment in knowledge and skills development programmes and initiatives to enable employees to increase their productivity level and efficiency.

It is here that we should note the correlation between a highly skilled workforce and high productivity. Improved talent productivity and performance are a function of organisational success. It is thus key for organisations to invest in the development of tailored opportunities for talent, in order to train, up-skill and re-skill their workforce as a means to improving their productivity.

Organisational policy and practice provide one route to addressing poor employee productivity, but more recent approaches shift the focus to an organisational culture and mindset as an enabler of improved productivity.

According to Michael Mankins, Organisation Practice Leader at Bain & Company, this can be achieved through the development and promotion of a 'productivity mindset' across the organisation, its leaders and employees. This mindset, according to him, highlights three crucial tenets, which can serve as enablers of increased employee productivity in organisations:

1. *Prevent organisational drag* – this relates to organisational structures and processes that consume valuable time and either slow down or prevent people from getting things done. The average organisation loses more than 20% of its productive capacity due to organisational drag.
2. *Avoid allocating star talent to roles that limit their effectiveness* – often organisations put 'difference makers' in roles that limit their effectiveness, as opposed to assigning this highly productive talent to business-critical roles and objectives.
3. *Unlock the discretionary energy of talent* – employees have considerable amounts of discretionary energy that they could devote to their work, yet many are not sufficiently inspired to do so. Inspired and motivated employees are 125% more productive than other employees. (*Harvard Business Review*, 2017)

Innovative organisations focus their efforts on using employee performance as a platform for organisational performance, growth and success. We discuss some examples of these approaches in the following section.

New organisational approaches and developments in productivity

A 2017 study by consulting firm Bain & Company found that organisations like Apple, Netflix, Google and Dell are 40% more productive than the average company. Attracting top talent is only one part of the equation – what has really contributed to their success in productivity is the approaches that these organisations have adopted to make the most of their highly productive talent.

Concentrating top talent in mission-critical roles and projects has made a true difference to highly productive organisations. Fast Company (2017) illustratively reports:

It took 600 Apple engineers fewer than two years to develop, debug, and deploy iOS 10 ... Contrast that with 10,000 engineers at Microsoft that took more than five years to develop, debut, and ultimately retract Vista.

This shows how highly productive organisations gain a competitive advantage through identifying and concentrating their high-performing talent on tasks and objectives of strategic importance to measuring and improving talent.

Let's consider Amazon, the world's largest online retailer, as another example. Amazon has patented a wristband called Wristband Haptic Feedback System, which has the ability to monitor the hand movements of its warehouse employees and direct them to items using small haptic vibrations. This wearable technology innovation will be deployed to monitor and improve the productivity of Amazon employees.

Amazon notes that when implemented across its warehouses, this innovation will significantly improve the productivity of its workforce tasked with picking items ordered through the company's website. Amazon's wearable technology innovation provides an insight into how large-scale organisations restructure their productivity management strategies in order to gain and sustain a competitive advantage in the global marketplace.

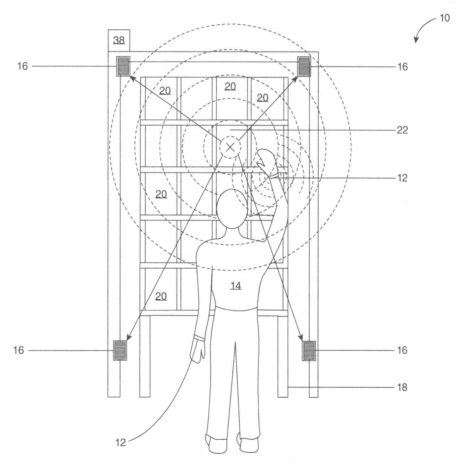

Figure 7.4 Amazon's wristband, which can inform an employee where a product is by vibrating

(Source: Dezeen, 2018)

Other organisational approaches focus on improving the wellbeing of talent as a means of tackling productivity challenges. By conducting an analysis of data from the Workplace Employment Relations Survey, Alex Bryson, John Forth and Lucy Stokes found that employee wellbeing and job satisfaction are positively correlated with talent productivity and the quality of output and service (CIPD, 2016).

Norway has been leading the way in this regard, with many organisations in the country switching to a 30-hour working week and 6-hour work days. In fact, over 10 years ago Toyota, one of the largest car manufacturers, reshaped its employment policies and practices at the firm's service centre in Gothenburg, Sweden to include a 30-hour working week. The key driver for this decision was the decreasing productivity of Toyota's workforce and poor customer service.

Not only did this change make Toyota's employees more productive, but the rise in productivity reflected in increased organisational productivity and profits at the service centre. Martin Banck, CEO of Toyota Centre Gothenburg, highlights the impacts that the introduction of a 30-hour working week has had on both the revenue of the organisation and talent retention (Kjerulf, 2016):

> In the first year sales grew by 30%, in the second by 25%. Profits grew too – by 25% in the first year and another 25% in the second year. Our employees are happier. That's easy to say but we can tell by a very low employee turnover.

Organisational performance records confirm the success of this approach – the mechanics at Toyota now get more work done in 30 hours a week than they had previously done in 40 hours. Not only is productivity higher, their actual total output has also been higher, according to Alexander Kjerulf, Chief Happiness Officer of Woohoo Inc., and one of the world's leading experts on happiness at work (Kjerulf, 2016). Other Swedish companies such as the internet start-up Brath and the app developer Filimundus have followed suit by adopting a 30-hour working week. Toyota, Brath and Filimundus illustrate the positive correlation between employee wellbeing and organisational productivity.

GLOBAL TALENT ANALYTICS
The case for the deployment of analytics

Technological developments and innovations such as the penetration of information technology, computing, smartphones, software solutions have reshaped the workforce and workplace, as we know it – something that we discussed in Chapter 4 of this text. These technological developments have also contributed to the emergence of global talent analytics or people analytics in talent management approaches.

People or talent analytics refers to the use of technology to gather rich data insights into employees, teams, departments and whole organisations, which enables senior leaders to better understand the people within their company – what drives and inspires them, what conditions are most conducive to their productivity, how they manage tasks and assignments, and what individual approaches and patterns they adopt to become more productive and improve their performance. Past approaches to using data have been very much focused on human resource-related tasks, operations and reporting, which serve the purpose of human resource departments but do not necessarily support the wider organisational priorities and objectives of more strategic importance. Proactive global talent management deploys a hybrid approach that brings together advancements in people analytics and elements of good practice in human resource-related analytics to respond to the wider business needs of modern-day organisations.

Talent analytics provide a powerful toolkit for organisations to identify, track and improve individual and organisational performance and productivity. They give organisations the opportunity to access a helicopter view of the state of their workforce and how the performance and productivity of individual employees align to organisational objectives and targets.

The 2017 Global Human Capital Trends study by global consulting firm Deloitte sheds light on the growing importance of people analytics – 71% of companies now see people analytics as a high priority in their organisations, a trend which has been depicted in Figure 7.5 (Deloitte, 2017b). Organisations with strong talent analytics strategies in place can boost their employee engagement, improve revenue and increase almost every business measure by making better people decisions.

Amid the opportunities for adoption, Deloitte found that many organisations are lagging behind in the adoption of employee analytics. It estimated that only 14% of companies have any form of talent analytics programme in place, yet more than 60% want to develop a strategy to capitalise on the organisational opportunities presented by talent analytics.

Global talent analytics can help organisations identify, measure and improve the performance and productivity of their talent. Yet, the success of employee analytics adoption depends on some fundamental factors that include the availability of data and talent data sets, the resources allocated to people analytics, and alignment with wider organisational objectives and priorities.

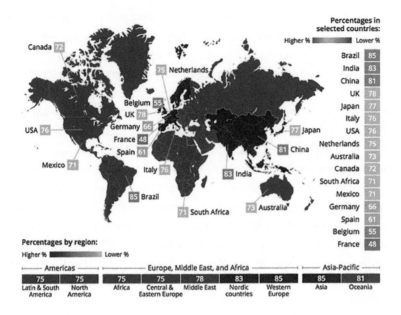

Figure 7.5 Importance of people analytics in organisations – a global perspective

(Source: Deloitte, 2017b)

Use of analytics to drive the performance and productivity of global talent

Josh Bersin, Founder and Principal at Bersin by Deloitte, notes that as the field of people analytics is expanding, there has been a fresh focus on identifying and measuring individual and organisational productivity. He argues:

> Companies can now study the behaviours of high-performers in greater detail to find out what percentage of their time is spent in meetings, how many e-mails they send to clients or internal staff, and even how much physical movement they experience each day. (2017)

According to Bersin, studying and measuring the productivity of high performers provide companies with the opportunity to utilise real productivity that would deliver impact at an organisational level. The application of people analytics to high-performing talent also allows organisations to mimic the behaviour of these highly performing and highly productive employees, and to apply this good practice across organisational levels, teams and other, less productive employees.

People analytics can also assist managers and executives in organisations with making informed decisions as regards the productivity of their workforce. According to Salesforce, an American cloud computing company, the latest talent analytics approaches allow for locating the cause of a loss in productivity such as process deficiencies in the organisation (Salesforce, 2018):

> Workforce analytics data allows you to go beyond the recognition that an employee is not working as productively as they could be, and begin to understand why that is and what can be done to correct it.

Despite its potential the uptake of people analytics in organisations remain low.

A study by the *Harvard Business Review* and Oracle made the case for innovation in the field of human resources and talent management and for deeper integration with transformative technologies used in the workforce and workplace (*HBR* & Oracle, 2014). The study found that only 42% of organisations use analytics to measure performance and productivity, as usage is focused on more traditional areas such as workforce headcounts and compensation and incentives (Figure 7.6).

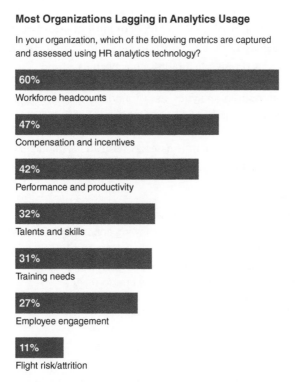

Most Organizations Lagging in Analytics Usage

In your organization, which of the following metrics are captured and assessed using HR analytics technology?

- 60% Workforce headcounts
- 47% Compensation and incentives
- 42% Performance and productivity
- 32% Talents and skills
- 31% Training needs
- 27% Employee engagement
- 11% Flight risk/attrition

Figure 7.6   Areas of use of people analytics across organisations

(Source: HBR & Oracle, 2014)

Only an estimated one third used analytics in areas such as measuring talents and skills or assessing training needs and employee engagement – despite the obvious benefits to organisational performance and productivity.

Developments in global talent analytics

The majority of organisations have yet to embark on people analytics strategies, equally there are a few examples of successful adoption by companies such as IBM and Salesforce. Organisations which have adopted global talent analytics direct their efforts at important talent and workforce-related functions of strategic importance, including:

- talent acquisition
- talent management
- learning and development
- workforce planning.

Paul Burrin, Vice President for People at Sage, has reflected on Google's innovative data-driven approach to 'people analytics' – a mix of quantitative and qualitative data analysis founded on the interplay between hard numbers and human feedback (Burrin, 2017). The organisation's focus on people analytics has been captured:

'At Google, we use people analytics as a foundational building block that informs everything we do to find, grow and keep Googlers'.

Its Project Oxygen is a platform that assesses its leaders/managers against 10 Oxygen behaviours that are linked to high performance and productivity:

1. Is a good coach
2. Empowers team and does not micromanage
3. Creates an inclusive team environment, showing concern for success and wellbeing
4. Is productive and results-oriented
5. Is a good communicator – listens and shares information
6. Supports career development and discusses performance
7. Has a clear vision/strategy for the team
8. Has key technical skills to help advise the team
9. Collaborates across Google
10. Is a strong decision maker. (re:Work by Google, 2018a)

Building on this, Google applies a similar methodology to the study of enablers of effective and highly productive teams at Google, entitled Project Aristotle.

The core purpose behind Project Aristotle was to answer the question: 'What makes a team effective at Google?' To assess productivity and performance at the team level, Google studied aspects of effectiveness across 180 teams through a mixed-method people analytics approach focused on:

- executive evaluation of the team
- team leader evaluation of the team
- team member evaluation of the team
- sales performance against quarterly quota. (re:Work by Google, 2018b)

Both projects at Google have been found to contribute significantly to the effectiveness, performance and productivity of leaders, teams and individuals across the organisation. Consequently, the organisation reported improvement in 75% of its underperforming managers after the completion of Project Oxygen. Multinational energy corporation Chevron provides another organisational perspective into the adoption of people analytics and their role in improving the productivity and performance of talent.

Chevron deployed analytics to understand the productivity of its analytics unit while maintaining its above-average profitability and revenue per employee. For this purpose, Chevron turned its analytics unit into a company-wide community of practice comprising of 295 members internationally from across all important divisions and operations to assume important people analytics roles, including the design of standardised metrics and the development of analytics programmes (Deloitte, 2017a).

This community of practice also developed an in-house workforce analytics curriculum with a view to developing core analytics skills and competencies. The rationale behind this initiative was to improve the productivity of Chevron's analytics unit, which enables it to make better, data-driven strategic decisions.

Two years after the adoption of the new people analytics model, the analytics unit has increased its capacity to develop and deliver projects for the organisation. This practice has reduced the time taken to complete an analytics project and lower end operating costs, yet achieves 30% higher productivity (Deloitte, 2017a). This example illustrates the power of people analytics in supporting talent and executives in improving the performance and productivity of their teams and units.

The field of global talent analytics is continually expanding and evolving. Thomas Davenport, Distinguished Professor in Management and Information Technology at Babson College and a research fellow at the MIT Initiative on the Digital Economy, notes the future potential for global talent analytics (*Harvard Business Review*, 2018):

We'll all be replaced by robots. I think there will be more and more metrics. At least right now I can envision that all aspects of human performance will be easily analysable. I think the creativity and intuition and human ability to think clearly, it's not something we're going to be able to delve into deeply with objective metrics anytime soon.

As Davenport notes, advanced artificial intelligence systems that connect and permutate behavioural and cognitive measures will enable greater future innovation in this area.

Another potential development is the integration of people analytics with predictive analytics. Predictive analytics is capable of identifying productivity and performance lags, estimating employee productivity and its alignment with future business targets and objectives, and predicting the future retention of employees through investment and talent development opportunities.

Next, we discuss LinkedIn and its approach to talent acquisition through the use of talent and people analytics as another illustrative example of our discussion in this chapter.

CASE STUDY 7.1

LinkedIn's approach to the deployment of people analytics

LinkedIn has a range of pioneering approaches to global talent analytics and many organisations use its services to access workforce intelligence. LinkedIn offers a truly international approach to sourcing talent as the company has over 500 million individual members from 200 countries (including 40 million students and graduates) and 3 million companies registered on its platform, enabling the connecting of global talent with opportunities on a global stage.

The previous Head of Talent Analytics at LinkedIn, Lorenzo Canlas, developed and adopted a comprehensive strategy to talent analytics. The organisation began its talent analytics journey by building a talent analytics team with the purpose of assisting LinkedIn's leaders to make evidence-based talent decisions that enabled the organisation to achieve its vision and mission and equally to expand in scale and scope. LinkedIn's talent analytics team consists of HE experts, data scientists and consultants and, as such, it benefits from a diversity of thought and expertise.

The company's talent analytics approach includes building its own HR data warehouse and working with a variety of partners for data visualisation and analytics, as opposed to outsourcing data storage and operations. LinkedIn's talent analytics team decision to develop its talent database in-house was based on its need to merge large sets of organisational performance data from multiple HR and finance systems with internal data that would not be a viable option to share with third parties.

Fusing talent analytics and predictive analytics

Starting from a problem landscape, in 2014 alone, LinkedIn grew by 40% and its talent acquisition team did not have the capacity to fill roles fast enough, making it unsustainable to meet its demand for talent (White, 2016). At the time, LinkedIn's talent acquisition team had no visibility of the headcount planning process, nor the ability to forecast the number of hires for the year and resource effectively.

In response, LinkedIn introduced a fresh approach founded on the fusion of people analytics and predictive analytics to estimate future talent demand in the organisation, and Rebecca White, a senior manager in Talent Analytics at LinkedIn, provided more insights into this problem landscape (White, 2016):

> Our goal was to build visibility and accountability into the hiring process and in a little over a year, we came up with a resourcing model that was able to predict hires within 5% of actuals (meaning we almost perfectly predicted how many hires would be made and how many recruiters were needed to make those hires that year) while more effectively staffing the recruiting team to meet business hiring demand.

This prediction model used organisational data on two levels, current and historic, to identify patterns and predict future talent demand from the organisation. LinkedIn collated data from the incremental hiring plan from its finance department and subsequently combined it with expected talent retirement and resignation rates and expected internal transfer rates to come up with the total expected hires for the year by business unit and region. Once LinkedIn had identified the total number of hires, it explored past data to identify patterns related to specific times when recruitment was likely to happen throughout the year.

Not only is LinkedIn innovative in the way it uses people analytics to enhance its talent acquisition operations, but also in the way its talent analytics team approaches key processes related to analytics. Lorenzo Canlas, Head of Talent Analytics at LinkedIn, pointed out that, commonly, companies will separate reporting, dashboards and analytics into different teams within an organisation (Canlas, 2015).

Within Talent Analytics at LinkedIn, all members of the team perform a combination of all three activities, regardless of their professional background and specialisation. Canlas notes that everyone in the team has to learn how to run regression in R, build a Tableau dashboard and liaise with the business. The advantage, according to Canlas, is that LinkedIn's HR partners do not always differentiate between a reporting, dash-

(Continued)

(Continued)

board or analytics request, and providing a single point of contact ensures efficiency in their response to business challenges coming from elsewhere in the organisation (Canlas, 2015):

> Providing a single point of contact allows us to iteratively frame what is needed to solve a business problem. Our generalist approach requires our team members to be more agile thinkers and grow skills they never imagined they needed.

Outcomes of talent analytics interventions

Because LinkedIn's Talent Analytics team was able to predict staffing needs, talent analytics interventions saved the Talent Acquisition team and the company 15% of its recruiting budget in the first year of adoption. LinkedIn noted that this move covered the cost of the investment in its Talent Analytics team for more than four years.

Further case study resources

Canlas, L. (2015). *How we built talent analytics at LinkedIn*. Available at: www.linkedin. com/pulse/how-we-built-talent-analytics-linkedin-lorenzo-canlas [Accessed 5 April 2018].

White, R. (2016). *How building out a talent analytics function saved LinkedIn recruiting considerable time and money*. Available at: https://business.linkedin.com/talent-solutions/blog/recruiting-strategy/2016/how-building-out-a-talent-analytics-function-saved-linked-in-recruiting-considerable-time-and-money [Accessed 5 April 2018].

REFLECTIVE EXERCISE

Global talent performance, productivity and analytics in practice quiz

This chapter discussed the importance of performance, productivity and analytics in global talent management in organisations. It also provided a case study of a global organisation's approach to implementing a fusion of people analytics and predictive analytics within its workforce. The 2017 Deloitte Global Human Capital Trends report, discussed earlier in this chapter, gathered the management perspectives of over 10,000 business and HR leaders from 140 countries, with a view to revealing 10 human capital trends for businesses to focus on to better organise, manage, develop and align their workforce. Workforce performance, productivity and analytics had a strong presence across Deloitte's global human capital trends.

Reflective exercise: Having read this chapter and the 2017 Deloitte Global Human Capital Trends report, take the following quiz, which will help you test your knowledge of current global human capital trends and the role of performance, productivity and analytics in driving individual and organisational success.

You can find the full 2017 Deloitte Global Human Capital Trends report on Deloitte's website at the following link: www2.deloitte.com/content/dam/Deloitte/global/Documents/HumanCapital/hc-2017-global-human-capital-trends-gx.pdf

Questions	Responses
1: For the last five years, companies have been experimenting with new performance management approaches that emphasise continuous feedback and coaching, reducing the focus on appraisals traditionally conducted once a year.	True/False
2: Performance management is the 5th most important global human capital trend with 78% of the 2017 Deloitte Global Human Capital Trends' 10,000 respondents identifying it as either important or very important.	True/False
3: High-performing companies develop strategies aimed at enriching the employee experience, which in turn leads to increased employee productivity and promotes purposeful and meaningful work.	True/False
4: The 2017 Deloitte Global Human Capital Trends report provides a global picture of the importance of implementing performance management across 16 key emerging and developed economies. Which of the following is not among the top five countries where organisations rated performance management as either important or very important for their workforce strategies? (A) Brazil, where 87% of HR leaders rate performance management as very important (B) India, where 91% of HR leaders rate performance management as very important (C) Germany, where 82% of HR leaders rate performance management as very important (D) China, where 85% of HR leaders rate performance management as very important (E) Mexico, where 86% of HR leaders rate performance management as very important	A B C D E

(Continued)

(Continued)

5:	Predictive analytics tools from many HR technology vendors have arrived, making it possible to analyse data regarding recruitment, performance, employee mobility and other factors.	True/False
6:	People analytics readiness remains a challenge. The 2017 Deloitte Global Human Capital Trends survey identified that only 15% of organisations have useable data to enable them to perform people analytics tasks and operations.	True/False
7:	The 2017 Deloitte Global Human Capital Trends survey identified some key recommendations for business and HR leaders to assist them with adopting forward-looking approaches and with better aligning their efforts in people analytics. Which of the following recommendations does not belong to the six put forward in the People Analytics chapter of the report? (A) Prioritise clean and reliable data across HR and the organisation (B) Increase people analytics fluency across the organisation (C) Bring together a specialist people analytics group from across the organisation (D) Develop a medium-term roadmap for investment in analytics programmes (E) Integrate HR, organisational and external data	A B C D E
8:	People analytics is the third most important global human capital trend with 71% of the 2017 Deloitte Global Human Capital Trends' 10,000 respondents identifying it as either important or very important.	True/False
9:	The 2017 Deloitte Global Human Capital Trends report provides a global picture of the importance of implementing people analytics across 16 key emerging and developed economies. Which of the following is not among the top five countries where organisations rated people analytics as either important or very important for their workforce strategies? (A) The UK, where 78% of HR leaders rate performance management as very important (B) Australia, where 85% of HR leaders rate performance management as very important (C) India, where 83% of HR leaders rate performance management as very important (D) Japan, where 77% of HR leaders rate performance management as very important (E) China, where 81% of HR leaders rate performance management as very important	A B C D E

10: The 2017 Deloitte Global Human Capital Trends report identified some key recommendations for business and HR leaders to assist them with adopting forward-looking approaches and with better aligning their efforts in performance management. Which of the following recommendations does not belong to the six put forward in the Performance Management chapter of the report? (A) Tailor performance management to strategic and organisational needs (B) Up-skill managers in coaching skills (C) Cascaded goals that help employees navigate through set activities (D) Identify a strategy and philosophy for performance management (E) Identify the design elements, tools and processes that are most effective for peers experimenting with performance management	A B C D E

Answers to questions

Q1: True

Q2: True

Q3: True

Q4: Option C – in Germany only 73% of HR leaders rate performance management as very important. With 82%, Spain is among the top five countries where HR leaders rate performance management as very important.

Q5: True

Q6: False – only 8% of organisations have usable data to enable them to perform people analytics tasks and operations.

Q7: Option C – bring together a multidisciplinary group from across the organisation. Contrasting considerations, such as data function, quality, business knowledge, data visualisation and consulting require multidisciplinary teams.

(Continued)

(Continued)

Q8: False – people analytics is the 7th most important global human capital trend. Talent acquisition is the 3rd most important global human capital trend with 81% of 2017 Deloitte Global Human Capital Trends' 10,000 respondents identifying it as either important or very important.

Q9: Option B – in Australia only 73% of HR leaders rate performance management as very important. With 85%, Brazil is among the top five countries where HR leaders rate performance management as very important.

Q10: Option C – instead of cascaded goals that lock employees into a set of activities, consider a more flexible, agile, transparent approach to goal setting.

Further reading and resources

AON (2017). *2017 trends in global employee engagement*. Available at: www.aon.com/unitedkingdom/attachments/trp/2017-Trends-in-Global-Employee-Engagement.pdf [Accessed 9 August 2018].

AON (2018). *2018 global employee engagement trends report*. Available at: www.aon.com/2018-global-employee-engagement-trends/index.html [Accessed 9 August 2018].

REFERENCES

Accenture (2015). *Accenture CEO explains why he is overhauling performance reviews*. Available at: www.accenture.com/gb-en/company-accenture-ceo-performance-review [Accessed 25 March 2018].

Albright, D. (2017). *10 proven strategies for increasing employee productivity*. Available at: https://blog.hubstaff.com/employee-productivity [Accessed 25 March 2018].

Bersin, J. (2017). *People analytics grows up: Healthy new focus on productivity*. Available at: https://joshbersin.com/2017/09/people-analytics-grows-up [Accessed 26 March 2018].

Bika, N. (2016). *What to measure in employee performance reviews*. Available at: https://resources.workable.com/tutorial/measuring-employee-performance [Accessed 24 March 2018].

Burrin, P. (2017). *Case study: How Google uses people analytics*. Available at: www.sagepeople.com/about-us/news-hub/case-study-how-google-uses-people-analytics [Accessed 26 March 2018].

Carroll, S. J. and Tosi, H. L. (1973). *Management by objectives: Applications and research*. London: Macmillan.

Chartered Institute for Personnel Development (CIPD) (2016). *Moving the employee well-being agenda forward*. London: CIPD.

Deloitte (2017a). *2017 Deloitte global human capital trends*. Available at: www2.deloitte.com/uk/en/pages/human-capital/articles/introduction-human-capital-trends.html#4 [Accessed 26 March 2018].

Deloitte (2017b). *People analytics: Recalculating the route*. Available at: www2.deloitte.com/insights/us/en/focus/human-capital-trends/2017/people-analytics-in-hr.html#endnote-sup-3 [Accessed 26 March 2018].

Dezeen (2018). *Amazon patents wristband to track productivity and direct warehouse staff using vibrations*. Available at: www.dezeen.com/2018/02/06/amazon-patents-wristbands [Accessed 24 March 2018].

Duggan, K. (2015). *Six companies that are redefining performance management*. Available at: www.fastcompany.com/3054547/six-companies-that-are-redefining-performance-management [Accessed 25 March 2018].

Dummies (2017). *How to measure individual employee performance*. Available at: www.dummies.com/business/human-resources/employee-engagement/how-to-measure-individual-employee-performance [Accessed 25 March 2018].

Fast Company (2017). *Why employees at Apple and Google are more productive*. Available at: www.fastcompany.com/3068771/how-employees-at-apple-and-google-are-more-productive [Accessed 25 March 2018].

Fletcher, C. (2002). Appraisal: an individual psychological perspective. In *Psychological Management of Individual Performance* (pp. 115–35). Chichester: Wiley.

Hanna, L. (2018). *7 steps for improving employee performance management programs*. Available at: https://blog.willis.com/2018/01/7-ways-to-improve-employee-performance-management-programs [Accessed 24 March 2018].

Harvard Business Review (2015). *GE's real-time performance development*. Available at: https://hbr.org/2015/08/ges-real-time-performance-development [Accessed 24 March 2018].

Harvard Business Review (2017). *Great companies obsess over productivity, not efficiency*. Available at: https://hbr.org/2017/03/great-companies-obsess-over-productivity-not-efficiency [Accessed 25 March 2018].

Harvard Business Review (2018). *Talent analytics: How do you measure up?* Available at: https://hbr.org/2010/09/talent-analytics-how-do-you-me [Accessed 26 March 2018].

Harvard Business Review (HBR) and Oracle (2014). *The age of modern HR*. Available at: www.oracle.com/webfolder/s/delivery_production/docs/FY14h1/doc7/18762-HBR-Oracle-Report-HR3-FINAL.pdf [Accessed 26 March 2018].

Houldsworth, E. and Jirasinghe, D. (2006). *Managing and measuring employee performance*. London: Kogan Page.

Hubstaff (2018). *Productivity measurement*. Available at: https://hubstaff.com/employee_productivity_measurement [Accessed 25 March 2018].

Kjerulf, A. (2016). *How Toyota Gothenburg moved to a 30-hour workweek and boosted profits and customer satisfaction*. Available at: https://positivesharing.com/2016/01/toyota-gothenburg-30-hour-work-week [Accessed 25 March 2018].

Kompaso, S. M. and Sridevi, M. S. (2010). Employee engagement: The key to improving performance. *International Journal of Business and Management*, 5(12), 89–96.

McKinsey (2016). *Ahead of the curve: The future of performance management*. Available at: www.mckinsey.com/business-functions/organization/our-insights/ahead-of-the-curve-the-future-of-performance-management [Accessed 25 March 2018].

Odiorne, G. S. (1965). *Management by objectives: A system of managerial leadership*. New York: Pitman Pub. Corp.

Office of Personnel Management (OPM) (2017). *A handbook for measuring employee performance*. Available at: www.opm.gov/policy-data-oversight/performance-management/measuring/employee_performance_handbook.pdf [Accessed 24 March 2018].

Perrin, O. (2017). *The difference between employee performance and productivity*. Available at: www.employeeconnect.com/blog/difference-employee-performance-productivity [Accessed 24 March 2018].

Public Health England (PHE) (2015). *Measuring employee productivity: Topic overview*. Available at: www.gov.uk/government/uploads/system/uploads/attachment_data/file/454172/20150318_-_Productivity_-_V3.0_FINAL.pdf [Accessed 25 March 2018].

re:Work by Google (2018a). *Great managers still matter: The evolution of Google's Project Oxygen*. Available at: https://rework.withgoogle.com/blog/the-evolution-of-project-oxygen [Accessed 26 March 2018].

re:Work by Google (2018b). *Introduction to Project Aristotle*. Available at: https://rework.withgoogle.com/print/guides/5721312655835136 [Accessed 26 March 2018].

Salesforce (2018). *7 ways workforce analytics will increase productivity and sales*. Available at: www.salesforce.com/hub/service/increase-productivity-sales-with-workforce-analytics [Accessed 26 March 2018].

Van Vulpen, E. (2016). *21 employee performance metrics*. Available at: www.analyticsinhr.com/blog/employee-performance-metrics [24 March 2018].

PART III

Global Talent Policy Perspectives

8
DEMOGRAPHIC DISRUPTIONS (RE)SHAPING THE GLOBAL TALENT LANDSCAPE

Chapter contents

Global demographic trends

- The scale of change
- The growing working-age population in developing countries
- The declining working-age population in developed economies
- Implications for the world of work

Global workforce challenges

- Demographic developments
- Educating and skilling the workforce in Asia, Africa and Latin America
- Challenges related to up-skilling and re-skilling the workforce in the West
- Policy implications

Global workforce opportunities

- Demographic trends
- Harnessing the demographic dividend in Africa and Southeast Asia

(Continued)

(Continued)

- Providing youth with the opportunity to join the global workforce
- Gender inclusivity and the workforce
- Over-65s in the global workforce
- Ideas and implications for policymakers

Case study 8.1: Contrasting demographic perspectives from China and India

The Human Capital Report 2016 Quiz

Learning objectives

After reading this chapter, you will be able to:

- understand key global demographic trends
- comprehend key global workforce challenges and opportunities
- develop an understanding of global policy responses to demographic trends and developments.

GLOBAL DEMOGRAPHIC TRENDS
The scale of change

Global demographic trends, including rapid growth in the youth demographic in low-to medium-income countries together with an upward trend in the ageing population in high-income economies, are shifting the workforce profile rapidly. In this chapter, we provide a critical perspective into some key challenges and opportunities that policymakers are faced with consequentially. We also provide policy insights and critical perspectives into how governments and policymakers have been responding to these challenges and opportunities.

Demographic shifts are high on the agenda for governments and employment policy around the world. The current world population of 7.6 billion is expected to reach 8.6 billion by 2030, 9.8 billion in 2050 and 11.2 billion in 2100, according to forecasts by the United Nations (UN). The UN's 'World Population Prospects:

The 2017 Revision', published by the UN Department of Economic and Social Affairs, provides a comprehensive overview of the latest global demographic trends and delivers future forecasts (UN, 2017a). The UN estimates that population growth worldwide is expected to continue as 83 million people join the world's population every year.

These trends are paving the way for an ageing population and workforce in many high-income countries. On the other hand is the growing proportion of youth in countries in Africa and Southeast Asia. Related global demographic trends such as higher life expectancy worldwide and the large-scale mobility of talent and migration are also redefining the profile of the global workforce and workplace.

The following sections explore the contrasting demographic trends in Asia/Africa with those of Europe/the USA and the West.

The growing working-age population in developing countries

The growing working-age population in countries in Asia and Africa in particular presents a global challenge. Over 50% of the world's population growth between 2017 and 2050 is expected to be concentrated in only nine, predominantly developing countries, most of which are located in these two continents. Furthermore, rapid population growth experienced by India, Nigeria, the Democratic Republic of Congo, Pakistan, Ethiopia, Tanzania, the USA, Uganda and Indonesia is expected to contribute to a significant increase in the working-age population globally. Together, these forces are intensifying the workforce dynamics for employment (Figure 8.1).

The UN highlights the role that Africa is projected to play (UN, 2017a):

> Africa's share of global population, which is projected to grow from roughly 17 per cent in 2017 to around 26 per cent in 2050, could reach 40 per cent by 2100. In all plausible scenarios of future trends, Africa will play a central role in shaping the size and distribution of the world's population over the next few decades.

In line with expected growth, the 2017 Africa Competitiveness Report by the World Economic Forum estimates that the working-age population in the young continent is expected to grow by close to 70% between 2015 and 2035. Consequently, a further 450 million people are projected to join Africa's current workforce by 2035 (WEF, 2017a).

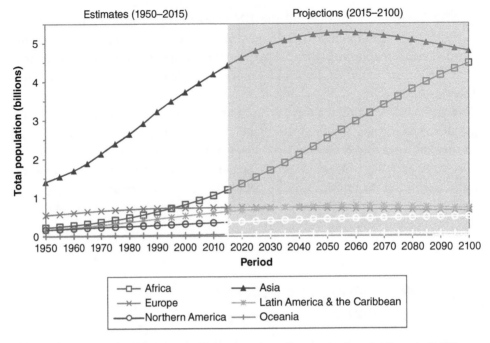

Figure 8.1   Population by region estimates and medium-variant projections to 2100

(Source: UN, 2017a)

Similarly many Asian countries are experiencing a growing working-age population. As Sterling Wong writes in Bloomberg, Southeast Asia will see its working-age population expand through 2020 at a time when other Asian countries, such as China, Japan and Hong Kong, have all experienced reductions in their workforce. The Philippines, for example, is projected to see a 1.9% expansion in its working-age population, while Malaysia's workforce is expected to rise by 1.6% on an annual basis (Bloomberg, 2017).

India, soon to be the world's single most populous country, is a prime example of the scale of rapid growth in Asia's working-age population. The Regional Human Development report by the United Nations Development Programme (UNDP) estimates that India's working-age population will grow to over a billion by 2050. As a result, over 280 million more people are expected to enter the workforce in India by 2050 (UNDP, 2016).

This global demographic trend provides some important policy implications related to an increase in demand for education and training. Policymakers are challenged to shape a response to this increased demand, which often remains unmet due to the sheer scale of the challenge and the lack of resources in low- to medium-income economies.

The declining working-age population in developed economies

In contrast to this is the emergent trend of a declining working age popultion in more developed and upper-income economies, mainly in Europe and North America and among countries labelled as the 'Asian Tigers' – Hong Kong, Singapore, South Korea and Taiwan. This decline is influenced by advancements in healthcare, workplace improvements and, more generally, access to a better lifestyle. These developments contribute to longevity in society, longer life expectancy and, ultimately, a rapidly growing proportion of the ageing workforce in developed countries.

In 2017, around 13% of the global population, or an estimated 962 million people, were aged 60 or over in the world, which represents a significant challenge for governments and policymakers. The UN notes that the world's population aged 60 or above is growing at a rate of about 3% per year. With 25% over the age of 60, Europe has the highest percentage of the population in this demographic. The UN's 'World Population Prospects: The 2017 Revision' concludes that ageing is turning into a truly global challenge whereby the majority of regions and countries across the world are projected to be affected by this emerging global demographic trend in the decades to come (UN, 2017a):

> Rapid ageing will occur in other parts of the world as well, so that by 2050 all regions of the world except Africa will have nearly a quarter or more of their populations at ages 60 and above. The number of older persons in the world is projected to be 1.4 billion in 2030 and 2.1 billion in 2050, and could rise to 3.1 billion in 2100.

South Korea is another example of a country facing a decline in its working-age population, which is expected to shrink significantly in the next two decades. According to the Health and Welfare Policy Forum report, compiled by the Institute for Health and Social Affairs, the number of people in the country aged 15 to 64 is projected to decline by 18.9% between 2017 and 2037 (*The Korea Times*, 2018).

The UK too is equally experiencing a rapid growth in the proportion of its population over the age of 65 in the country. This leads to a reduction in the country's workforce due to a declining working-age population. A report by the Institute for Public Policy Research, 'Future Proof: Britain in the 2020s', concludes that the country's over-65 population is projected to surge from 11.6 million in 2016 to 15.4 million by 2030, while the working-age population is expected to increase by only 3% or an estimated one million (IPPR, 2016).

Even China, the world's most populous country at the time of writing this text, is starting to experience the consequences of an ageing population. This country-level demographic trend has been influenced by a rise in China's middle class, together with improvements in lifestyle and healthcare provision. Allan Zhang, a Chief Economist at PwC China and Hong Kong, noted that China's working-age population, aged 16 to 59, has declined for three straight years since 2012, with the over-60 population reaching 222 million in 2015 (PwC, 2017). Zhang concludes that the total workforce in the country is predicted to decline to about 700 million people by 2050 when one in three people in China is projected to be over the age of 65. Hence, countries like China will need to find innovative approaches to shaping workforce policy and practice as the significant reduction in working-age population may well result in limited productivity, economic performance and competitiveness. We discuss the different demographic perspectives between China and India in more detail in our case study section of this chapter.

Implications for the world of work

These demographic trends, together with an increased talent mobility worldwide, are expected to significantly influence the worldwide talent pool profile. In fact, over 30% of the global workforce by 2050 is now projected to come from China and India alone. Negative growth in the working-age population in some parts of the world is expected to create the conditions for a more significant movement of talent across borders, mainly from countries seen as a source of global talent such as Nigeria and India to advanced economies that suffer from a talent shortage and ageing workforce, including Japan and the UK.

Ageing societies are already tapping into this opportunity to rebuild a younger workforce, which is the case with Japan and India who adopted a win-win policy approach to the issue. India and Japan signed a Memorandum of Cooperation (MoC) on a Technical Intern Training Programme (TITP) in November 2017 to provide technical education and skills to 300,000 Indian youths in Japan (MSDE, 2017). After the successful completion of their training, over 50,000 Indian trainees are expected to be allocated a job in Japan, to deal with the acute manufacturing and technical talent shortages in the country.

Singapore is yet another case of creating a favourable national policy to attract global talent and improve the profile of its ageing population and workforce. The country's

Employ-ment of Foreign Manpower Act (EFMA) regulates the employment of non-Singapore-born employees and protects their wellbeing, while exercising employment rights in the country (Ministry of Manpower, 2017). The Employment Act sets a wide range of rules and regulations that concern global talent in Singapore, including entitlements, roles and responsibilities related to salary, hours of work, overtime and rest days, public holidays, annual leave and sick leave. We discuss Singapore's approach to attracting and retaining global talent in more detail in Chapter 9 of this textbook.

Policy initiatives set at a regional, city and even national levels, such as those in Japan and Singapore, are expected to ease the pressure on countries facing a talent shortage due to an ageing workforce, while leading to a more diverse and culturally rich workforce globally.

Other countries will also ultimately develop new policy frameworks that will enable them to address challenges related to their shrinking working-age populations.

These trends present both challenges and opportunities that you, as global talent, will be required to navigate as you find your own place in the global workforce and work-place. We discuss some of these considerations in the section that follows.

GLOBAL WORKFORCE CHALLENGES
Educating and skilling the workforce in Asia, Africa and Latin America

The youth population is on the rise in many low- to middle-income countries across the world, and this contributes to a significant challenge related to skilling, up-skilling and re-skilling the workforce of these countries. In many of these developing states, the demand for higher education and training has been positively correlated with a grow-ing youth population. Low- to middle-income countries are, however, often unable to allocate resources, nor do they have the capacity to address this challenge.

Countries in Southeast Asia, for example, face significant challenges related to the provision of skills development and training opportunities for their often large work-force where the demographic dividend is, in fact, seen as a demographic challenge. We take India as an example. With a population of 1.29 billion people (WEF, 2017b), India is the second most populous country in the world. More than half of the country's popula-tion is under the age of 25. It is projected that India will be among the world's youngest nations by 2020. India's demographic dividend is predicted to have enormous implica-tions for the future workforce, not just in India but also on a global scale. The country adds 12 million people to its workforce every year, and it is estimated that by 2030, a third of the world's working population will be from India alone.

With as many as 711 million people in the working-age group of 15–59, India hosts the largest workforce in the world. While economic and demographic changes are leading to a growing demand for education in the country, the skill development and capacity building of Indian talent have been at the forefront of Indian government policy. Amid India's demographic dividend and large-scale young workforce, the opportunities for scalability and sustainability of the provision of skills development interventions remain low.

A recent report, 'Global Talent in India – Challenges and Opportunities for Skills Development in Higher Education', provides insights from the employer perspective into the challenges faced by India in the provision of quality skills development interventions targeted at its future workforce (Minocha et al., 2018). The report concludes that only 33% of Indian employers surveyed are satisfied with the entry-level skills and knowledge of graduates as employees. Additionally, policymakers raised issues with quality and only 30% of those surveyed agreed that universities have the necessary academic and professional staff to provide students with industry-relevant knowledge and skills.

Similar challenges present themselves in the African context. Jakaya Kikwete, former president of Tanzania, has written about the skills challenges faced by African countries as he noted that, by 2050, Africa would be home to a billion young people. If current trends persist, Kikwete (2017) estimates that only one in ten young people will be on track to gain the necessary secondary-level skills in low-income countries in Africa by 2030. With as many as 50% of African graduates being unemployed, the continent is facing challenges regarding reaping its demographic dividend. Graduate unemployment in African countries is a widespread issue. In Nigeria, the unemployment rate is as high as 23.1% for those with undergraduate degrees, while in South Africa this figure stands at 11.5% (British Council, 2015).

South Africa is illustrative of the wider African challenge wherein the quality and capacity of the country's skills development and training provision have been jeopardised by limited resources and a rapidly growing youth population. A British Council report with a focus on South Africa highlighted the importance of quality teaching and learning opportunities in developing skills and attributes, but also noted the fragmented evidence of knowledge application opportunities for students (British Council, 2015). Another key challenge in the context of South Africa has been the slow massification of higher education whereby demand for higher education far outstrips the existing capacity, quality and infrastructure in the country. This relatively slow expansion of the higher education system, together with declining state funding for universities, and colleges, presents further challenges for the growing proportion of the population aged 16 to 24 to access education, training and skills development opportunities that prepare them for the world of work.

Challenges related to up-skilling and re-skilling the workforce in the West

In contrast to the Asian and African context, advanced economies such as those in Europe, Japan and North America are facing the challenge of up-skilling and re-skilling their working-age population.

Challenges include the need for further investment in training to tackle the lower productivity of an ageing workforce, particularly with technology adoption in the workplace, increased life expectancy and longer working lives, among other trends.

Let's take the example of Japan. The Japanese government recognises the vital contribution of an ageing workforce to the country. It noted that 'older people's participation in the labour force will also be increasingly essential for Japan's sustained growth as the low birth rate and ageing of society lead to a decline in the working-age population' – an agenda promoted by the Japan Institute for Labour Policy and Training (2016: 16).

The Japan Institute for Labour Policy and Training highlighted in its report 'Labour Situation in Japan and Its Analysis: General Overview 2015–16' the need to utilise the knowledge and experience of the rapidly growing ageing workforce in the country. This requires a fresh approach to the inclusion of over-65s in the workforce that will benefit the economy and society and ensure the future sustainability of Japan's social security system. Despite its commitment to up-skill and re-skill its older workforce, the Japanese government's initiatives are likely to require substantial further resources and thus present another challenge in providing development opportunities for its growing proportion of over-65s in the workforce.

The Japan Revitalisation Strategy, implemented by the government in 2014, sets out the policy of promoting the active social participation of seniors to achieve an ageless society. The Strategy sets a bold target of attaining a labour force participation rate of 65% among those aged 60–64 by 2020 (Japan Institute for Labour Policy and Training, 2016).

The UK is in a similar position to Japan, where 10% of the population aged 65 and over are in employment. Amid recent projections that a third of people in the UK born in 2017 will live to the age of 100, the UK's Institute for Employment Studies highlighted that longer life expectancy necessitates longer working lives (IES, 2017).

The Department for Work and Pensions' (DWP) Fuller Working Lives initiative has been developed with the intention of improving the participation levels of over 50s in the workforce. There is evidence of impact following the implementation of this initiative whereby 69.6% of people aged 50–64 were in employment in 2015 (DWP, 2017). This figure nevertheless remains below the current employment rate of 74.5% for those aged 16–64, and the government is expected to be taking further steps to improve the numbers.

The UK government recognises the need to up-skill and re-skill the country's growing older workforce with initiatives such as apprenticeships and professional and career development loans (PCDLs), and, more generally, with efforts aimed at reforming the adult skills system. Employees aged 50–64 years are less likely to participate in training than younger employees, and the DWP highlights the importance of addressing the skills gap in employees that fall within this age bracket. To date, PCDLs have supported the development and training of around 300,000 adults in the UK. Equally, in 2015–16 alone over 57,700 or 11% of those starting an apprenticeship in the UK were aged 45–59 (DWP, 2017). Less than 1% of individuals accessing apprenticeships were over the age of 60, and a more proactive approach needs to be adopted to engaging this demographic in training and re-skilling initiatives.

The UK faces similar challenges to Japan with regard to providing adequate resources to deliver scalable training and skilling solutions to its senior workforce – solutions which are often in the hands of multiple stakeholders. Despite a proactive partnerships approach promoted by the DWP, a government-led, concerted effort combined with channelled resources will ensure that organisations, communities and individuals themselves make the most of the opportunities provided by the growing proportion of over-60s in the workforce. This fresh approach includes the need to adopt an inclusive policy that promotes and enables active workforce participation and builds on the skills and abilities of over-65s in the workforce.

Policy implications

We have explored a number of economies, both developing and developed ones, facing challenges in adapting to shifting demographic trends on a global level. We offer some insights and ideas for future policy making in these areas:

- **Create large-scale entrepreneurship opportunities for the graduate demographic.** The recommendation here is that skills development, especially in the youth and graduate populations, requires a concerted policy effort. The scale of the issue, particularly in economies like that of Africa, requires intervention at a state level to ensure that education-to-employment pathways address the problem at the roots. Providing large-scale enterprise and entrepreneurship opportunities would be necessary too in addressing the youth unemployment challenge in these economies.
- **Support the development of social entrepreneur educators and NGOs to provide education and skilling solutions, especially for youth.** Education and training

challenges faced by countries such as India are often driven by the limited capacity and quality of the provision of related interventions. Social entrepreneurship innovations from countries in Asia and Africa already provide scalable skills development and employment opportunities for youth but further good practice backed up by state policy is also required. NGOs also have the potential to provide scalable education and skills development solutions, particularly for youth from disadvantaged backgrounds.

- **Build education and training capacity to improve quality and provide scalable interventions aimed at the transition of youth into the world of work**. There is a real opportunity for developing countries to scale up their education and training systems through establishing mechanisms to develop and up-skill trainers who will then go on to skill and educate the youth. Capacity-building initiatives related to teacher training require resources and government backing and provide sustainable solutions due to the multiplier effect of these interventions.

In this chapter, we also offer some indicative ideas for high-income, developed economies that face an ageing population and a growing proportion of over-65s in the workforce:

- **Develop a comprehensive government-led approach to the provision of up-skilling and re-skilling opportunities for the ageing workforce**. Some countries have already embarked on policy interventions to up-skill and re-skill the over-65s as they recognise the opportunities for a wider inclusion of this demographic in the workforce. Skills development interventions nevertheless require the inclusion of training elements, including exposure to a cross-generational environment, technology adoption in the workplace and cross-cultural communication.
- **Place adult learning and lifelong learning at the heart of government policy and practice concerning the workforce and employment**. This recommendation highlights the importance of scaling up good practice in the skilling, re-skilling and up-skilling of over-65s in the workforce and developing learnability as a core attribute. Employment and workforce policy thus require a focus on developing lifelong learning modules that cater for the over-65s, many of whom might be engaged in the workforce for a number of years before they retire. Such initiatives would support wider workforce inclusion of the over-65s in countries experiencing relatively low workforce participation of this demographic.
- **Establish good practice for employers and industry organisations, including mechanisms for the over-65s to be fully integrated into the workforce**. Policy should enable a higher participation rate of over-65s into the workforce through a proactive engagement with employers. This requires regional support for industry engagement aimed at the development of agile and adaptive talent management models to fully unlock the potential of over-65s in the world of work. As industry would be required to cater for an ever-growing pool of employees over the age of 65, the mindset of this demographic can be understood through the provision of mechanisms to engage it in the workforce more fully.

GLOBAL WORKFORCE OPPORTUNITIES
Demographic trends

Amid our discussion of global demographic trends in the first part of this chapter, and some of the challenges surrounding these trends, in this section we critically reflect on some key opportunities related to the changing profile of the global workforce. We provide a national policy perspective on approaches that have been developed and delivered at country level to capitalising these opportunities.

Harnessing the demographic dividend in Africa and Southeast Asia

The UN estimates that the overall increase in global population between now and 2050 is projected to occur either in high-fertility countries, mostly in Africa, or in countries with large but relatively young populations, such as China and India. This demographic dividend may play an essential role in improving the state of economies and societies through an increased workforce participation of youth. A policy-driven integration of youth into the workforce leads to higher economic productivity and improved levels of societal wellbeing.

The demographic dividend, according to the Bill and Melinda Gates Institute for Population and Reproductive Health at the Johns Hopkins Bloomberg School of Public Health, provides opportunities for accelerated economic growth. Such opportunities are the result of improved reproductive health, a rapid decline in fertility and the subsequent shift in population age structure (Bill & Melinda Gates IPRH, 2018):

> With fewer births each year, a country's working-age population grows larger relative to the young dependent population. With more people in the labour force and fewer children to support, a country has a window of opportunity for economic growth if the right social and economic investments and policies are made in health, education, governance, and the economy.

Countries that have experienced high fertility rates in the past few decades, such as Nigeria and India, are now starting to evidence a change in the profile of their population whereby a significant proportion is under the age of 25 – 62% and 50% respectively. A youthful population, which is fully integrated into the workforce, provides a range of opportunities to support economic development and productivity in low- to medium-income countries and improve the state of societal wellbeing.

Despite a recognition of and the opportunities provided by this demographic dividend, youth unemployment worldwide is on the rise with over 13% of the global youth population being unemployed, in both developed and developing countries. The International Labour Organisation (ILO) notes that the global youth unemployment rate was estimated to reach 13.1% in 2017 – up from 12.9% in 2015 (UN, 2017b). The ILO's Global Employment Trends for Youth (GET Youth) report estimates that 73.3 million of the 200 million people globally who are unemployed are young people falling within the 15–24 demographic (Ryder, 2016).

What does the future of youth involvement in the global workforce look like? The World Employment and Social Outlook, which is an ILO report focused on challenges related to the world of work, notes that over 475 million jobs need to be created within the next decade. This large-scale job creation intervention would significantly reduce the number of unemployed youth and provide employment opportunities for around 40 million of them who enter the global labour market annually (ILO, 2015). This opportunity for a wider inclusion of youth in the workforce would nevertheless require policy initiatives implemented on a national level, and evidence suggests that both high- and low- to medium-income economies have been unable to fully integrate this growing demographic into the workforce.

Providing youth with the opportunity to join the global workforce

Global youth unemployment data provides an insight into the missed opportunity of involving talent aged 16 to 24 in the workforce in both developing and developed economies. According to World Bank (2016) data, over 12% of youth in the UK and Australia are unemployed, while the proportion of this demographic which is not in any formal employment in China and India, is over 10%. The presence of high youth unemployment figures across both low- and high-income countries highlights the importance of developing policy and good practice aimed at harnessing this demographic dividend and the broader inclusion of youth in the workforce.

Opportunities related to the demographic dividend have frequently been pronounced in countries in Africa and Southeast Asia where youth unemployment has been considerably higher than the global average of 13%. Data from the Africa Competitiveness Report 2017 (WEF, 2017a) highlights that Africa is the only region in the world where youth and subsequently the working-age population are expected to continue expanding well beyond 2035, particularly in sub-Saharan Africa.

This growth in the continent's youth population and working-age population presents challenges concerning education and training but also opportunities related to the integration of this fast-growing demographic into the workforce. Authors of the report highlight that a young workforce tends to be more productive and that a growing share of young adults participating in the workforce leads to increased productivity – an opportunity that certainly needs further attention from policy and practice, particularly in the context of sub-Saharan Africa.

Haroon Bhorat, Professor of Economics at the University of Cape Town, South Africa reflects on the challenges surrounding youth unemployment across sub-Saharan Africa. Youth unemployment in sub-Saharan Africa is four times higher than the region's aggregate unemployment level. According to Bhorat, in Nigeria alone, 45% of youth are unemployed (Brookings Institute, 2017). High levels of youth unemployment together with low-wage income are thought to act as a barrier to accelerating sub-Saharan Africa's ability to reap the benefits of its demographic dividend and enable its further economic and societal development.

What do governments in sub-Saharan Africa do to capitalise on the opportunities provided by a rapidly growing young workforce? The Federal Government in Nigeria, for example, has made job creation one of the primary objectives of its Economic Recovery and Growth Plan (ERGP). Job-creation initiatives are set to prioritise the involvement and integration of youth across a range of strategic sectors for the Nigerian economy, such as construction, manufacturing and agriculture (*The Guardian*, 2017).

These trends and policy interventions are also present across countries in Southeast Asia. We critically reflect on India as an example where half of the country's 1.3 billion population is under the age of 25. India adds 12 million people to its workforce every year and the majority of this talent entering the world of work is formed of the 16–24 demographic. An Ernst & Young (2013) study, 'Reaping India's Promised Demographic Dividend', emphasised the importance of adopting an inclusive policy to ensure India's youth have access to skilling opportunities, gain employment in the formal economy and engage in the country's growing workforce more fully.

What does the Indian government do to include more youth in the workforce and prepare them for meaningful employment? Education, alongside employment and skills development, is among the pillars of India's National Youth Policy, launched in 2014 by the Indian government and the Ministry of Youth Affairs and Sports. This government-led initiative delivers different training and workforce integration initiatives aimed at India's youth, such as targeted employment provision in rural areas where there are limited opportunities for them (Ministry of Youth Affairs and Sports, 2014).

Evidence from Nigeria and India suggests that governments need to step up and create large-scale opportunities for this demographic to engage in the workforce with a view to supporting the economic development in these countries. In turn, opportunities will improve the economic wellbeing of low- to middle-income countries and regions, particularly in Africa and Southeast Asia, where the productivity and inclusion of youth in the workforce have been fragmented and uncoordinated from a policy perspective.

In low- to medium-income economies, one needs to acknowledge the importance of partnerships in skills development and the integration of youth into the workforce. India and the UK provide an example of how a bilateral partnership in education and skills development can positively influence workforce integration and economic development in both countries. Hence, we provide a partnership insight into the projected benefits of bilateral initiatives in skills development and of workforce-integration initiatives.

PARTNERSHIP INSIGHT

Global Indian talent

India's demographic dividend is predicted to have enormous implications not only for the country's future workforce, but also on a global scale. India is a nation categorised by rapidly shifting demographics. More than half of its population are under the age of 25, and it is projected that India will be among the world's youngest countries by 2020. India aspires to become a global talent hub by skilling its workforce both to serve the country and fill talent gaps in other countries across the world. The following are some of the key recommendations from the 2014 FICCI 'Higher Education 2030: Making It Happen' summit. Together, these present a range of opportunities for the UK.

The employability of Indians graduating from Indian HEIs is nevertheless low. As many as 75% of university leavers in the country are considered unemployable. The UK, through its higher education, can support India's aspirations to become a global talent hub by addressing the gap between the quantity and quality of talent graduating from Indian colleges and universities. As India becomes younger, Britain sees its highest level of ageing than at any time in recent history, with one in every six people now aged over 65.

(Continued)

(Continued)

The UK is already experiencing global talent shortages – as an illustration, 745,000 additional workers with digital skills were needed to meet the rising demand of UK employers in 2017 alone. Equally, the UK is evidently slipping down prominent skills and talent indices due to the talent shortages the country is experiencing.

An education and skills development partnership between India and the UK can help the former country fulfil its aspirations to become a global hub for talent and the latter to address its talent shortages. Evidence of the UK's transformative impact in education and skills development on India is the 250,000 graduates from UK universities who have joined the workforce of India since 2004. But, equally, the contribution of Indian talent to the UK should not be underestimated as Indians fill skills gaps in critical sectors of the economy and represent over 40% of the highly skilled international workforce in the UK.

Gender inclusivity and the workforce

Alongside policymakers' efforts to integrate youth into the workforce, another equally important global opportunity that is high on the agenda in many countries has been the wider representation and inclusion of women in the world of work.

The gender pay gap and female representation have been subject to numerous debates and discussions in the past decade, particularly in advanced, middle- to high-income economies in Europe, Asia and North America. What we nevertheless observe in the rest of the world, particularly in Southeast Asia and Africa, is a more profound, socio-economic challenge related to the lack of female representation in the workforce. It is a lost opportunity and is often evident in countries with a historically low participation rate of women in the world of work. As Guy Ryder, Director-General of the International Labour Organization writes, women are less likely to participate in the workforce, and when they do so, they are less likely to secure employment opportunities.

The World Economic Forum's 2017 Global Gender Gap Index and report estimates that it could take another 217 years before the world achieves universal gender parity through economic, political, health, educational and workforce participation (WEF, 2017c). The report concludes that while the gap is now almost closed in education, with 94% gender parity at the tertiary education level, this does not extend to the workplace where gender parity is only 67% (Figure 8.2).

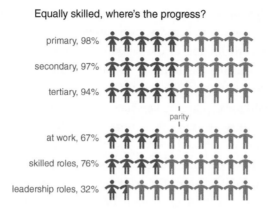

Figure 8.2   Global gender parity in the workforce

(Source: WEF, 2017c)

This WEF data points to an urgent need for large scale interventions to achieve gender parity. We will discuss three country-level perspectives from China, India and Saudi Arabia in this regard.

China is one example of a country that, despite its recent economic boom, is struggling to integrate women into the workforce and realise the benefits of doing so, due to the lack of favourable policy. Catalyst, a global organisation tasked with accelerating progress for women through workplace inclusion, highlights the scale of female misrepresentation in the Chinese workforce where only 63.3% of women in the country are in employment compared to 77.9% of men. Norms and policies in the Chinese workforce often disadvantage women, and they have fewer employment opportunities and policy-driven employment protections should they decide to start a family or have children. Catalyst data also highlights that China's current employment policy, which promotes an early retirement age for women, contributes to unrealised workforce participation and career development opportunities (Catalyst, 2018).

There are nevertheless other, perhaps more notable, examples of the misrepresentation of women in the workforce from developing countries. We take a look back at the WEF's Global Gender Gap Index and track India's performance in gender parity. In 2017, India was ranked 108th out of 144 countries on the Index, slipping from 87th in 2016. This downward trend is complemented by recent World Bank data suggesting that India has one of the lowest female workforce participation rates in the world. Building on these hard facts and figures, we would like to reiterate the words of Christine Lagarde, the International Monetary Fund's (IMF) CEO, who highlighted that India needs to focus urgently on the inclusion of women in its economy and workforce. Female integration into the workforce, according to Lagarde, provides immense opportunities for the country. Boosting female participation in the workforce of India, to achieve a level playing field with men, would enable the Indian economy to grow by 27%, according to a study by the IMF (*Indian Express*, 2018). Despite the projected benefits of wider female inclusion in the Indian workforce, policymakers have yet to develop interventions that would enable gender parity at work that can contribute to the realisation of the economic opportunities related to it.

Both India and China are illustrative sites for the opportunities that could unfold through the inclusion of women in the workfoce. However, we need to note that the integration of women into the workforce is not only a challenge faced by low- and medium-income countries in Asia and Africa; high-income states in the Middle East have also been struggling to enable more women to participate in the workforce, again often due to a lack of favourable national workforce policy. Female inclusion in the Kingdom of Saudi Arabia's workforce has been seen as a taboo for centuries due to the conservative culture of the country. This includes the socio-cultural characteristics of the Islamic state whereby the role of women has long been regarded as that of looking after the family and engaged in domestic work. This is, however, expected to change by 2030 as recent Saudi policy aspires to include more women in the workforce of the country.

Saudi Arabia's Prince Mohammed bin Salman's economic reform plan, Vision 2030, aims to diversify the country's economy and reduce its dependence on oil and oil-related revenue and growth. One of Vision 2030's primary targets is to increase female participation in the workforce from 22% to 30% over the next 15 years (Kingdom of Saudi Arabia, 2018). This policy, which aims to facilitate the wider representation of women in Saudi Arabia's workforce, is projected to boost the economic development of the country and create new employment opportunities and sectors of the economy.

These examples, from both developing and developed nations across the world, demonstrate how favourable, government-led employment policy can contribute to the development of opportunities for the inclusion of more women in the world of work, and accrue the socio-economic benefits of this integration for cities and countries.

Over-65s in the global workforce

This chapter has provided a discussion of the challenges related to the integration of the ageing population into the workforce and offered insights into how some governments have approached this challenge through tailored policy interventions and innovations.

However, alongside these challenges, the growing proportion of over-65s globally provides a range of opportunities for organisations, industries and nations.

As discussed in Chapter 3 of this text, finding four or more generations in the workplace is no longer unusual; it is the new norm. With an increased life expectancy and improved healthcare and social welfare globally, we expect to see an ever-growing proportion of the world's population over the age of 65 engaged in the workforce.

While being widespread, the workforce participation of the over-65s is fragmented globally and the level of involvement of seniors in the workforce is very different in different countries. A study conducted by the Organisation for Economic Co-operation and Development (OECD) places Indonesia as the country with the highest rate of people working beyond the age of 65. OECD data highlights that 50.6% of Indonesians aged 65–69 are engaged in the workforce (Figure 8.3). The OECD (2017) suggests that workers over the age of 65 are prevalent in other Asian countries. In South Korea, 45% of this demographic is engaged in employment, while in Japan the figure stands at 42.8%. Spain and France have the lowest engagement of over-65s in the workforce. The low workforce engagement of over-65s may not be sustainable in the long term and may place a burden on the health and social welfare system, currently being experienced by countries such as Japan.

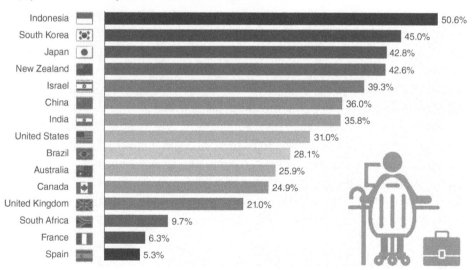

Where People Are Working Beyond 65

Employment rate for 65–69 year-olds in selected countries in 2016

Country	Rate
Indonesia	50.6%
South Korea	45.0%
Japan	42.8%
New Zealand	42.6%
Israel	39.3%
China	36.0%
India	35.8%
United States	31.0%
Brazil	28.1%
Australia	25.9%
Canada	24.9%
United Kingdom	21.0%
South Africa	9.7%
France	6.3%
Spain	5.3%

Figure 8.3   Employment rate for those aged 65–69 in selected countries

(Source: OECD, 2017)

Taking into account the rapid expansion of ageing societies globally, the lack of a more comprehensive inclusion of over-65s in the workforce seems to be a missed opportunity that needs to be addressed by governments across the world. In our discussion of global workforce challenges, we provided policy insights into how some governments enable the ageing workforce to re-skill and up-skill to remain gainfully employed over a longer term. Here, we provide an overview of policy responses from some countries and governments around the world to tap into the opportunity to provide employment to the expanding proportion of over-65s globally.

While Japan is increasing its retirement age to 65 by 2025, other countries, such as Canada, are implementing bolder policies to tap into the opportunities presented by an inter-generational workforce. The Government of Canada policy, 'Age-friendly Workplaces: Promoting Older Worker Participation', provides good practice examples and a guiding framework for organisations and individuals to improve the level of involvement of over-65s in the country's workforce (Government of Canada, 2012). In the UK, Andy Briggs, CEO of Aviva UK Life, the government's business champion for older workers, has set a challenge to employers in the UK to increase the proportion of older workers in the workforce by 12% by 2022. Briggs (2017) estimates that this measure would result in the workforce participation of a million more 50- to 69-year-olds in the UK.

The USA is also being challenged to evolve its approach to the inclusion of elderly workers as the share of people aged 65 and over in the country is estimated to rise from 19% in 2017 to 29% in 2060. Briony Harris, a senior WEF Agenda contributor, highlights that large-scale employers in the USA, including Barclays, Ford and Booz Allen Hamilton, have developed and implemented tailored interventions to engage older workers in the workforce (Harris, 2017). She goes on to suggest that older workers are an untapped solution to the ageing population. Equally, government-led interventions, including employment and training programmes for the over-65s, provide Americans with the opportunity to be fully engaged in the workforce and to develop additional skills and abilities to make them more employable. There are three main federal employment and training programmes in the USA that are suitable for older workers, in addition to two additional programmes targeted at the over-65s. One example is the Senior Community Service Employment Programme (SCSEP) run by the US Department of Labour, which offers employment and skills development opportunities for those over the age of 55, with a view to preparing them to re-enter and fully engage with the workforce (OECD, 2018).

Ideas and implications for policymakers

Our discussion in this chapter highlights the need for a concerted effort to capitalise on the demographic dividend globally. An ageing workforce could be seen as a burden, but 'smart nations' would see this as an opportunity to optimise and diversify the workforce.

With this perspective, policymakers could foster greater inclusivity and improved opportunities as follows:

- **Develop bilateral training and employment partnerships with a focus on the mobility of talent either between countries experiencing oversupply or nations with a shortage in their skilled workforce**. This mutually beneficial approach can follow successful policy initiatives such as the Japan–India model, which is seen as good practice in the provision of training and employment opportunities for the youth demographic. This would require from governments the development of talent mobility policy frameworks alongside good practice guidelines to enable these bilateral partnerships to flourish.
- **Create an empowering environment that would encourage more women to join leadership roles in the workplace**. Government policy could play an active role in improving the state of female participation in the workforce through leadership and empowerment. Effective policy and practice enable women to take up decision-making roles, leading to the development of further employment opportunities for this demographic. Parallel to this is the importance of developing country-specific integration programmes for women to enable more meaningful workforce and workplace participation.
- **Provide opportunities for the over-65s to up-skill and re-skill through development interventions informed by sectors of the economy experiencing a skills deficit**. This would require a deeper and more meaningful integration of the over-65s in areas of the economy and society where they can deliver a substantial contribution. The alignment of talent over the age of 65 with employment opportunities and organisations where their skills and abilities are in demand is one example. The development of flexible, gig-economy approaches for the engagement of over-65s in the workforce is another opportunity for future policy.

CASE STUDY 8.1

Contrasting demographic perspectives from China and India – China's ageing population versus India's youth–dominant society

Different countries across the globe are at differing stages of their demographic cycle. The two most populous countries in the world, China and India, are able to provide

(Continued)

(Continued)

contrasting perspectives into how major demographic trends fundamentally reshape the structure and composition of a country's workforce and have the potential to influence the global workforce. With a population of well over 1 billion in each country, China and India can truly influence and impact the profile and composition of the global workforce (Shirley, 2016).

India and China alone contribute to 37% of the global population but the two countries are very different when it comes to the profile of their workforces. Both countries provide evidence of significant national-level demographic trends fuelled by population profile differences. These include a growth in the youth population in India and increased life expectancy in China.

However, while China's population is forecast to level out at around 1.4 billion towards 2025, India's population is expected to grow further, according to the United Nation's World Population Prospects report (United Nations, 2017). These shifting demographics are most evident in the youth demographic. In addition, these trends are projected to have significant implications for the future world of work due to shifts in the profile and composition of the global workforce. We will discuss national-level demographic perspectives from China and India in more detail before we explore what the future holds for both countries.

China's ageing population

China has a population of 1.4 billion people. The country's demographic profile, however, is already on the verge of assuming some of the patterns and characteristics of populations and workforces in developed economies in Europe and North America. Trends evident in high-income countries include the rise of the middle classes alongside improved lifestyle and healthcare, which collectively contribute to an increased life expectancy. These trends are likely to push up median age in the country, unlike India, and current evidence already suggests a downward trend in the proportion of its youth demographic. China is the only country in the world where there is evidence of a steep reduction in its tertiary-age population, which is aged 18–24 (Universities UK, 2017). The proportion of youth in China is projected to decrease from 176 million in 2010 to 105 million in 2025, according to World Bank data.

At the same time, China's ageing population is quickly becoming a significant social and economic challenge, with the number of seniors set to soar. The proportion of over-65s in the country is forecast to grow to 167 million by 2020. This figure has nearly doubled when compared to 1995 data, according to United Nations estimates. In only 20 years between 2017 and 2037, China's over-65 population is expected to double from 10% to 20%. The next country, which is closest to China regarding rapid ageing population processes, is Japan, where it took 23 years for its over-65 population to double. In other developed economies, such as Germany and Sweden, this figure is 61 and 64 years respectively. Therefore, what we note in China is a rapid growth in the population over the age of 65, which develops much faster than many middle- to high-income countries.

India's youth on the rise

With a population of 1.29 billion people, India is the second biggest country in the world after China. Unlike China's downward trend related to the growth of its youth population, more than half of India's population in 2018 is under the age of 25. Following this rapid expansion in its youth population, it is projected that India will be among the world's youngest countries by 2020 (Shirley, 2016). In recent years, India has experienced a rapid increase in its tertiary age population, which is aged 18–24. It is estimated that this demographic is likely to grow further by 2025. The size of the 18- to 24-year-old population in India is forecast to grow from 161 million in 2010 to more than 175 million in 2025.

India's demographic dividend is projected to have profound implications for the future workforce, not just in India but also on a global scale. The country adds 12 million people to its workforce every year, and it is estimated that by 2030, a third of the world's working population will be from India alone. With as many as 711 million people in the active working age of between 15 and 59 years, India is already the largest workforce in the world. While these demographic changes are leading to a growing demand for education in the country, the skill development and capacity building of the Indian workforce have been at the forefront of government policy.

The way forward – China consolidating its workforce while Indian talent grow to supply talent abroad

These contrasting perspectives from China and India bring about many challenges and opportunities for the workforces in both countries. China is likely to consolidate its workforce and increase the retirement age of its population. Recently, China relaxed its one-child policy, which represents a move that could, in the short to medium term, mitigate the pressure on its labour market and social welfare services by reshaping the profile of the workforce. This policy intervention is projected to contribute to a steep rise in global population growth towards 2050, but it is also expected to lead to a younger Chinese workforce.

(Continued)

(Continued)

As more than half of its population is under the age of 25, India's aspirations to become a global talent hub through skilling the country's young workforce present an immense opportunity for the country. Earlier in this chapter, we discussed the fact that ageing and skills shortages are challenges that are experienced by many middle- and high-income economies in Europe, Asia and North America. This points to a demographic opportunity and a trend that is already evident through the size of the Indian diaspora in North America of over one million and its role in addressing skills shortages in the US workforce. Indian talent are thus expected to join the workforces of many other countries that experience talent shortage due to an ageing population and other socio-economic factors such as the relatively low participation of women and youth in the workforce.

Alongside these opportunities, various challenges lie ahead for both India and China. At present, these challenges are likely to be greater than the opportunities and, as such, they require targeted government and policy interventions to cater for the future needs of the population, workforce and labour market requirements in both countries.

One of the critical challenges for China going forward is related to its adaptation and response to its inevitably ageing population and workforce. China's ageing population will have significant implications for the composition of the national workforce, where at least four generations with different needs, skills and abilities are expected to work together. Increased life expectancy will mean a longer working life and employers will have to rethink their talent attraction, development and retention strategies for this increasingly multi-generational workforce.

Implications for government and policymakers are also projected to be on a significant scale. China's ageing population will have a profound impact on the workforce of the country, where substantial investment will need to be channelled into up-skilling and re-skilling a significant proportion of the older workforce. An ever-growing population of over-65s is also likely to put a strain on the healthcare and pension budgets of the country.

India, on the other hand, is projected to face very different challenges, mainly related to the expansion of the quality and scale of its education and skills development infrastructure due to its inability to cater for its ever-growing youth population that will need targeted skills development initiatives to respond to labour market trends. Skills development and capacity building have been put in practice through recent policy moves in skills development in the country, such as Skill India. Such interventions are, nevertheless, expected to put a considerable strain on the country's balance sheet due to the size of its youth population and the scale of the interventions that are needed.

Fast forward and the United Nation's World Population Prospects report suggests that an increased life expectancy in India is likely to lead to a rapid increase in the median age in the country as it approaches 2050 – from 26.6 to 37.3 years. India's projected median age in 2050 will be in line with China's current median age of 37. This comparative data suggests that young India is projected to experience demographic challenges in the future that are similar to those that China experienced in 2017 (United Nations, 2017).

This comparative case study provides evidence of the importance of the development and delivery of national-level policy that recognises the challenges and opportunities related to shifting demographics in countries, and adopts a long-term approach that nurtures sustainable economic and societal development through the deeper and more meaningful workforce integration of youth, women and senior talent.

Further case study resources

Shirley, A. (2016). *India's population will soon be bigger than China's. And the economic implications are huge.* Available at: www.weforum.org/agenda/2016/06/when-will-india-have-more-people-than-china [Accessed 5 April 2018].

United Nations (2017). *World population prospects: The 2017 revision.* Available at: www.un.org/sustainabledevelopment/blog/2017/06/world-population-projected-to-reach-9-8-billion-in-2050-and-11-2-billion-in-2100-says-un [Accessed 5 April 2018].

Universities UK (2017). *Patterns and trends in UK higher education 2017.* Available at: www.universitiesuk.ac.uk/facts-and-stats/data-and-analysis/Documents/patterns-and-trends-2017.pdf [Accessed 5 April 2018].

REFLECTIVE EXERCISE

The Human Capital Report 2016 quiz

Identify the top three trends from your perspective that influence global human capital

The World Economic Forum's 'Human Capital' report (at http://reports.weforum.org/human-capital-report-2016) ranks 130 countries on how well they are developing and deploying their talent. The index takes a life-course approach to human capital,

(Continued)

(Continued)

evaluating the levels of education, skills and employment available to people in five distinct age groups, starting from under 15 years to over 65 years. The aim is to assess the outcome of past and present investments in human capital and offer insight into what a country's talent base looks like today and how it is likely to evolve in the future.

Reflective exercise: Having read this chapter and the World Economic Forum's Human Capital report, take the following quiz, which will help you test your knowledge of key demographic, socio-economic and technological developments and their impact on the global workforce and in selected talent source countries.

Question	Response
1: The Human Capital report provides nine demographic and socio-economic drivers of change, which influence the state of human capital in the world. Which of the following drivers does not belong to the nine demographic and socio-economic drivers discussed in the report? (A) Young demographics in emerging markets (B) Changing nature of work and flexible work (C) Longevity and ageing societies (D) Artificial intelligence	A B C D
2: Digital disruptions, together with demographic and socio-economic drivers of change are on course to transform traditional employment. It is predicted that some disruptions to industries will necessitate a shift in employees' skillsets, while others will lead to wholly new jobs or make particular roles redundant.	True/ False
3: With 77,670,000 degree holders among its population, China has the largest number of people with higher education degrees in the world.	True/ False
4: The Human Capital report provides nine technological drivers of change, which have influence over the state of human capital in the world. Which of the following drivers does not belong to the nine technological drivers discussed in the report? (A) Sharing economy and crowdsourcing (B) Mobile internet and cloud technology (C) Rapid urbanisation (D) Robotics	A B C D

5:	China and India alone account for over half of the world's total graduate talent pool in Science, Technology, Engineering and Mathematics (STEM) subjects.	True/ False
6:	Some jobs have a higher degree of transferability across different industries, which makes some job-specific skills more universal than others. Which three of the following are the top three jobs with the highest skills transferability across industries? (A) Digital marketing specialist (B) Lawyer (C) Web developer (D) HR business partner (E) Journalist	A B C D E
7:	On average, the world has developed 81% of the human capital potential of the youngest members of the global population in the age bracket 1–14 years old.	True/ False
8:	The global level of unemployment for the 15–25 year-old demographic stands at 13.7% of the economically active population in this age group.	True/ False
9:	Globally, nearly 35% of our human capital potential remains undeveloped, due to a lack of learning or employment opportunities or both.	True/ False
10:	While current education systems seek to develop cognitive skills, non-cognitive skills that relate to an individual's capacity to collaborate, innovate, self-direct and problem-solve are becoming increasingly important.	True/ False

Answers to questions

Q1: Option D

Q2: True

Q3: False – India has the largest number of higher education degree holders among its population – 77,950,000. China comes second with 77,670,000 degree holders among its population.

(Continued)

(Continued)

Q4:   Option C

Q5:   True

Q6:   A, C and D; options B and E are incorrect.

Q7:   True

Q8:   True

Q9:   True

Q10: True

Further reading and resources

United Nations (2017). *World population prospects: The 2017 revision – further resources.* Available at: https://esa.un.org/unpd/wpp [Accessed 21 February 2018].

REFERENCES

Bill & Melinda Gates Institute for Population and Reproductive Health (IPRH) (2018). *What is a demographic dividend?* Available at: www.demographicdividend.org [Accessed 22 February 2018].

Bloomberg (2017). *Young workers herald the rise of Southeast Asia.* Available at: www.bloomberg.com/news/articles/2017-05-09/young-workers-herald-rise-of-southeast-asia-as-growth-leader [Accessed 21 February 2018].

Briggs, A. (2017). *Ageing workers are key to filling skills gaps.* Available at: www.hrmagazine.co.uk/article-details/ageing-workers-are-key-to-filling-skills-gaps [Accessed 22 February 2018].

British Council (2015). *Soft skills, hard challenges.* Available at: www.britishcouncil.org/sites/default/files/china_skills_gap_report_final_web.pdf [Accessed 14 March 2017].

Brookings Institute (2017). *Increasing employment opportunities: Navigating Africa's complex job market.* Available at: www.brookings.edu/wp-content/uploads/2017/01/global_2017 0109_foresight_africa_chapter-2.pdf [Accessed 22 February 2018].

Catalyst (2018). *Women in the workforce: China*. Available at: www.catalyst.org/knowledge/women-workforce-china [Accessed 22 February 2018].

Department for Work and Pensions (DWP) (2017). *Fuller working lives: A partnership approach*. Available at: www.gov.uk/government/uploads/system/uploads/attachment_data/file/587654/fuller-working-lives-a-partnership-approach.pdf [Accessed 22 February 2018].

Ernst & Young (2013) *Reaping India's promised demographic dividend: Industry in driving seat*. Available at: www.ey.com/Publication/vwLUAssets/EY-Government-and-Public-Sector-Reaping-Indias-demographic-dividend/$FILE/EY-Reaping-Indias-promised-demographic-dividend-industry-in-driving-seat.pdf [Accessed 22 July 2018].

Government of Canada (2012). *Age-friendly workplaces: Promoting older worker participation*. Available at: www.canada.ca/en/employment-social-development/corporate/seniors/forum/older-worker-participation.html#tc2 [Accessed 22 February 2018].

Guardian, The (2017). *Government committed to youth employment, says Udoma*. Available at: https://guardian.ng/appointments/government-committed-to-youth-employment-says-udoma [Accessed 22 February 2018].

Harris, B. (2017). *Older workers are an untapped solution to the ageing population*. Available at: www.weforum.org/agenda/2017/11/this-is-why-the-job-market-is-booming-for-older-workers [Accessed 22 February 2018].

Indian Express (2018). *India should focus on women's inclusion in economy: IMF chief*. Available at: http://indianexpress.com/article/business/economy/india-should-continue-with-reforms-imf-chief-5035916 [Accessed 22 February 2018].

Institute for Employment Studies (IES) (2017). *The challenges of an ageing workforce*. Available at: www.employment-studies.co.uk/news/challenges-ageing-workforce [Accessed 22 February 2018].

Institute for Public Policy Research (IPPR) (2016). *Future proof: Britain in the 2020s*. Available at: www.ippr.org/files/2017-07/future-proof-dec2016.pdf [Accessed 21 February 2018].

International Labour Organisation (ILO) (2015). *World employment and social outlook: The changing nature of jobs*. Available at: www.ilo.org/global/research/global-reports/weso/2015-changing-nature-of-jobs/WCMS_368640/lang--en/index.htm [Accessed 22 February 2018]

Japan Institute for Labour Policy and Training (2016). *Labour situation in Japan and its analysis: General overview 2015/2016*. Available at: www.jil.go.jp/english/lsj/general/2015-2016/2015-2016.pdf [Accessed 21 February 2018].

Kikwete, J. (2017). *In 2050, Africa will be home to 1 billion young people. And they'll need educating*. Available at: www.weforum.org/agenda/2017/04/in-2050-africa-will-be-home-to-1-billion-young-people-and-theyll-need-educating [Accessed 21 February 2018].

Kingdom of Saudi Arabia (2018). *Vision 2030*. Available at: http://vision2030.gov.sa/en/foreword [Accessed 22 February 2018].

Korea Times, The (2018). *Working age population to drop by 19% over two decades*. Available at: www.koreatimes.co.kr/www/nation/2018/01/119_241836.html [Accessed 21 February 2018].

Ministry of Manpower (2017). *Employment of Foreign Manpower Act*. Available at: www.mom.gov.sg/legislation/employment-of-foreign-manpower-act [Accessed 21 February 2018].

Ministry of Skills Development and Entrepreneurship (MSDE) (2017). *Signing of MoC on Technical Intern Training Programme (TITP) between India and Japan*. Available at: http://pib.nic.in/newsite/PrintRelease.aspx?relid=171789 [Accessed 21 February 2018].

Ministry of Youth Affairs and Sports (2014). *National youth policy 2014*. Available at: www.rgniyd.gov.in/sites/default/files/pdfs/scheme/nyp_2014.pdf [Accessed 22 February 2018].

Minocha, S., Hristov, D. and Sreedharan, C. (2018). *Global talent in India: Challenges and opportunities for skills development in higher education*. Available at: https://issuu.com/globalbu/docs/global_talent_in_india_online_versi [Accessed 21 February 2018].

Organisation for Economic Co-operation and Development (OECD) (2017). *Pensions at a glance 2017: OECD and G20 indicators*. Available at: www.keepeek.com/Digital-Asset-Management/oecd/social-issues-migration-health/pensions-at-a-glance-2017_pension_glance-2017-en#.WigBDcYqWUk#page1 [Accessed 22 February 2018].

Organisation for Economic Co-operation and Development (OECD) (2018). *Working better with age and fighting unequal ageing in the United States*. Available at: www.keepeek.com//Digital-Asset-Management/oecd/employment/ageing-and-employ ment-policies-united-states-2018_9789264190115-en#.WqEouq2cZTY#page5 [Accessed 8 March 2018].

PricewaterhouseCoopers (PwC) (2017). *The long view: How will the global economic order change by 2050?* Available at: www.pwc.com/gx/en/world-2050/assets/pwc-the-world-in-2050-full-report-feb-2017.pdf [Accessed 21 February 2018].

Ryder, G. (2016). *3 ways we can tackle youth employment*. Available at: www.weforum.org/agenda/2016/01/3-ways-we-can-tackle-youth-employment [Accessed 22 February 2018].

United Nations (UN) (2017a). *World population prospects: The 2017 revision*. Available at: www.un.org/development/desa/publications/world-population-prospects-the-2017-re-vision.html [Accessed 21 February 2018].

United Nations (UN) (2017b). *Global youth unemployment is on the rise again*. Available at: www.un.org/youthenvoy/2016/08/global-youth-unemployment-rise (Accessed 16 March 2017)

United Nations Development Programme (UNDP) (2016). *Human development report 2016*. Available at: http://hdr.undp.org/en/2016-report [Accessed 21 February 2018].

World Bank (2016). *Unemployment, youth total*. Available at: http://data.worldbank.org/indicator/SL.UEM.1524.ZS [Accessed 18 May 2017].

World Economic Forum (WEF) (2017a). *The Africa competitiveness report 2017*. Available at: www3.weforum.org/docs/WEF_ACR_2017.pdf [Accessed 21 February 2018].

World Economic Forum (WEF) (2017b). *The global competitiveness report 2016–2017*. Available at: www3.weforum.org/docs/GCR2016-2017/05FullReport/TheGlobal CompetitivenessReport2016-2017_FINAL.pdf [Accessed 21 February 2018].

World Economic Forum (WEF) (2017c). *Global gender gap report 2017*. Available at: http://reports.weforum.org/global-gender-gap-report-2017 [Accessed 22 February 2018].

9

ECONOMIC COMPETITIVENESS
AND THE ROLE OF
GLOBAL TALENT

Chapter contents

The relationship between global talent and global economic competitiveness

- Global talent competitiveness
- The role of global talent and organisations as hubs for global talent
- An international perspective on the current evidence
- Global talent as an indicator of global competitiveness

Evidence from national policy in developing and developed countries

- Socio-economic development plans and policies of countries in relation to talent
- Progress in national-level plans for global talent
- Challenges in facilitating talent development and economic policy development

Evidence from global indices and the place of global talent

- The GTCI and the effectiveness of talent policy
- Learning and implications for organisations and policymakers

Case study 9.1: Singapore as an Asian hub for global talent

The Global Talent Competitiveness Index 2018 quiz

Learning objectives

After reading this chapter, you will be able to:

- understand the relationship between global talent and economic competitiveness
- discuss examples of national policy and practice on global talent
- appraise the Global Talent Competitiveness Index and its role in measuring global talent competitiveness.

THE RELATIONSHIP BETWEEN GLOBAL TALENT AND GLOBAL ECONOMIC COMPETITIVENESS

Global talent competitiveness

Beyond the development of future individuals, global talent has broader implications and impacts, which include a positive contribution to economic growth, sustainability and competitiveness alongside societal wellbeing. Developing industry-relevant skills, attributes and abilities future-proofs workforce productivity and capacity. Both workforce productivity and capacity are critical ingredients of competitiveness and competitive organisations, cities, regions and countries on a global stage.

Global talent are seen as global human capital, which implies a significant yet often underestimated feature of the global workforce – value! Human capital is key to unlocking innovation and nurturing sustainability.

Despite recent developments in the 4th Industrial Revolution, as discussed in Chapter 4, human talent is still ahead of the machines on many fronts. Opportunities for automation and the adoption of robotics and artificial intelligence improve the productivity of organisations and provide value, but they are not yet as advanced as the inherent human capacity.

It should not therefore come as a surprise that global talent is increasingly seen as a competitive advantage; they are the currency that countries and organisations gamble on when they shape their strategies and plans to elevate their global standing and improve their competitiveness in a highly saturated market of products, services and experiences. Seen from an international perspective, global talent is a key source of competitiveness. This is an opportunity for governments and policymakers to put the role of talent first through the development of favourable policies that capitalise on the relationship between global talent and global economic competitiveness.

The role of global talent and organisations as hubs for global talent

Individuals as global talent are the building blocks of competitiveness that unlock higher productivity and value through the skills, attributes and abilities they develop, demonstrate and apply in the world of work. Indeed, global talent, alongside its management and productivity, is now among the five forces reshaping the global economy, according to the international think tank and consulting firm McKinsey Global Institute (2010). Global talent individuals bring diverse knowledge, experience and expertise that enable them to transform organisations and improve their global standing and competitiveness.

The role of organisations as hubs for global talent and their contribution to global economic competitiveness is critical. Organisations are key agents in the attraction, development and retention of talent. In so doing they are a nation's key agents for global talent.

An international perspective on the current evidence

We now go on to explore some international and cross-sectoral perspectives on how global talent becomes a source of competitive advantage in national-level policy making. *Talent Economy*, a Human Capital Media publication that reports on the evolving dynamic around the role a global workforce plays in the modern economy, highlights that talent is the world's most valuable resource (*Talent Economy*, 2016). What the world operates in today, therefore, is a talent-driven economy. In fact, global talent, which is aligned with workforce requirements in the world of work, can contribute $150 billion to the global economy, according to research commissioned by PwC and LinkedIn (PwC, 2014).

It is clear that global talent is driving global competitiveness upward and outward. We now provide examples from critical global industries and sectors of the economy.

In the UK, the motor industry contributed £15.8 billion to the economy through a strong talent pool of 155,000 skilled individuals across the country. Equally, global talent in the creative industries in the UK contributed a total of £90 billion to the economy in 2016 alone. In Hong Kong, a global talent network of over 2 million employees in the country's booming financial and professional services sector adds over $160 billion to the economy of the country. Equally, over $310 billion is the contribution of 12% of India's total workforce which is engaged in employment in the country's rapidly expanding manufacturing sector.

This is why global talent is well recognised in national plans, policies and strategies in both low- to medium-income economies and advanced ones. In fact, China released its first talent strategy – the National Medium- and Long-term Talent Development Plan (2010–20) – back in 2010. Canada has also recently launched a national-level talent plan that recognises the contribution of a skilled workforce to national economic competitiveness. These examples, from both developing and developed economies, indicate a transition in the position of talent. Traditionally seen through a corporate lens, talent is now moving into the policy space and is poised to gain further recognition in national economic development plans and strategies.

Microsoft, the established global software firm and tech giant, urged the US government to develop and implement a National Talent Strategy to secure the country's competitiveness and future economic growth (Microsoft, 2012). The proposcal was triggered by the need to strengthen America's STEM talent pipeline and reform highly skilled immigration policies toward improving the productivity, capacity and competitiveness of the national economy.

What do these global talent policy propositions and interventions tell us? Global talent as a notion is gaining traction in policy circuits and is now on the radar of governments aspiring to secure a competitive and sustainable future for their economies. The policy perspective on global talent competitiveness is something that we discuss in more detail in the second section of this chapter.

EVIDENCE FROM NATIONAL POLICY IN DEVELOPING AND DEVELOPED COUNTRIES

Socio-economic development plans and policies of countries in relation to talent

Building on the introductory policy discussion, we go on to provide an insight into the socio-economic development plans and policies of countries, which are either nations with large-scale global talent pools or those that serve as well-known hubs and destinations for global talent. We also discuss how ambitious and aligned economic development plans and policies are with a country's core talent objectives.

A number of economies, both developing and developed ones, have been recognised as important players with the potential to reshape the global talent landscape, according to the WEF's Human Capital report of 2017. Our discussion of selected developing and developed countries is thus informed by this report. We begin by providing an insight into India and China – the two most populous countries in the world, projected to hold over 30% of the global talent pool by 2050.

The Government of India has ambitious plans to transform the country into a competitive, high-growth, high-productivity, middle-income state. As India embraces globalisation and international links in shaping a more competitive and open economy and society, the country needs a well-rounded, future-ready workforce which is capable of contributing to increased productivity and capacity building across key setors of the country's economy.

India's Twelfth Five-Year Plan, 2012–17, implemented by the Planning Commission to the Government of India, highlighs government priorities focused on the opportunity to develop and attract top talent that will improve the country's competitiveness on a global stage. The Plan focuses on research and development talent, an entrepreneurial talent base and job-creation potential (Planning Commission, 2012). The 13th Five-Year Plan has not been published at the time of writing this text, but it is expected that talent and its relationship with national competitiveness will have an even stronger policy footprint amid the country's transition from an agricultural and manufacturing society to a high-productivity knowledge and innovation economy.

The People's Republic of China has also recognised the importance of attracting, developing and retaining global talent in its 13th Five-Year Plan for Economic and Social Development of The People's Republic of China, 2016–20. The Plan includes aspirations for China to become a talent-rich country of innovation and attract talent from other countries to sustain its economic development.

The Communist Party in Beijing has made an explicit statement in its Plan emphasising this sentiment (Central Committee of the Communist Party of China, 2016):

> We will treat talented people as the number one support for development, move faster to make innovations in the systems and policies for human resource development, create an internationally competitive personnel system, improve the calibre and structure of human resources, and work faster to make China one of the most talent competitive countries in the world.

China aims to achieve this competitive talent positioning by revamping its current policy and practice on how the country attracts, develops and retains talent for productivity and competitiveness. When compared to India, China's Plan provides a more comprehensive and future-proof vision for global talent and its role in supporting national economic competitiveness. We will revisit this in detail later in this chapter.

Like China and India, strengthening Australia's competitiveness is the key to the country's future prosperity, according to the Australian government's recently launched Industry Innovation and Competitiveness Agenda: An Action Plan for a Stronger Australia. Australia aims to better prepare for the jobs and industries of the future through policy interventions that include increasing the skills level of its workforce, revamping its education and training system and the opportunity to attract highly skilled talent from abroad. The Australian Agenda and proposed policy interventions recognise the importance of facilitating the interplay between talent and economic competitiveness (Australian Government, 2014): 'In an increasingly globalised economy, it will be critical that all businesses have the people and skills to innovate, the networks to remain competitive in domestic markets, and the know-how to identify opportunities in global markets.'

Australia is not the only high-income economy that recognises the importance of talent in improving national productivity and driving economic competitiveness. Singapore, one of the global champions in attracting global talent, is reshaping its policy for talent and skills. The Future Economy, a master plan led by Singapore's Ministry of Finance, aims to drive the growth and transformation of the country's economy for the future and a highly skilled workforce is seen as imperative to future-proofing people, organisations and communities.

A report by the Singaporean government's Committee on the Future Economy highlights the country's aspirations to expand its pipeline of entrepreneurial and technical talent and offers key recommendations to achieve this vision. In its pursuit to equip its workforce with skills for the future, the Singaporean government highlights the importance of developing global skills and capabilities and attracting overseas talent so that the country's industries and the economy remain competitive globally (Committee on the Future Economy, 2017):

> To grow key nascent industries where there are fewer Singaporeans with existing expertise, Singapore must augment local talent with foreign talent possessing specialised skillsets. Concurrently, Singapore must develop global-minded local talent who can acquire specialised skills and assume leadership roles in large enterprises.

Singapore's policy response is an example of a balanced approach to talent attraction, development and retention, which recognises the contribution of both home-grown and international talent through establishing mechanisms that harness both pipelines. In doing so, the country's over reliance on talent from abroad to realise its growth ambitions is expected to be reduced through national-level policy aimed at up-skilling and internationalising the Singaporean workforce.

POLICY INSIGHT

China's Thousand Talents Plan

In addition to China's National Talent Plan charting a vision for talent towards 2020, the country released its Thousand Talents Plan in the wake of the 2008 global economic downturn, with a view to attracting top international talent to the country and supporting its research and innovation base.

China's Thousand Talents Plan, initiated as the Recruitment Program of Global Experts, has its focus on the recruitment of an extensive network of established and experienced global talent, including scientists, researchers and innovators who can deliver breakthroughs across key technology-enabled sectors, which is a priority for the country and enhances China's established and emerging high-tech industries. The Plan is currently being carried out through the inclusion of six strategic global talent areas:

- The Recruitment Program for Innovative Talents (Long-Term)
- The Recruitment Program for Entrepreneurs
- The Recruitment Program for Young Professionals
- The Innovative Talents Recruitment Program (Short-Term)
- The Recruitment Program for Foreign Experts
- The Recruitment Program for Top-notch Talents and Teams. (The Thousand Talents Plan, 2018)

China's Thousand Talents Plan is inspired by the increased mobility of talent globally and sees talent from abroad as a competitive advantage through the attraction and retention of skills, knowledge and experience acquired internationally. The Plan has been developed to support the country's aspirations to become a leading global economy driven by a transition from agriculture and manufacturing to innovation and technology adoption.

Canada, a high-income economy, also recognises the role of talent in driving economic competitiveness through specific talent-driven policies. Digital Talent: Road to 2020 and Beyond is a national strategy to develop Canada's talent in a global digital economy – a vision that has been shaped by the Information and Communications Technology Council (ICTC) in collaboration with industry, education, government and professionals in the information and communications technology (ICT) sector (ICTC, 2017). Canada's strategy provides practical recommendations that aim to position the country's talent as a comparative advantage in the increasingly global and rapidly evolving digital landscape. (Figure 9.1).

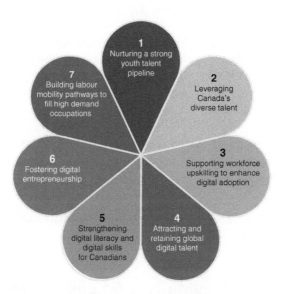

Figure 9.1   Strategic recommendations for building Canada's digital talent base
(Source: ICTC, 2017)

Middle- to high-income economies in Asia are also rethinking the interplay between talent and economic competitiveness. One example is Malaysia and its aspiration to become a competitive hub for global talent. The aspiration behind TalentCorp, a government-led talent initiative, is to turn Malaysia into a top 20 global talent destination by 2020.

TalentCorp was established in 2011, under the Department of the Prime Minister, to formulate and facilitate initiatives to address the availability of talent in line with the needs of the country's economic transformation, development and future growth. Serving as the national agency that drives Malaysia's talent strategy towards becoming a dynamic talent hub, TalentCorp developed and rolled out a range of talent attraction, development and retention initiatives. Implemented between 2011 and 2017, these initiatives have been tailored to professionals, students, employers, industry and academia (TalentCorp, 2018).

In 2012, TalentCorp developed and implemented a comprehensive roadmap to talent development, attraction and retention initiatives to 2020. Talent Roadmap 2020 is designed to address the underlying issues affecting talent availability in Malaysia, while delivering a pool of skilled talent needed by economic sectors that are key to the country's competitiveness and future growth.

Talent Roadmap 2020 and TalentCorp focus on three strategic domains driven by national, government-led policy initiatives (Figure 9.2):

- *Optimise Malaysian talent* – designed to ensure home-grown talent secure fulfilling careers
- *Attract and facilitate global talent* – implemented to attract talent from abroad that complements the Malaysian talent pool
- *Build networks of top talent* – developed to connect top talent to leading employers and vice versa. (TalentCorp, 2012)

Malaysia's approach showcases the country's forward-looking strategy for the attraction, development and retention of both Malaysian and foreign-born talent, while also facilitating a better integration between talent and opportunities in the job market. Comprehensive talent policies, such as the Malaysian one, enhance opportunities for future-proofing labour markets, narrowing the talent mismatch and further supporting economic competitiveness through talent.

Progress in national-level plans for global talent

The preceding discussion provides evidence that both low- to medium-income and high-income countries have developed tailored policy interventions for the development, attraction and retention of home-grown and global talent. The importance of talent and its global dimension, as we discussed earlier in this chapter, has also been recognised in national economic plans and strategies as a source of sustained economic competitiveness and as a key enabler for the future success and sustainability of key sectors of the economy in these countries.

But how successful are these plans and strategies? In this section, we provide an international policy insight into the performance of some national-level talent policies and what they have achieved since their inception. We take China's Thousand Talents Plan, as an example. Hepeng Jia, a science writer in Beijing for the global science magazine *Nature*, highlights that a decade after its inception, the Thousand Talents Plan has attracted over 7,000 individuals that can be classified as highly skilled scientific talent from abroad. Yet, in a country with over 2500 colleges and universities and with a working-age population of over 900 million, the attracted pool of international talent represents a tiny fraction of the country's workforce. As such, the Thousand Talents Plan may need further expansion in scale and scope to enable China to fulfil its ambition to become a global science and technology powerhouse.

However, there is another policy hurdle that may be argued to be preventing China from attracting more talent from abroad. Jia notes that China issued only 1,576 permanent residencies to talent engineers from abroad in 2016, while the USA, a country whose workforce is less than 20% that of China, has issued around one million certificates to global engineering talent (*Nature*, 2018). This complex employment and immigration policy landscape, coupled with a shrinking working-age population, which is forecast to experience a reduction of 225 million by 2050, may warrant a fresh approach to sustaining its talent ambitions.

Another example is Malaysia's Talent Roadmap 2020 driven by the national agency TalentCorp, which we discussed earlier in this chapter. The World Bank undertook a review of TalentCorp's two key initiatives – the Returning Expert Programme (REP) and the Residence Pass-Talent (RP-T) programme – to evaluate its efficacy. While Malaysia's success in implementing vital talent-driven policy interventions is acknowledged, the World Bank audit recommended a revision to TalentCorp's current direction of travel to enable the country to better compete in the global war for talent and to strengthen the competitiveness of its economy through the attraction and retention of talent (World Bank, 2018).

One reason for the fragmented evidence of success in talent development, attraction and retention performance across countries may be that developing economies in Asia and Africa occasionally emulate models seen as successful in high-income economies in Europe and North America with a highly skilled workforce. Developing economies that aspire to a global talent advantage may require newer forms of policies and frameworks to facilitate the interplay between global talent and economic competitiveness. For example, the current level of graduate unemployment across Africa, which totals 50%, may not be resolved by emulating talent attraction, development and retention frameworks that have been implemented in advanced economies such as the UK or Australia – countries that experience significantly lower graduate talent unemployment levels.

Some African countries, traditionally low- to medium-income economies, such as Kenya, are also taking the lead on crafting policy for global talent and have established policy initiatives to recognise the role and contribution of talent in national competitiveness. The Government of Kenya's Presidential Digital Talent Programme aims to develop leadership and information and communications technology (ICT) capabilities in Kenya's home talent (Opportunities for Africans, 2017). This is seen as a source of competitiveness, providing opportunities for the sharing of good practice which can be tailored to specific socio-economic characteristics and national development plans.

South Africa is another example from the sub-continent, which places central importance on talent development in realising the country's long-term economic and societal development. It recently launched its National Development Plan 2030: Our Future – Make it Work, which recognises that South Africa will work towards enhancing its positioning and competitiveness in sectors of the economy through job creation, education, skills and talent development (National Planning Commission, 2017). Yet, like Kenya, South Africa will need to provide a more enabling environment for the development and retention of both home-grown talent along with skilled overseas talent to support the country's growth ambitions.

These examples signify the need for an organic, grassroots approach that centres specific national characteristics of the socio-cultural, economic and environmental context of the economy in building a contextualised model of talent competitiveness. Alongside embracing international good practice, developing nations would need to channel their efforts into shaping sustainable, resourceful and future-proof approaches that facilitate both the development of home-grown talent and the attraction and retention of talent from abroad. This comprehensive approach to policy development is necessary to secure a sustainable approach to economic competitiveness, enabled through a skilled and sustained pool of both home-grown and international talent.

Challenges in facilitating talent development and economic policy development

The adoption of talent driver models of competitiveness still presents a number of challenges especially in the policy content of emerging economies.

For example, in low- and medium-income countries across the African continent, in Southeast Asia and in South America, there are often many competing national priorities such as access to education, infrastructure and development, pollution and urban sustainability, to name a few. As a result, strategic themes that include workforce development and the attraction of global talent are often left behind when national-level policy and planning are either crafted or implemented.

How does one facilitate talent attraction, development and retention interventions that contribute to economic competitiveness at a time when many countries in South America and Africa, in particular, are still facing some fundamental challenges, such as corruption and law and order?

A good example with regard to reflecting on the grand challenges facing developing economies that aspire to be at the forefront of talent, is Brazil. With a population of over 210 million and a territory that spreads across South America, Brazil is the largest and most populous country on the continent. Yet its workforce development aspirations have been jeopardised by persistent corruption scandals and political shake-ups, together with the country's poor economic performance over the past few years. Brazil's recession of 2016 was reportedly the country's worst economic crisis since the Great Depression. It also led to an inability to plan long term for the development of its future workforce and the attraction and retention of talent to improve the competitiveness of the Brazilian economy.

Dr Oliver Stuenkel, Professor of International Relations at the Getúlio Vargas Foundation (FGV) in Sao Paulo, has argued that Brazil is missing a golden opportunity. According to Stuenkel (2015), the country has been slow in the development of an enabling policy environment. He says: 'Brazil does far too little to actively attract international talent. The shortage of skilled labour significantly hampers Brazil's capacity to compete internationally. It also makes services in Brazil unnecessarily expensive, thus contributing to rising inflation.'

Brazil is not an isolated case and more needs to be done in low- to medium-income countries so that states, public bodies, businesses and communities can realise the benefits of a national policy aimed at the attraction, development and retention of global talent and, importantly, to realise the effect policy interventions might have on the economic competitiveness and global positioning of countries.

This section provides a critical perspective on a range of policy approaches aimed at the attraction, development and retention of global talent – policies that recognise the impact of a skilled workforce on economic productivity and competitiveness. Challenges driven by the complexity of national priorities, including economic, socio-cultural, political and environmental concerns dominate the agenda. Future policy making requires innovative ideas and interventions to shape a productive and competitive global workforce for the future.

EVIDENCE FROM GLOBAL INDICES AND THE PLACE OF GLOBAL TALENT

The GTCI and the effectiveness of talent policy

Global talent indices have emerged in the past decade both as evidence of the importance of global talent globally and as a reliable approach for countries to benchmark their performance in the attraction, development and retention of global talent. Global talent indices reflect a strategic-level, independent assessment of the effectiveness of national policy and practice focused on global talent.

The Global Talent Competitiveness Index (GTCI), compiled by INSEAD, The Adecco Group and TATA, which ranks 119 countries and 90 cities based on their ability to attract, develop and retain global talent is a leading bechmark. Global talent, according to the developers of GTCI, is the most powerful resource for driving economic competitiveness, at country, city and organisation levels, and this, understandably, has become a policy priority for governments (GTCI, 2018):

> Countries are competing globally to grow better talent; attract the talent they need; and retain those workers who contribute to competitiveness, innovation, and growth. Countries seek to put economic and social policies in place that will facilitate this.

GTCI comprises six pillars or indicators of global talent competitiveness that make up the Index (Figure 9.3). Hence, measuring global talent competitiveness includes indicators such as a country's ability to enable, attract, grow and retain global talent alongside the profile and quality of its workforce through the availability of vocational, technical and global knowledge and skills:

1. *Enable* – looks at the regulatory, market, business and labour frameworks in countries and whether relevant policies and practices help attract talent (or not)
2. *Attract* – assesses how open a country or city is to talent from abroad, both highly skilled workers and productive businesses, and also looks to remove labour market entry barriers to those from underprivileged backgrounds, women and older people
3. *Grow* – examines how well a country or city develops its workforce; for example, through a good education system, the provision of training opportunities, apprenticeships and lifelong learning interventions
4. *Retain* – looks at the quality of life in global talent destinations and is key to ensuring sustainability, not just in the provision of a steady talent pipeline but also in its links to productivity and economic competitiveness
5. *Vocational and technical skills* – measures the availability of global talent with vocational and technical skills that are sought after by priority sectors of the national economy
6. *Global knowledge skills* – looks at the availability of global knowledge and skills, including the availability of workers in professional, managerial or leadership roles that require creativity, innovation and problem solving.

The GTCI is computed as the simple arithmetic average of the scores registered on each of the six pillars discussed above. The Index indicators of global talent competitiveness emphasise the importance of a country's ability to attract, retain and develop global talent, through national level policies on talent, workforce development and economic competitiveness.

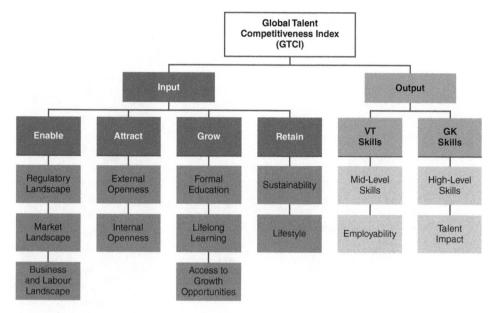

Figure 9.2   The six input and output pillars of the GTCI

(Source: GTCI, 2018)

Countries with the highest GTCI scores demonstrate strong performance across each of the six pillars of the GTCI, as depicted in Figure 9.2. There are several key characteristics that top-ranking countries on the GTCI have in common:

- a flexible regulatory and business landscape
- employment policies which combine flexibility and social protection
- external and internal openness. (INSEAD, 2018)

We now take a look at the top five countries in the 2018 GTCI and examine how they have secured their prime GTCI position through the development and implementation of policy aimed at the attraction, development and retention of global talent. Switzerland and Singapore occupy the first two positions in the overall GTCI (Figure 9.3). Switzerland, according to the GTCI, excels at the development and retention of its home-grown talent base. It does so by offering a favourable economic environment characterised with a talent-centric regulatory, market, and labour policy and practice. Singapore has emerged as the leader in the Enable pillar of the GTCI, as the small but highly competitive state that has been the best performer in attracting talent from abroad. This is a result of its proactive national-level policy directed at the attraction and retention of global talent. The USA, Norway and Sweden have secured the third, fourth and fifth place respectively, owing to their favourable policies in promoting practices that develop its home-grown talent and secures the attraction and retention of talent from abroad.

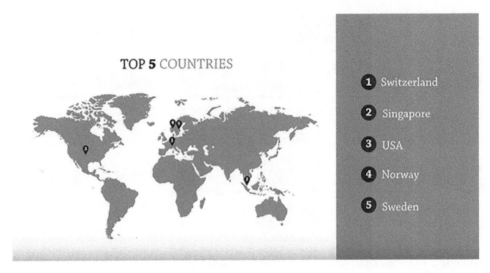

Figure 9.3   Five top-performing countries on the GTCI

(Source: GTCI, 2018)

If we examine the top 50 best GTCI performers, we note a relatively low representation from countries in Africa and Latin America. Only five Latin American countries feature in the top 50 entries in the GTCI – Chile (33rd), Costa Rica (35th), Uruguay (44th), Panama (45th) and Argentina (49th). If we look at Africa, only one country from the continent makes it into the top 50 on the Index – Mauritius being 46th. In fact, the majority of African and Latin American countries are located towards the 3rd and 4th quartile of the Index and thus occupy relatively low Index positions, between 80th and 119th. This poor representation of African and Latin American countries provides a wake-up call for governments and policy-makers regarding the importance of creating an enabling infrastructure and environment to develop and grow their existing pool of talent. The performance of countries in Africa and Latin America in the attraction and retention of talent from abroad is another indicator of the need for underperformers on the GTCI to rethink their policy approach. The development of a comprehensive workforce policy aimed at the development, attraction and retention of home-grown and international talent is key to improving the economic competitiveness and social wellbeing of countries that have demonstrated a poor performance on the GTCI.

The 2018 edition of the Index has its focus on diversity and particularly the role of diversity in the talent pipeline, which leads to innovation and brings improvements in the competitiveness of cities, regions and nations. We discussed in Chapter 3 the importance of global talent's ability to navigate through an increasingly cross-cultural workforce. You as a future global talent should also be able to reflect critically on the enablement of diversity of thinking and policy making necessary for diving talent centric competitiveness.

GTCI is a powerful tool for policymakers to measure and benchmark the national efficacy of their policies from a talent perspective.

Learning and implications for organisations and policymakers

What is the effectiveness of national-level policies and plans for global talent? Country level performance data drawn from the GTCI suggests that the implementation of global talent policy may not always deliver policy objectives focused on the attraction, development or retention of a highly skilled workforce. In Figure 9.4, we note that some countries such as Singapore, Qatar and the United Arab Emirates (UAE) have lost their positions on the GTCI over the past few years, particularly in the Retain pillar. This is despite initiatives in these countries to elevate the role of talent in national economic competitiveness, and the adoption of approaches and mechanisms to facilitate talent development, attraction and retention across key sectors of the economy.

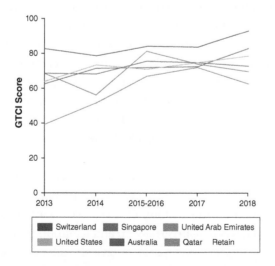

Figure 9.4   Comparison of countries on the Retain pillar of the GTCI

(Source: GTCI, 2018)

A shift in these countries' workforce policies in favour of the development of home-grown talent and of combatting the overreliance on talent from abroad is likely to have played its part in shaping their performance on the GTCI (Figure 9.5). The GTCI provides an important benchmarking tool for policymakers, which evaluates the impact of their policy interventions on the attraction, development and retention of global talent.

This section provides some indicative considerations that have been informed by our examples in this chapter so far. First and foremost, our discussion of international workforce policies and practices demonstrates that the creation of an enabling environment and infrastructure is key to the attraction, development and retention of global talent. This includes both physical infrastructure related to the quality of life and cognitive infrastructure to enable talent to further develop and provide opportunities for lifelong learning and personal development. TalentCorp's strategic policy approach to optimising the performance, productivity and competitiveness of Malaysian talent through the provision of developmental opportunities is just one example of such an infrastructure.

Governments could also work towards positioning global talent at the heart of policy planning and development related to economic competitiveness. We explored a number of national development policies and plans where global talent and the development of a skilled workforce are considered of prime importance, including those of Canada and China. Examples of government-led policy and practice, which are specifically targeted at the attraction, development and retention of global talent, are less common. Our discussion highlighted the case of Malaysia as one of the few examples of national-level global talent policy. Favourable and targeted national-level policy to enable the development of home-grown talent and the attraction and retention of overseas talent provides the basis for a sustainable, forward-thinking approach to talent-driven competitiveness.

Policymakers and government bodies can also utilise impact studies as a tool to evaluate the socio-economic impact of talent on local and national economies as a whole. The GTCI, as discussed in this chapter, is a useful tool but sector-level impact studies can provide deeper comparative insights to enable the development of targeted policy initiatives to attract, develop and retain talent.

Countries like Singapore and Switzerland are role models for other states on a journey to shape policy and practice related to talent-driven national competitiveness. This was evident in our discussion on the position of these two countries on the GTCI. While good practice in talent development, attraction and retention from high-income economies can provide learning for developing nations, the adoption of this good practice needs to be tailored to the social, economic, political and social characteristics of the state it is being implemented in as illustrated through the case of Africa.

Policymakers and governments in countries that experience either an oversupply or undersupply of talent can identify win-win approaches enabled through cross-country talent mobility initiatives. This approach is thought to work particularly well for countries considered as sources of global talent and of an abundant workforce, such as China and India, as well as for those that experience talent shortages fuelled by a negative demographic growth, in the likes of the UK, Japan and Canada. In Chapter 8 we discussed the case of the Japan–India partnership in training and employment provision as an example of this win-win approach to talent attraction and retention. We now provide an in-depth insight into Singapore's government policies and practices aimed at the attraction, development and retention of talent in one case study.

CASE STUDY 9.1

Singapore as an Asian hub for global talent

An Insight Into Singapore's Competitive Labour Market

Singapore is a thriving high-income economy in Southeast Asia with a relatively small population for the continent of 5.54 million people. Singapore's labour market is of modest size when compared to other Southeast Asian countries and this accounts for 3,672,800 people. However, a significant 38% of its workforce comes from other countries in the world, according to 2017 figures from the Singaporean Ministry of Manpower. The 1,393,000 foreign workers fill skills gaps across key sectors of the Singaporean economy, such as construction, financial and professional services and maritime industries (Ministry of Manpower, 2018).

Singapore's competitive position in attracting talent from abroad has been recognised across the world as the country frequently ranks among the best-performing states on the performance and competitiveness of its workforce. Singapore has long served as an attractive destination for global talent due to its reputation for being Asia's hub for global talent. This success has been achieved through the development and implementation of a competitive government policy aimed at the attraction

(Continued)

(Continued)

of global talent. This, together with pioneering industry practice which seeks to retain and develop further foreign-born workers, will contribute to the continued growth of Singapore's economy.

Recent policy moves of the Singaporean government, however, involve the development of home-grown talent in an attempt to respond to the challenge of over-reliance on talent from abroad and explore opportunities to scale up the productivity of Singapore's native workforce. Singapore, nevertheless, remains the most attractive destination for highly skilled workers in Asia and is second only to Switzerland in the world, when ranked on its ability to attract, develop and retain global talent in global indices benchmarking the talent competitiveness of individual countries.

Government policy aimed at attracting global talent

The importance and contribution of global talent have been highlighted through a number of key initiatives by the Singaporean government to further strengthen the competitiveness of the country on a global stage. The Singaporean government's approach lies in what the Japan Research Institute calls 'a comprehensive approach to recruitment' whereby national efforts to attract highly skilled manpower are conducted in a concerted fashion, including the attraction of foreign businesses, students, scholars, tourists and international events.

Recent government initiatives have moved to the introduction of more niche interventions that address specific country needs and opportunities. In late 2017, the Start-up SG Talent initiative, a key enabler to develop a strong start-up ecosystem in Singapore, has evolved alongside its EntrePass scheme to enable the attraction of global start-up talent to build innovative businesses and enterprises in Singapore.

The Ministry of Manpower announced that from 3 August 2017, the EntrePass scheme would be enhanced to facilitate the entry and stay of promising foreign start-up talent who are keen to establish innovative businesses in Singapore. This enhanced government-led scheme is projected to strengthen and add vibrancy to tech start-up ecosystems with a view to positioning Singapore as a leading innovation and entrepreneurship destination. Enhancements to the Start-up SG Talent initiative and the EntrePass scheme aim to attract a large pool of highly skilled global start-up talent at an early stage of the formation or realisation of their business and enterprise ideas (Ministry of Manpower, 2017).

The effectiveness of the Singaporean government policy and planning for global talent has been recognised by independent audits and global indices, such as the GTCI. The country has been given a maximum score of 100 in the GTCI for 'government effectiveness' in enabling the attraction, development and retention of global talent (GTCI Singapore, 2017). It is only recently that the government has announced its plans to address the overdependence on a foreign workforce across key sectors of the economy, with the intention to increase the productivity of Singapore's home-grown workforce. This is a policy focus, which has been echoed in the OECD's 'Structural Policy Challenges for Southeast Asian Countries' report. The government aims to address this opportunity to nurture home-grown talent through initiatives targeted at the provision of up-skilling, re-skilling and education opportunities, such as Skills Future Singapore (SSG) and Workforce Singapore (WSG).

Singapore in comparative perspective

How does Singapore compare to other global hubs for talent? The GTCI ranks 118 countries according to their ability to compete globally to grow better talent, attract the talent they need and retain those workers who contribute to competitiveness, innovation and growth in these countries.

Ranked second in the 2018 GTCI, Singapore is the regional leader in the Index, being the only Asian country in the top 10. Singapore is only second to Switzerland, where the latter has benefitted from its geographic proximity to a number of highly skilled labour markets, such as Germany, France and the Nordic countries. A number of key common characteristics exist among top-performing countries, such as in the case of Singapore. As the Index highlights (GTCI Singapore, 2017):

> High ranking countries share key traits, including educational systems that meet the needs of the economy; employment policies that favour flexibility, mobility and entrepreneurship; and high connectedness of stakeholders in business, education and government as well as high level of technological competence.

Singapore is a success story, ranked second for a fourth consecutive year. It leaves countries such as Australia (11th), New Zealand (12th), Japan (20th), Malaysia (27th) and South Korea (30th) behind. Singapore is also well ahead of Asia's emerging economic superpowers, China (43rd) and India (81st) (GTCI Singapore, 2017). This is due to both countries' inability to attract talent, while also facing severe 'brain drain' where highly skilled home-grown talent leave the country to work abroad, often attracted by more favourable working conditions such as competitive pay packages and a high standard of living.

The future of Singapore as a hub for global talent

Increased competition from other, both established and emerging players serving as hubs for global talent has the potential to disrupt the global talent policy landscape in a number of countries, including Singapore. China and only recently India have provided channelled investment and resources in academic talent and skills

(Continued)

(Continued)

development initiatives that will help both countries scale up their efforts to establish cities, such as Beijing, Shanghai and Mumbai, as global talent hubs and competitors of Singapore.

Despite its strong reputation as a hub for global talent, Singapore faces an acute shortage of highly skilled workers across many sectors of its economy, which may partly be attributed to the pertinent skills mismatch in the country – an issue that has been brought up by Hays, one of the world's leading global recruiting firms with operations in 33 established and emerging labour markets (Hays Singapore, 2017):

> Singapore's shortage of highly-skilled professionals has reached a point where it is now a hindrance to the effective operation of businesses in the city-state. Given the intensity of demand, salaries in high-skill industries outpace those in low-skill industries. Government initiatives that endorse local Singaporean hires have seen the demand for talented local candidates reach new heights. As employers react quickly to ensure they have the right proportion of local, permanent resident and work pass holders in their headcount, the ability to secure the right talent – whether that is a highly valued locally experienced candidate or a specialist from overseas – will remain employers' greatest challenge.

The country would need to stay abreast of developments on a global level and identify approaches to constantly adapt to the competitive global labour market landscape to retain its top position in a highly competitive and volatile global labour market. As we discussed, one recent move in this direction involves Singapore's efforts to develop its own workforce as a global and future-ready one.

It has been given a maximum score of 100 in the GTCI for business–government relations in enabling collaboration to maximise the opportunities presented by global talent attraction, development and retention between both sectors. Further evidence is, nevertheless, needed in the form of good industry practice to demonstrate a continuous commitment to global talent development and retention, which complements government policy.

Not only is Singapore implementing initiatives to reduce its reliance on a global talent workforce and to create a cluster of highly skilled domestic and foreign human resources that complement each other, but the country also aims to develop Singaporeans as global, future-ready workers. The Singaporean government has recognised the importance of developing global competencies and attributes that will strengthen the country's talent competitiveness amid the opportunities and challenges brought about by the globalisation of markets and industries. International Enterprise (IE) Singapore unveiled new initiatives in 2017 with the vision of building a large pool of Singaporean talent keen and able to work internationally, such as in other countries in Southeast Asia. These initiatives will seek to nurture a pool of Singaporeans that understand international business practices and the operating conditions of the key markets in Southeast Asia and India in particular. IE aspires to develop a global network of youthful Singaporean talent with aspirations to work abroad and in regional growth engines such as emerging economic growth regions like India. Singapore provides an interesting case for policymakers as the workforce policy adaptation of the country, amid global disruptions and opportunities, is projected to provide valuable lessons and good practice for other countries challenged to rethink their national policy approaches to the development, attraction and retention of global talent.

Further case study resources

GTCI Singapore (2017). *Singapore ranks first in Asia Pacific in the Global Talent Competitiveness Index (GTCI) 2017*. Availale at: www.insead.edu/news/2017-singapore-ranks-first-in-AP-GTCI2017 [Accessed 5 April 2018].

Hays Singapore (2017). *Singapore overview*. Available at: www.hays.com.sg/global-skills-index/HAYS_227897 [Accessed 5 April 2018].

Ministry of Manpower (2017). *Startup SG talent initiative*. Available at: www.mom.gov.sg/newsroom/press-releases/2017/0803-enhanced-entrepass-to-attract-global-startup-talent-to-build-innovative-businesses-in-singapore [Accessed 5 April 2018].

Ministry of Manpower (2018). *Foreign workforce numbers*. Available at: www.mom.gov.sg/documents-and-publications/foreign-workforce-numbers [Accessed 5 April 2018].

REFLECTIVE EXERCISE

The Global Talent Competitiveness Index 2018 Quiz

The Global Talent Competitiveness Index (GTCI) 2018 ranks 118 countries according to their ability to compete globally to grow better talent, attract the talent they need and retain those workers who contribute to competitiveness, innovation and growth in these countries. The 2018 GTCI and report are focused on the relationship between diversity and competitiveness. Diversity is seen as both a consequence of and a contributor to success and prosperity. In light of this, countries, cities and enterprises are advised to do more to harness the full power of diversity, according to the GTCI.

(Continued)

(Continued)

Reflective exercise: Having read the Global Talent Competitiveness report for 2018, take the following global talent competitiveness quiz, which will help you test your knowledge of what makes a country competitive in attracting, growing, retaining and enabling talent.

Question	Answer
1: The Global Talent Competitiveness Index is founded on six distinctive pillars that collectively provide an aggregate score for each country ranked on the Index. Which of the following actions is not a pillar in the Index? (A) Enable (B) Promote (C) Grow (D) Attract	A B C D
2: Attracting talent, in the context of global talent competitiveness, as a concept involves luring valuable resources from abroad, including people with sought-after high-level skills and competencies, while removing barriers to entering the talent pool.	True/False
3: Growing talent, in the context of global talent competitiveness, as a concept has broadened beyond education to include apprenticeships, training and continuous education, as well as experience of or access to growth opportunities.	True/False
4: Retaining talent, in the context of global talent competitiveness, as a concept reflects key interventions to ensure the sustainability of the talent pipeline in times when highly skilled talent can find competitive opportunities elsewhere in the world.	True/False
5: Enabling talent, in the context of global talent competitiveness, as a concept includes the regulatory bodies, markets and businesses within a country that serve to facilitate the attraction and growth of talent.	True/False
6: Which of the following countries is not featured in the top five best-performing countries in the Attract pillar of the Global Talent Competitiveness Index? (A) Switzerland (B) Australia (C) Singapore (D) United Arab Emirates (E) Qatar	A B C D E
7: The top five positions in the Global Talent Competitiveness Index are dominated by both developing and developed countries from three continents.	True/False

8:	Which of the following countries is not featured in the top five best-performing countries in the Global Knowledge Skills pillar of the Global Talent Competitiveness Index? (A) Iceland (B) USA (C) UK (D) Singapore (E) Switzerland	A B C D E
9:	With talent and diversity becoming increasingly valuable for business performance, there is a competitive advantage for companies seeking to get ahead. One of the key recommendations of the report is that companies should implement effective integration and inclusion policies that embrace diversity in the workplace.	True/False
10:	The report suggests that employment policies in countries should change to accommodate and make the most of diversity in the workforce and workplace. Learning through exposure to different cultures and being challenged by different systems stimulate deeper and more complex thinking, problem solving, flexibility and creativity that ultimately lead to an improved competitiveness.	True/False

Answers to questions

Q1: Option B

Q2: True

Q3: True

Q4: True

Q5: True

Q6: Option B

Q7: False – the top five positions in the Global Talent Competitiveness Index are dominated by developed countries.

Q8: Option E

Q9: True

Q10: True

Further reading and resources

Gray, A. (2018). *These are the best countries and cities for attracting and developing talent.* Available at: www.weforum.org/agenda/2018/02/these-are-the-best-countries-and-cities-for-attracting-and-developing-talent [Accessed 9 August 2018].
INSEAD (2018). 2018 *Global Talent Competitiveness Index: Talent diversity and competitiveness will fuel the future of work.* Available at: www.insead.edu/news/2018-gtci-talent-diversity-competitiveness-fuel-future-of-work [Accessed 9 August 2018].

REFERENCES

Australian Government (2014). *Industry innovation and competitiveness agenda: An action plan for a stronger Australia.* Available at: https://industry.gov.au/industry/Pages/Industry-Innovation-and-Competitiveness-Agenda.aspx#header [Accessed 24 February 2018].

Central Committee of the Communist Party of China (2016). *The 13th five-year plan for economic and social development of the People's Republic of China 2016–2020.* Available at: http://en.ndrc.gov.cn/newsrelease/201612/P020161207645765233498.pdf [Accessed 24 February 2018].

Committee on the Future Economy (2017). *Report of the Committee on the Future Economy.* Available at: www.gov.sg/~/media/cfe/downloads/mtis_full%20report.pdf [Accessed 24 February 2018].

Global Talent Competitiveness Index (GTCI) (2018). *Global Talent Competitiveness Index 2018: Diversity for competitiveness.* Available at: https://gtcistudy.com [Accessed 24 February 2018].

Information and Communications Technology Council (ICTC) (2017). *Digital talent: Road to 2020 and beyond.* Available at: www.niagaraknowledgeexchange.com/wp-content/uploads/sites/2/2017/09/ICTC_DigitalTalent2020_ENGLISH_FINAL_March2016.pdf [Accessed 24 February 2018].

INSEAD (2018). *2018 Global Talent Competitiveness Index: Talent diversity and competitiveness will fuel the future of work.* Available at: www.insead.edu/news/2018-gtci-talent-diversity-competitiveness-fuel-future-of-work (Accessed 26 February 2018).

McKinsey Global Institute (2010). *Five forces reshaping the global economy: McKinsey global survey results.* Available at: www.mckinsey.com/business-functions/strategy-and-corporate-finance/our-insights/five-forces-reshaping-the-global-economy-mckinsey-global-survey-results [Accessed 23 February 2018].

Microsoft (2012). *A national talent strategy: Ideas for securing US competitiveness and economic growth*. Available at: https://news.microsoft.com/download/presskits/citizenship/MSNTS.pdf [Accessed 24 February 2018].

National Planning Commission (2017). *Our future – make it work: National development plan 2030*. Available at: www.dac.gov.za/sites/default/files/NDP%202030%20-%20Our%20future%20-%20make%20it%20work_0.pdf [Accessed 26 February 2018].

Nature (2018). *China's plan to recruit talented researchers*. Available at: www.nature.com/articles/d41586-018-00538-z [Accessed 26 February 2018].

Opportunities for Africans (2017). *Government of Kenya presidential digital talent programme 2017–18 (12-month ICT programme for Kenyan graduates)*. Available at: www.opportunitiesforafricans.com/government-of-kenya-presidential-digital-talent-programme-2018-for-kenyan-graduates [Accessed 26 February 2018].

Planning Commission (2012). *Twelfth five year plan 2012–17*. Available at: http://planningcommission.nic.in/plans/planrel/fiveyr/welcome.html [Accessed 24 February 2018].

PricewaterhouseCoopers (PwC) (2014). *Talent mismatch costs global economy $150 billion*. Available at: https://press.pwc.com/News-releases/global-economy-misses-out-on-150bn-due-to-talent-mismatch/s/c433d953-6669-41c1-9225-fd63ac9298d6 [Accessed 24 February 2018].

Stuenkel, O. (2015). *How Brazil loses the battle for international talent*. Available at: www.postwesternworld.com/2015/05/11/brazil-international-talent [Accessed 26 February 2018].

TalentCorp (2012). *Talent roadmap 2020*. Available at: www.talentcorp.com.my/resources/publications/reports/talent-roadmap-2020 [Accessed 26 February 2018].

TalentCorp (2018). *Visioning Malaysia's future of work: A framework for action*. Available at: www.talentcorp.com.my/Homepage Accessed 26 February 2018].

Talent Economy (2016). *Welcome to Talent Economy*. Available at: www.talenteconomy.io/2016/12/02/talent-valuable-resource [Accessed 23 February 2018].

The Thousand Talents Plan (2018). *Recruitment program of global experts: The thousand talents plan*. Available at: www.1000plan.org/en/plan.html [Accessed 26 February 2018].

Wang, H. (2010). *China's national talent plan: Key measures and objectives*. Available at: http://robohub.org/wp-content/uploads/2013/07/Brookings_China_1000_talent_Plan.pdf [Accessed 24 February 2018].

World Bank (2018). *Closing the skills gap*. Available at: www.talentcorp.com.my/clients/TalentCorp_2016_7A6571AE-D9D0-4175-B35D-99EC514F2D24/contentms/img/publication/Focus%20Malaysia%2029082015.pdf [Accessed 26 February 2018].

10

THE ROLE OF GLOBAL TALENT IN SHAPING CITIES, REGIONS AND ECONOMIES

Chapter contents

The role of global talent in shaping cities

- The relationship between global talent and cities
- The economic, socio-cultural and demographic contribution of global talent to cities
- The Global Cities Talent Competitiveness Index as evidence of impact
- City-level policy for developing an enabling global talent infrastructure
- The role of private-sector initiatives in shaping talent
- New forms of talent in the context of cities

The role of global talent in shaping regions

- The relationship between global talent and regions
- The economic, socio-cultural and demographic contribution of global talent to regions
- Evidence from the Silicon Beach on the contribution of global talent

The role of global talent in shaping economies

- The relationship between global talent and economies

- The economic, socio-cultural and demographic contribution of global talent to countries
- Ideas and implications for organisations and policymakers

National, regional and city-level policy as an enabler of global talent

- The role of immigration policy and Brexit
- Policy that enables the attraction and retention of talent

Interview: The contribution of global talent to UK regions – Dorset, with Nuno Almeida, NourishCare

Reflective exercise: The most important contributions of global talent to cities, regions and countries – essay or discussion

Learning objectives

After reading this chapter, you will be able to:

- understand the role of global talent in shaping cities, regions and countries
- recognise the economic, socio-cultural and demographic contribution of global talent
- critically appraise current policy trends and developments regarding global talent.

THE ROLE OF GLOBAL TALENT IN SHAPING CITIES
The relationship between global talent and cities

Michael Bloomberg, businessman, philanthropist and former Mayor of New York, writes that the success of global cities depends, to a large extent, on global talent. He highlights that, as a result of this close relationship between talent and cities, competitive urban economies must continuously innovate in the way they respond to the future demands of a talent-driven market (*Financial Times*, 2012). There is undoubtedly a strong correlation between cities and global talent. Cities often serve as global talent magnets through the facilitative policy and infrastructure that they establish in order to attract, develop and retain a highly skilled workforce.

Building on the premise of this text, it is important to note that global talent in the context of cities, regions and countries is not just about highly skilled talent from abroad. 'Global talent' is also about developing and retaining home-grown talent and – more importantly – enabling both to collaborate and learn from each other in co-creating competitive cities, regions and countries. This facilitates a diverse talent pipeline of home-grown talent, with strong local knowledge and talent and a global mindset, who were born or lived, studied and worked abroad.

The economic, socio-cultural and demographic contribution of global talent to cities

Evidence suggests that global talent is a source of economic competitiveness for cities. Our discussion and indeed selection of global cities are informed by the 2018 Typology of World Cities, developed by JLL, a leading professional services firm. In its latest research, JLL, in collaboration with The Business of Cities, has identified 10 city groups, each playing a distinct role on the global stage (Figure 10.1). Cities within each group share a range of strengths and challenges that deserve the attention of businesses and policymakers (JLL, 2018).

London, one global city and a hub for global talent featured in the 'big seven' list by JLL, provides an insight into the economic, socio-cultural and demographic contribution of talent to cities. Global talent are key to the city's booming financial and professional services sector and London's workforce is among the most international in the world. The capital of the UK has a strong home-grown and international talent pool of over 5.2 million and over 37% of this talent were born outside the country. Equally, in Shenzhen, China, global talent are central to fulfilling the city's vision to become the high-tech capital of the country through a strong pool of global talent of 7 million, including a large proportion of talent from abroad.

However, it is not just the economic contribution of global talent to cities. Global talent have a socio-cultural footprint and often a wider demographic contribution to the cities they live and work in. Through their socio-cultural footprint, global talent make urban places more diverse and vibrant and, again, London is an excellent example of a city where talent from over 120 countries flock and make the city one of the most international in the world. Melbourne in Australia is another example of a city that acts as a talent magnet with its large-scale Chinese and Indian diaspora reshaping the socio-cultural footprint of the city. Identical socio-cultural trends and developments driven by talent can be observed in many other cities across the world, including Singapore, Zurich, San Francisco and Barcelona.

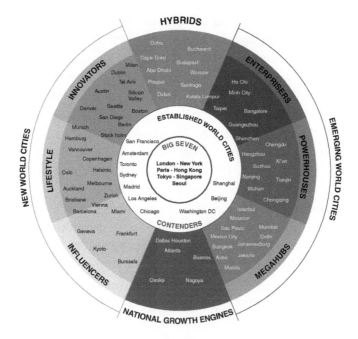

Figure 10.1   JLL's Typology of World Cities 2018

(Source: JLL, 2018)

In addition to the economic and socio-cultural impact of global talent in cities, they often make an important demographic contribution. As the increasingly mobile global talent are often in their 20s and 30s, they reshape the demographic profile of cities by making them younger. Global examples of cities with a rapidly growing population of talent in their 20s and 30s are Hong Kong, Sydney and Mumbai, among many others.

This wide-ranging economic, socio-cultural and demographic contribution highlights the significance of identifying and measuring key factors and indicators that enable cities to become more competitive and vibrant. Benchmarking the success of talent-driven cities enables policymakers and urban planners to develop and access a body of good practice to strengthen further the profile of their cities as competitive destinations that attract, develop and retain global talent.

The Global Cities Talent Competitiveness Index as a measure of impact

Chapter 9 of this text provided a brief insight into the Global Talent Competitiveness Index (GTCI), which ranks countries on their ability to grow, attract and retain talent.

In 2017, the GTCI and report expanded to include the inaugural edition of the Global Cities Talent Competitiveness Index (GCTCI). In its refined version, launched in 2018, the Index measures the competitiveness of 90 cities of different sizes located in all parts of the world, and represented a mix of national capitals and regional centres as well as up-and-coming urban destinations in the talent competitiveness space (Figure 10.2). The figure provides evidence of the diverse geographic representation of cities on the GCTCI. Cities featured on the Index include Sao Paulo in Brazil, Washington, DC in the USA, Seoul in South Korea, Kuala Lumpur in Malaysia, Nairobi in Kenya, alongside a further 85 destinations for global talent. The GCTCI is made up of most of the performance indicators included in the GTCI, as discussed in Chapter 9.

Talent competitiveness has become key to cities, and cities are becoming key to talent competitiveness. The GCTCI serves as evidence of this interdependency. The development of competitive cities is not only about the attraction of global talent. It is also about the opportunities that cities provide for talent to develop, and grow. The opportunity to retain global talent is largely dependent on the development of an enabling environment and an urban infrastructure that will attract, keep and enable talent to flourish in cities.

City-level policy for developing an enabling global talent infrastructure

In this section, we provide illustrative examples of initiatives and strategies, especially across Asia and Europe, into city-level policy making for talent attraction and retention.

Singapore, ranked 33rd on the GCTCI, provides a forward-thinking approach to policy and practice aimed at the development of urban spaces and infrastructure to support talent attraction to and retention in the city. Singapore's Committee of the Future Economy published in its 2017 report its vision to develop 'a vibrant and connected city of opportunity' through pioneering, integrated and interconnected urban solutions. The latter include advanced transportation, agile urban spaces, economic partnerships and ICT innovations, among other urban solutions and interventions. Some proposed urban interventions aligned with strategic themes in Singapore's urban-level policy include the opportunity to:

* strengthen Singapore's status as a global air-transport hub by investing in new international connections and infrastructure
* introduce more specialised spaces that improve land productivity and support growth and develop innovative ways to create new urban environments
* enhance Singapore's physical landscape, alongside the city's cultural and lifestyle offerings to strengthen its identity and distinctiveness.

Figure 10.2   Geographic distribution of GCTCI-ranked cities

(Source: GTCI, 2018)

The Committee report has also recognised the importance of building a thriving urban environment that attracts global talent and provides enriched professional and personal life opportunities, experiences and services. The small island city-state projected that the development of this urban infrastructure will, in turn, contribute to Singapore's future economic growth and further enrich its vibrant society (Committee on the Future Economy, 2017):

> One of Asia's most liveable cities today, Singapore should also build on our strong posi-
> tion to create a city distinguished by the dynamism of our environment and uniqueness
> of our culture. Singapore should be a great place not only for work, but also to live, learn
> and play. This will also allow us to attract and retain talented individuals – both local and
> global – to contribute to Singapore's economy and society.

One example of Singapore's master plan to create an urban space for living, learning and innovation for over 100,000 people is Jurong Innovation District. This is a government-led initiative to encourage more innovation through the development of an enabling talent infrastructure where the first phase of the grand urban scheme is projected to be completed by 2022. The District aims to bring together a diverse group of researchers, students, innovators and businesses with a view to developing the products and services of the future (Figure 10.3). With this project, the Singaporean government aspires to develop a prototype of talent infrastructure that showcases what the future of live-work-learn-play urban spaces and environments might look like (Committee on the Future Economy, 2017).

Compared to Singapore, Mumbai, which is now the largest and most populous city in India, has also taken steps towards the implementation of city-level policy to improve the quality of urban life, providing amenities and facilities such as improved transportation and housing. One of the key objectives of this government-led initiative is the attraction and retention of talent to the city. With a population of over 22 million, Mumbai is the fourth most populous city in the world. This growth of the talent pool in Mumbai has led to a rapid expansion of the city, providing both challenges and opportunities for policymakers and urban planners.

Mumbai Development Plan (DP) 2014–2034 is an important policy initiative to improve the state of urban spaces in the city. This is an ambitious detailed plan, which is being implemented by the Indian government at the time of writing this text. Mumbai Development Plan (DP) 2014–2034 has its focus on areas of strategic importance for the city and its future as a hub for global talent. Strategic areas include the development of more affordable housing, sustainability and urban life quality, transport, communications and infrastructure (Municipal Corporation of

Jurong Innovation District

Figure 10.3   Jurong Innovation District

(Source: Committee on the Future Economy, 2017)

Greater Mumbai, 2017). Mumbai's growing technology, maritime, consumer goods and financial and professional services sectors emphasise the strategic importance of an enabling environment to support the attraction and retention of talent. The Plan's proposed intervention areas aim to address the need for the creation of a more talent-centric environment and urban spaces.

Another example of the future vision of the Indian government for Mumbai includes the large-scale transport project for the greater urban area. Mumbai's Urban Transport Project is a grand initiative which commenced in 2016 and aims to improve the state of the urban transport infrastructure. Mumbai's transport infra-structure has been facing capacity and quality challenges due to rapid urbanisation, inward investment and a growth in housing construction in India's urban hub for technology, innovation and start-ups (Figure 10.4). Over eight million passengers commuting to work on a daily basis use the suburban rail system of 2,900 train services, which is in need of upgrade and expansion. Mumbai's Urban Transport Project is a long-term initiative jointly funded by the Government of Maharashtra and the World Bank, which is now in its third phase and has a budget of $1.6 billion. This third phase has wider scope for transportation improvement interventions, including the development of additional railways, waterways and airport infrastructure (Phadke, 2018). However, the city is still ranked 89th out of 90 cities on the GCTCI, which indicates that further action is needed to enable Mumbai to improve its global talent standing.

In Europe, Barcelona has become a popular spot for global talent and business start-ups in the mainland, due to the enabling environment the city has created through making its urban spaces smarter through technology and talent. Barcelona has been

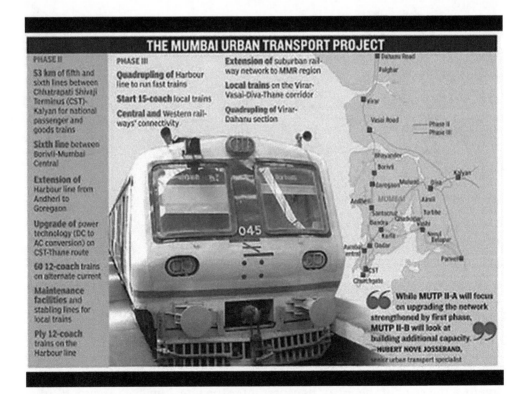

Figure 10.4 The Mumbai Urban Transport Project)

ranked 30th out of 90 cities on the GCTCI, which indicates its relatively strong standing as an urban hub for global talent.

Barcelona's Smart City strategy adopts a holistic approach to urban planning and the wellbeing of its talent and communities through 22 targeted programmes, each containing different initiatives, projects and strategies, to engage public, private and non-profit parties in the city (Figure 10.5). This smart urban environment, led by the City Council of Barcelona and its citizens, is central to increased inward investment in the city and the sustained attraction of talent. The environment has turned Barcelona into a talent hotspot – over 17% or 280,000 of the city's overall population of 1.6 million are now foreign-born talent.

1	Telecommunications networks	12	Citizenship
2	Urban Platform	13	Open Government
3	Smart Data	14	Barcelona in the pocket
4	Smart Light	15	Smart Garbage Collection
5	Energy self-sufficiency	16	Smart Regulation
6	Smart Water	17	Smart Innovation
7	Smart Mobility	18	Health and Social Services
8	Renaturation	19	Education
9	Urban Transformation	20	Smart Tourist Destination
10	Smart Furnishings	21	Infrastructure and Logistics
11	Urban Resilience	22	Leisure and Culture

Figure 10.5 Barcelona's 22 smart programmes

(Source: Ferrer, 2017)

It embraces technology as a tool to manage the city's resources and services in a way that is both efficient and effective. The strategy promotes sustainability in social, economic and urban development and is committed to improving the quality of life of citizens and communities in Barcelona.

Chinese cities are also increasingly adopting urban policies to enable them to attract, develop and retain global talent. Shenzhen, China's high-tech and hardware capital, is a well-known hub for global talent. In fact, 90% of the world's electronics now come from Shenzhen, which is now well known as 'the world's factory', producing everything from air conditioning units and toys to smartphones and drones. Shenzhen was selected by the government in Beijing as China's first special economic zone, having the opportunity to pilot the country's efforts to open up to overseas talent, entrepreneurs and investors through a favourable inward investment policy. Shenzhen, nevertheless, faces a strategic challenge to build more housing in an effort to attract (and retain) talent to the city. According to Xu Jinguang, president of Shenzhen IMT Industry Group, housing is one of the most important elements of a city's attractiveness to foreign talent (*China Daily*, 2016).

With this consideration in mind, the world's factory developed an ambitious and forward-looking approach to urban policy and practice targeted at improving urban spaces and the attraction and retention of talent. Key to Shenzhen's urban transformation has been Shenzhen Investment Limited, the largest listed property developer under the Shenzhen State-owned Assets Supervision and Administration Commission in China. The government-led organisation has been engaged in a range of high-profile residential and commercial urban re-development projects in response to the shortage of housing and office space experienced by the fast-expanding city of Shenzhen (Figure 10.6). One example of a commercial project is Chegongmiao, which is projected to deliver 416,000 square metres of innovation and incubation space for new businesses, talent entrepreneurs and start-ups in the city of Shenzhen. Noble Times is another large-scale talent infrastructure project driven by Shenzhen Investment Ltd. It aspires to develop an enabling talent environment of over 280,000 square metres of residential, education and healthcare space in Pingshan New District – an area with a high demand for housing (Shenzhen Investment Ltd, 2018).

Another important aspect of Shenzhen's strategy is its policy around the development of a more open and collaborative culture of research and innovation in the city. According to Briony Harris, a senior WEF Agenda contributor, Shenzhen attracts thousands of freelance mechanical and electrical engineers who often collaborate to innovate due to the lack of intellectual property rights and the promotion of an open-source culture in China (Harris, 2017). This talent, however, need access to a more sophisticated environment with housing often high on the agenda. Shenzhen is

Figure 10.6 Key residential and commercial development projects in Shenzhen

(Source: Shenzhen Investment Ltd, 2018)

ranked 73rd out of 90 cities included on the GCTCI indicating the unrealised potential that policies may target in the future.

The role of private-sector initiatives in shaping talent

We have explored the city perspective and the role of government-led policy in shaping competitive cities that are able to attract, grow and retain global talent. However, the private sector plays an equally important role in the talent shaping dynamic. For example, IBM, a tech giant based in Silicon Valley, has been pioneering industry-led work on technology and data-enabled urban transformations that create future-proof, sustainable and innovative cities, which have the capacity to attract and retain global talent.

IBM established the Smarter Cities challenge – a signature initiative that contributes IBM technology and the skills and expertise of teams of IBM experts to engage with urban leaders and policymakers in addressing key challenges facing cities around the world (IBM, 2018). These challenges include transportation, the environment, social services, public safety, administration and other areas of strategic importance to cities, should they want to be successful in the attraction, development and retention of global talent.

IBM's Smarter Cities challenge approach involves the deployment of a team of five to six IBM experts working closely with the city leadership and urban policymakers for a three-week period on their proposed challenge. Equally, IBM cognitive computing and big data capabilities have the opportunity to provide deep, data-driven insights into urban challenges and to enable urban policymakers to generate and evaluate options that may have an effect on future policy development and decision making with regard to overcoming these challenges. IBM's initiative is just one example of the role played by industry in shaping competitive and talent-driven cities.

New forms of talent in the context of cities

Urban innovations and collaborations between government, policymakers and industry organisations are a driving factor in strengthening the relationship between talent and cities. This interaction between 'people and cities' and its increased importance in the 21st century create new forms of talent that you, as a global talent, should critically reflect on and understand the role of. Some of these new forms of talent are urban problem-solvers, city shapers and innovators, start-up space architects and urban infrastructure engineers.

These new forms of roles, skills and talent have mushroomed, thanks to the advanced interaction and interdependency between talent and cities. Most of these roles are key to the future of cities but are yet to be fully defined and recognised by urban planners, governments, businesses and education establishments, who collectively hold responsibility for educating and training the next generation.

While there is a handful of academic degrees on urbanism, the relationship between urban studies and contemporary urban phenomena such as smart cities, shaping sustainable urban spaces, developing competitive urban features remains under-researched. We need to see further evidence of the development of education and training opportunities that put the spotlight on contemporary challenges and opportunities that our cities have faced, are currently facing or will face in the future. This would allow new jobs and roles to be imagined and created in and for a talent centric city of the future.

THE ROLE OF GLOBAL TALENT IN SHAPING REGIONS
The relationship between global talent and regions

Global talent contributes to regions economically and socially and supports the development of competitive and culturally rich regional economies. Studying the link between global talent and regions, we can see the impact of human capital on, and its contribution to, large-scale administrative and economic geographies, which boast one or more cities. International examples of such regions include the Multimedia Super Corridor in Malaysia, the Bay Area in Southern China, and the San Francisco Bay Area in the USA.

Let us explore China's Greater Bay Area and the contribution of global talent to this fast-growing region. For Amanda Lee from the *South China Morning Post*, China's new Bay Area can be compared with the bay areas of San Francisco, New York and Tokyo, due to its rapid growth and economic success (Lee, 2017). In 2017, the Chinese government announced a plan for the development of a cluster of 11 cities – Hong Kong, Macao, Guangzhou, Shenzhen, Zhuhai, Foshan, Zhongshan, Dongguan, Huizhou, Jiangmen and Zhaoqing – spanning 56,500 sq. km – that collectively contribute to China's Greater Bay Area.

The GDP of China's Greater Bay Area reached US\$1.36 trillion in 2016, supported by a strong pipeline of global talent engaged in the technology, manufacturing, maritime and services sectors of the regional economy. With an estimated population of 66.71 million, the region has a strong pipeline of talent. Along with this talent, the region boasts a sustainable flow of inward investment. The influence of talent on the region and vice versa is evidenced by the fact that four of the world's top 100 universities and 16 of the Top 500 Fortune companies are now located in China's Greater Bay Area (Lee, 2017).

Malaysia provides another Asian perspective on the contribution of global talent to specific regions. The Multimedia Super Corridor (MSC), located in close proximity to Kuala Lumpur, Malaysia's capital, is a Special Economic Zone and high-technology business district with a business footprint of over 3,800 companies that can be traced back to more than 40 countries. With more than 150,000 high-income knowledge workers who collectively contribute to over 1.3% of Malaysia's GDP, the MSC is an important talent hub for Malaysia.

There is also a significant cultural contribution of global talent to the Malaysian high-tech region which complements their economic impact. Facilitated by a favourable government policy that welcomes skilled migration and encourages international talent mobility, numerous non-Malaysian-born talent have moved into the area from countries such as Australia, the UK and the USA. This inward flow of talent has also been enabled due to the boom in satellite cities in the region such as Cyberjaya – the science and innovation capital of the country. Over 15% of the workforce in the MSC region was born outside Malaysia, according to the country's Digital Economy Corporation (Malaysia Digital Economy Corporation, 2017).

Our discussion of China and Malaysia surfaces the rapid economic growth, diversification and internationalisation of regions across Asia fuelled by global talent. There are other examples of global regions benefitting economically, socially and culturally from global talent in high-income economies in Europe and North America as we explore the next section.

The economic, socio-cultural and demographic contribution of global talent to regions

The combination of a government-led policy approach to the attraction of global talent and large-scale inward investment in technology-enabled businesses and innovative start-ups has positioned the San Francisco Bay Area in the USA as a global talent destination. Both home-grown talent from other cities and regions in the USA and overseas talent have been attracted to Silicon Valley and other popular talent hotspots in the San Francisco Bay Area as a result.

Small cities and urban conurbations in the region, such as Palo Alto – Google's home, Cupertino – Apple's home, and San Jose hosting many other tech giants, make up most of Silicon Valley and, indeed, the San Francisco Bay Area.

Talent has been driving the success of the San Francisco Bay Area, where its economy is growing three times faster than the national average in the USA. The workforce of the area boasts over two million home-grown and foreign-born talent. The Area's combined economic output contributed $781 billion to the economy of the USA in GDP in 2016 (McDermid, 2017).

A LinkedIn analysis from 2018 highlights the attractiveness of the Area both to talent from the USA and to talent born outside the country (Figure 10.7). By using its own global talent big data, LinkedIn estimates that the San Francisco Bay Area has been able to attract workers in the last 12 months both from US cities, such as New York, Boston and Chicago, and Indian cities such as Bangalore and Hyderabad (LinkedIn, 2018).

February 2018

Cities that San Francisco Bay Area Has Gained the Most Workers From

Rate per 10,000 Members

Top Three

1) New York City, NY
2) Boston, MA
3) Chicago, IL

Boston, MA
4.11

Chicago, IL
3.64

Detroit, MI
1.25

San Francisco
Bay Area, CA

New York City, NY
5.57

Los Angeles, CA
2.22

Pittsburgh, PA
1.63

Washington, D.C.
3.10

Bangalore, India
2.22

Houston, TX
1.16

Hyderabad, India
1.33

We define migration as a member changing their location on their LinkedIn profile. To develop the list of cities that San Francisco Bay Area gained the most workers from, we identified the cities the most LinkedIn members moved to San Francisco Bay Area from in the past 12 months. For every 10,000 LinkedIn members in San Francisco Bay Area, 5.6 moved to the city in the last 12 months from New York City.

Linked in.

Figure 10.7   Global talent migration to the San Francisco Bay Area

(Source: LinkedIn, 2018)

Sharon Simonson, Founder and Editor-in-Chief of Silicon Valley's *One World*, notes that more than 238,000 foreign-born people alongside Americans returning from abroad have moved to the San Francisco Bay Area in the last five years (Simonson, 2016). The Area, according to Simonson, relies heavily on foreign-born technical and engineering talent to fuel its expanding technology-enabled sectors. The contribution of foreign-born talent to the Area is immense. One example is the fact that nearly 70% of all software engineers based in San Francisco Bay Area cities, including Santa Clara, San Mateo and San Francisco, were born outside the country.

Farhad Manjoo writes that talent born outside the USA has largely shaped Silicon Valley (*The New York Times*, 2017):

> One of Google's founders is an immigrant from Russia, and its current chief executive is an immigrant from India. Microsoft's chief executive is also from India. EBay and Yahoo were started by immigrants. Facebook's largest subsidiaries, Instagram and WhatsApp, were both co-founded by immigrants. Apple was started by a child of immigrants.

This has been enabled by a growth in global talent mobility internationally and by the San Francisco Bay Area's welcoming policy towards skilled migration. Sharon Simonson highlights that the growing pool of foreign-born talent in the Area contributes to its diverse outlook through international festivals, celebrations and food outlets. Such international community celebrations include the San Jose Vietnamese Tet Festival and India Day. Similarly, new Indian and South Asian food outlets have been launched in the Area to showcase the cuisines of the world and enrich the local hospitality and evening economy offering. This socio-cultural demographic contribution of talent in the Area affirms its position as a hub for talent.

Evidence from Silicon Beach on the contribution of global talent

San Francisco is not the only region in advanced economies that has benefitted from the economic, socio-cultural and demographic contribution of global talent. Its lesser known 'cousin' the Silicon Beach on the south coast of England, in the county of Dorset has become famous for its thriving digital industry that specialise in the provision of technology solutions, digital advertising and internet services.

The digital sector contributes significantly to the UK economy. More than 1.6 million people work within the digital sector, or in digital tech roles across other sectors, as highlighted by Theresa May, the current UK prime minister (at the time of writing). It is widely known that the number of jobs in the digital technology sector across the UK has grown at more than twice the rate of non-digital tech sectors. Silicon Beach and its main contribution in Bournemouth illustrate this. Tech Nation, the largest community-driven research project of the UK's digital tech industries, highlights that the Bournemouth area saw new digital start-ups rising by 212% between 2010 and 2013, making it the fastest-growing tech economy in the UK.

The area is home to over 400 companies and start-ups in the digital sector with a combined contribution of £352 million to the economy. Talent are central to the success of this region in the south of England, which has recently seen the opening up of over 15,000 jobs in the digital sector in Bournemouth and Poole alone (Tech Nation, 2017).

The Silicon Beach area benefits from a strong graduate talent pool, further and higher education institutions in the region. Equally, a new wave of overseas talent entrepreneurs and technology experts have either launched many of the digital start-ups and joined the workforces of technology-enabled businesses in the region.

Now that you know more about the UK's Silicon Beach on the south coast of England, we would like to give you a policy perspective on the contribution of global talent to Dorset's region, which has been provided by the Head of Economic Development and Sustainability at Bournemouth Borough Council (BBC), at the time of writing this text.

POLICY INSIGHT

Bournemouth Borough Council on the contribution of global talent to Dorset

The Economic Development and Sustainability Unit at Bournemouth Borough Council (BBC) focuses on key sectors in Bournemouth. The Council has appointed dedicated sector managers, particularly in sectors of prime importance to the economy, such as the Financial and Professional Services sector, Digital and Creative, and Retail. According to the Head of Economic Development and Sustainability, talent is a defining feature of the success of the economy of Bournemouth and the wider region:

> Across those sectors, when we engage with businesses, we find that talent is one of the biggest drivers. So whether it is finding it, keeping it, attracting it, it is one of the big things that come out in our discussions, whether it is in Finance and Professional Services or the Digital and Creative sector.

(Continued)

(Continued)

Alongside the impact of talent on the region in general terms, the Head of Economic Development and Sustainability highlighted the important contribution that talent born overseas make to many of the key sectors of Bournemouth's economy.

What sectors of Dorset's economy do overseas talent tend to be employed in?

BBC Head: I would say that overseas talent is in every sector we touch – definitely Digital & Creative, definitely Advanced Engineering and also definitely Financial & Professional Services. You will find that companies from these sectors are pulling talent from elsewhere – mostly because they are businesses with a global reach themselves. Sectors such as Hospitality and Healthcare are also important as they are large-scale sectors and they do attract workforce and much of that workforce is talent from overseas. Another sector with a high concentration of global talent, particularly for Bournemouth, is International Education. By this sector I don't only mean universities but actually language schools and other international education establishments.

What is the socio-cultural contribution of overseas talent to Bournemouth and Poole?

BBC Head: Diverse communities are something that England is based on and that we should continue to support and encourage. I think overseas talent have a great contribution to the region both socially and culturally. I will give you a few examples: initiatives such as restaurants opened by overseas talent, international festivals, languages – these are great and I feel like we are in a place where the education sector particularly embraces that.

Both Silicon Valley in the USA and Silicon Beach in the UK are illustrations of the immense economic section of global talent to their local economy. Global talent also make a socio-cultural contribution through events and festivals that promote diversity and enrich the cultural profile of regions. A key enabler within this context is the development and implementation of a tailored regional-level policy focused on harnessing the economic, socio-cultural and demographic contribution made by global talent.

THE ROLE OF GT IN SHAPING CITIES, REGIONS AND ECONOMIES

THE ROLE OF GLOBAL TALENT IN SHAPING ECONOMIES
The relationship between global talent and economies

We have explored the role of global talent in shaping cities and regions and the challenges and opportunities they face in utilising global talent as a source of competitiveness. We now take a holistic, country-level approach to exploring the economic, socio-cultural and demographic contribution of global talent through a number of international case studies.

The economic, socio-cultural and demographic contribution of global talent to countries

The economic contribution of global talent to cities, regions and countries has been well covered by many authors and publications. Fewer accounts discuss the socio-cultural and demographic contribution of global talent to countries. Here we provide an insight into the policy development perspectives of Canada, New Zealand and Japan, with a particular focus on the demographic and socio-cultural contribution of global talent to these three countries.

Canada has long been praised as a country which adopts a welcoming attitude to skilled migration and global talent arriving from all parts of the world. The country's declining population and the rapid ageing of its society and workforce have been the drivers of recent policy interventions aimed at reversing these negative demographic developments. Canadian policy recognises the fact that global talent serve two important functions in the country – a demographic function and a socio-cultural one.

Government data indicates that Canada is experiencing negative demographic growth. In 1971, there were 6.6 people of working age for each senior citizen. By 2012, the ratio between people in work and retirees had gone down to 4.2 to 1. According to 2017 estimates by the Canadian government, only two people of working age will support one senior citizen by 2036. With this negative demographic growth in mind, Canada's immigration minister, Ahmed Hussen, also predicted that by 2036 most, if not all, of the country's population growth will be as a result of immigration, and recognised the important demographic function immigration serves in the country:

> Our government believes that newcomers play a vital role in our society ... Why do we need immigration? Well, five million Canadians are set to retire by 2035. And we have fewer people working to support seniors and retirees.

Canada's immigration minister's predictions are grounded in recent government initiatives where policymakers are preparing a flagship strategy – Canada's Immigration Plan – with the aim of welcoming nearly one million non-Canadian-born talent to the country over the next few years (Government of Canada, 2017) (Figure 10.8).

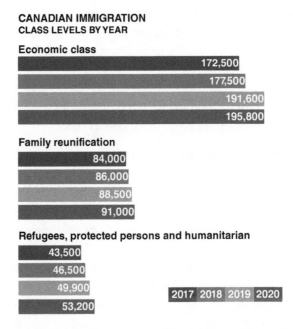

CANADIAN IMMIGRATION
CLASS LEVELS BY YEAR

Economic class
- 172,500
- 177,500
- 191,600
- 195,800

Family reunification
- 84,000
- 86,000
- 88,500
- 91,000

Refugees, protected persons and humanitarian
- 43,500
- 46,500
- 49,900
- 53,200

2017 2018 2019 2020

Figure 10.8   Canada's plan to welcome one million immigrants over three years
(Source: Government of Canada, 2017)

These initiatives by the Canadian government recognise the importance of developing long-term strategies and policy interventions that welcome global talent and enable their demographic and socio-cultural contribution, particularly for countries experiencing negative population growth and a declining workforce.

New Zealand provides another example of the wider recognition of global talent and the contribution they make in balancing the effect of a declining working-age population in the country. Over the next 50 years, New Zealand's population will age substantially and this will have important implications for the economic wellbeing of the country, according to a New Zealand Treasury Working Paper published back in 2003 (New Zealand Treasury, 2003). Sustained immigration into the country is seen as an opportunity to address challenges related to a progressive ageing and declining workforce. Government policy has been encouraging immigration, though through a more balanced and cautious approach than Canada, say. According to New Zealand government statistics, the country saw a net gain of 70,700 migrants for the year ending October 2017 and future targets have yet to be announced.

Our Futures Te Pae Tāwhiti: The 2013 census and New Zealand's changing population provides a review of the changing demographics and its implications for the country's social cohesion, economy, education and health. The New Zealand's Royal Society (2014) report acknowledges the role of immigration in population growth and in reversing the rapid ageing the country has experienced in recent years. For example, it predicts that there will be one million more young workers from Melanesia, who are expected to join New Zealand's workforce by 2050 (The Royal Society, 2014). From a socio-cultural perspective, talent migration is deeply engrained in New Zealand's history and the country recognises diversity's role in reshaping and enriching its cultural fabric (The Royal Society, 2014): 'New Zealand has always been an ethnically diverse society, but in the last twenty years the country has become diverse in new ways: increasing migration from Asia and a growing proportion of the population born overseas.'

One example is the city of Auckland, with its population of 1.4 million, which has seen a rapid growth in its non-New Zealand-born citizens – 39% of Aucklanders were born overseas.

Japan provides another country-level perspective on how global talent are shaping and are likely to shape its future. Jamil Anderlini, the Asia editor for the *Financial Times*, notes that Japan's population shrank by 403,000 in 2017 alone and is projected to drop further by 2115 – from 126.5 to 51 million (*Financial Times*, 2018).

On the other hand the foreign share of the overall population in Japan has grown from 0.7% in 1990 to 1.8% in 2016. While that proportion is relatively low when compared to other high-income countries, the population has risen in absolute numbers from 900,000 in 1990 to approximately 2.3 million as of mid-2016. This represents an increase of 160% in real terms (Migration Policy Institute, 2017).

David Green, Professor of Political Science at Nagoya University in Japan, acknowledged that the Japanese government has implemented a variety of programmes to attract non-Japanese-born talent to the country. One example is a new Highly Skilled Foreign Professional (HSFP) visa launched in 2012, aiming to recruit scientists, researchers, engineers and entrepreneurs to the country.

Moving forward, Japan needs a targeted policy to welcome more non-Japanese-born talent to the country in response to negative demographic growth and skills shortages experienced across key sectors of the national economy. According to Toshihiro Menju,

Managing Director and Chief Program Officer at the Japan Center for International Exchange, developing a forward-looking immigration policy is key to the long-term sustainability of the Japanese economy in the long term (East Asia Forum, 2017).

Ideas and implications for organisations and policymakers

As this chapter embeds a number of international examples from policy and practice in its text, you, as a global talent, have been able to broaden your understanding of the ways in which global talent shape cities, regions and countries and understand the complexity of shaping policy responses to the opportunities provided by global talent.

To accompany these international policy perspectives, we provide a summary of key considerations for individuals, organisations and policymakers on the role of global talent in shaping competitive and culturally rich cities, regions and countries. Our proposed considerations are grounded in the three primary ways that global talent make a contribution to cities, regions and countries – economically, socio-culturally and demographically.

First, global talent have a vital economic contribution to make through the knowledge, skills, abilities and diverse approaches they may bring to an organisation or region. The cases of Shenzhen and Mumbai, discussed earlier in this chapter, illustrated this potential. Such a contribution can be harnessed through policy that prioritises the attraction of foreign-born talent, alongside the development of home-grown talent, for sectors of national priority that experience skills shortages and/or an insufficiently skilled workforce.

Second, global talent make an important socio-cultural contribution to the communities and societies they become part of. The socio-cultural contribution of global talent to regions can be harnessed through the adoption of policy that prioritises the development of globally minded and open societies through the integration of foreign-born talent and the opportunities for learning from them.

Third, global talent have an important demographic contribution to make, particularly to countries experiencing negative demographic growth and a shrinking workforce due to an overall ageing population. Our discussion of the cases of Canada, New Zealand and Japan provide insights into the demographic contribution of talent to these countries. Such a contribution can be harnessed through a tailored immigration policy to address workforce declines, and also through initiatives aimed at the retention and development of home-grown talent.

NATIONAL, REGIONAL AND CITY-LEVEL POLICY AS AN ENABLER OF GLOBAL TALENT

The role of immigration policy and Brexit

A text on Global Talent Management, written in 2018, is incomplete without a discussion of a key phenomenon of our times – Brexit, and its implications for talent management.

Brexit, together with the UK government's stance on immigration, has had a substantial negative impact on Brand Britain and the country's soft power in the rest of the world. The country aspires to bring net migration figures to tens of thousands, while it still experiences skills shortages across many sectors of the economy. Alastair Cox, CEO of global recruiting firm Hays, notes that borders need to be open to global talent, and emphasises the opportunity for skilled migration to secure the UK's longer-term prosperity, economic growth and sustainability (Hays, 2017): 'One of the key points that must be made is that prosperity and growth depend on people and that without the right talent and skills, businesses and therefore societies can flounder rather than flourish.'

The UK has all the building blocks to be able to benefit from overseas talent but this opportunity is not utilised at present due to the complex immigration and visa policy landscape in the country. In one of our interviews with pioneers in Bournemouth's digital sector, we had the opportunity to hear the CEO of a leading digital agency Bright Blue Day's perspective on the importance of developing a policy framework that favours the attraction of a skilled workforce and indeed global talent to the UK.

INDUSTRY INSIGHT

Attracting global talent to the UK – interview with the CEO of Bright Blue Day

How can advanced economies such as the UK benefit from global talent?

CEO: I think the idea of limiting people to move into the UK because we don't want to have a net influx of immigrants is just not viable. I see the government has to do it

(Continued)

(Continued)

for political reasons. But this is actually crippling our economy. Developed economies should keep their doors open to talent from countries like Brazil, China or India. In other words, we should be welcoming them to the UK. Don't just close the doors and say you can't come because there is a massive talent mismatch across the UK. So the only problem that's going to stop us from growing is not having enough talent and we often cannot attract UK-born talent because everybody else in the UK is desperate for it. So actually the obvious way to go forward is to hire someone non-EU who is very keen to come to the UK – what a fantastic talent source for us and what a great way of getting a younger population, a more diverse population, with different skills, different cultures and building a much more cosmopolitan Dorset.

How does global talent benefit your organisation?

CEO: When you have overseas talent in your business, they are actually very good. They add a really strong dimension to the organisational culture. A much more diverse mix of people working in digital and creative adds to the culture, the knowledge, the experience, the reach – it is a very valuable dimension. And also when we are trying to deal in global markets, then you have different languages and cultures – so just bringing people in who have this cultural sensitivity in a digital and creative culture is really important because that's not something you can just pick up on the internet or read about.

What would post-Brexit Britain look like? Would immigration policy in the UK change amid skills shortages? These are some key questions that still remain unanswered. The answers to these questions depend on the development of an open, welcoming and thriving global talent policy in the UK. There will be a lot of uncertainty going forward, as Brexit and its consequences are still unfolding at the time of writing this text.

London, as the global financial capital of the world and, indeed, a global hub for talent, is set to be impacted by the consequences of Brexit. There has been extensive reportage on the interplay between Brexit developments and global talent, with overseas organisations' talent set to leave the capital en masse. This is a worrying trend, particularly as global talent in London often take up employment in sectors and organisations that require high specialisation or high-level skills. An estimated 40% of the 1.1 million European Union (EU) talent in London who come from the group of 14 older EU member states, including Sweden, Finland and Denmark, work in highly skilled jobs in the UK's capital.

This over-dependence on global talent is likely to impact the city should these individuals decide to seek employment opportunities elsewhere due to an unfavourable immigration policy and the ongoing Brexit rhetoric around migrants in the UK. Hence, the city and its mayor, Sadiq Khan, have been advocating for the implementation of post-Brexit policies that demonstrate the openness of London to investment and talent and that contribute to its long-term competitiveness and economic growth.

Policies for the attraction and retention of talent

London is not the only city where a fresh global talent policy is needed to retain its talent. We are likely to see more global cities, particularly megacities in Southeast Asia, which will join the global race for talent through the introduction of favourable city-level policies aimed at the attraction and retention of a highly skilled global workforce. However, we see a rapid evolution of models of development due to the complexity and specificity of different urban contexts.

We know that countries like Singapore and Switzerland have successfully implemented policies to attract talent from abroad. Nevertheless, in shaping cities, regions and economies, it is not just about attracting global talent, but also about keeping them there and enabling them to grow and amplify their impact and contribution. Hence, we expect to see new models and frameworks, alongside new approaches and policies aimed at the attraction, development and retention of global talent to cities, regions and countries.

Whether the global talent policy frameworks are ready at such a meta-level is something that is less clear. The complexity of creating a talent centric environment requires a forward-thinking approach and vision to global talent policy and practice to harness the economic, socio-cultural and demographic dividend of global talent to our cities. Global talent policymakers will find new ways to make that contribution more evenly distributed across the world, as more cities, regions and countries benefit from the impact generated by global talent.

Interview: the contribution of global talent to UK regions – Dorset, with Nuno Almeida, Founder and CEO of Nourishcare (Technology, Health and Social Care)

Q: Can you tell us more about yourself and your company?

I was born in Coimbra, Portugal in a lower-middle-class family, which probably made me more ambitious. I was the first person from my family who actually had the opportunity to go to university. I was, nevertheless, lucky enough to start setting up businesses very early, from the age of 16. I graduated from a university outside the UK – Universidade de Coimbra, with an MSc in Automation and Robotics. I started my journey in the UK in 2003 and I have been living in Dorset for the past 12 years.

So there is that case with NourishCare that came outside of the UK. We grew a subsidiary here quite successfully and created a number of jobs and we generated something which is a net exporter. So, at the end, we contributed positively to the GDP of Dorset. I sold my stake in that successful business in 2009. Then after I sold my previous company in 2009, I thought of establishing another business in Dorset. My main ambition for setting up is that we wanted a Dorset-established business which delivers an impact locally – a business which even when it grows, we won't feel the need to move our headquarters to London or somewhere else.

I started my company NourishCare in 2012. In 2014, we launched our first product, which became very successful and attracted a lot of investment. We currently employ 17 people and we have over 60 clients in the UK alone. We wanted to do something that is meaningful to the local economy. The Health and Social Care sector is definitely a key priority for the local enterprise partnership in Dorset. This provides a clear message that this is a relevant industry.

Q: What were the motivations for you to pursue a career in Dorset, UK?

The first people I met in Dorset were extremely welcoming. So I became embedded in the context very quickly and I decided to stay and live in Dorset. I like the ecology and the environment and I wanted to live in such a society, which values this. So Dorset has a mix of really well-managed landscapes and resources. It is also a matter of connectivity – living here, I can be in France in four hours and that makes me feel connected. I am also less than two hours away from Heathrow.

I also love the fact that you can balance a hectic professional life with the ability to take a 12-mile walk along the beach. You wouldn't be able to do that in London. I think this puts Dorset in a fairly unique position. Another pull factor for me was that the region is so crowded with high-tech companies. You have a heritage of engineering companies as well and this interests me. Another reason is that despite being in the middle of the countryside you can still access all sorts of creative and innovative people.

Q: Do you believe that talent from overseas have a role to play in boosting the economic activity in Dorset? If yes, what is the role of overseas talent in this process?

I think that there is no simple answer to this question. We probably have at least three degrees of contribution that overseas talent can provide the economy of Dorset:

Contribution number one is the opportunity for overseas talent to fill skills gaps across the UK. That is a very strong contribution and probably the most obvious one. This is about meeting requirements for labour and skilled labour in areas across the UK, where we clearly do not have the required skills in place. And I think in our sector we see that on two levels. Every time I walk into a hospital I think it is fair to say that if you take out all non-UK-born members of the workforce in our sector, then hospitals just wouldn't be able to run. This goes without saying. In our sector we try to have a much more significant intervention around social care. So I don't think we could have a social care sector without talent from overseas. Then, when we go into highly paid skills, we have some of the best universities in the UK, churning out high-quality engineers, for example, and still there are not enough for the health and social care sector. And, of course, talking only about engineering (that's a very broad subject), there are areas in software engineering that we just cannot recruit in the UK as we are not able to find the right kind of skills in the workforce. So we experience a shortage of skilled workers.

Then there are two other contributions, which are smaller, but not irrelevant. One is overseas talent who are based in the UK and have links to other countries and cultures across the world. Such people contribute on a certain level to make UK companies more prepared for undertaking international business. If you, for example, have a company where everyone was born and grew up in the UK, your employees may not realise what they don't know about other cultures. So for me this is a really key aspect of teams that I have built in the past. So, if you don't build that degree of diversity, companies will struggle to become international by nature.

Then there is a third angle, which I think is very relevant and this is inward investment. We live in a very desirable part of the world. A number of people from overseas decide to buy property here in the UK and put quite a significant amount of money into the local economy. There are very significant pots of money moving around people, who are from overseas and who are often also very experienced business people.

(Continued)

(Continued)

So having that combination of contributions of overseas talent to Dorset has, I think, a massive impact and this goes without saying. If you look at bigger businesses here, they are all owned by large entities from outside the UK. Look at JP Morgan, for instance, and the number of talent from overseas employed by that company – these businesses would not otherwise be there and the contribution of these businesses to the economy of Dorset is considerable.

Q: Do you believe that overseas talent have a role to play in filling skills gaps across sectors in Dorset experiencing skills shortages? If yes, which skills?

I think areas where the UK is lagging behind are those in terms of creating the right quantity of talent, where somehow the UK created the perception that there are careers which are not worthy. There is a public perception that they are not as important as other careers. Clearly, the Health and Social Care sector is one of those areas that suffers to a significant degree.

The sector partly has itself to blame, because there is a very obvious shortage of role models. That makes it difficult to encourage young talent to take Health and Social Care as a career route. There is also a misconception that the sector is not well paid. But, yes, the sector provides significant career opportunities, you can progress with your career, and feel very respected in the professional community you contribute to. But, for some reason, these opportunities are not perceived as such across the UK and most young people making career choices at an early stage will often exclude our sector.

Then I also think that engineering is not as highly valued as it should be for a country which invented the industrial revolution. Therefore, we find that it is consistently easier to recruit someone who comes from outside the UK for highly specialised engineering skills. The UK is, nevertheless, pretty good at creating a talent environment which is very mixed up and diverse. So putting a team together that has to involve people with the right skills, people with the right entities and then making teams work is where I think overseas talent does have a significant role to play in that.

Q: What are the key skills, competencies or qualities that you, as overseas talent, bring to your organisation?

First, I think it is the diverse background. I think it is also being someone who doesn't accept stereotypes lightly (for me, we are all equal). I don't accept limitations lightly. So, one thing I like about the UK is that the law is pretty simple and most of the things that people think they cannot do, they can actually do. When people say that something is impossible, I would always question that and I don't accept things lightly. I would also like to say that I have global vision and I am proud to be living in Dorset.

Q: What is the role of residents born overseas in enriching Dorset's socio-cultural landscape?

Dorset has two very different demographics. We have the conurbation, where you have a very high concentration of overseas talent and then you have the rural area, where this concentration of talent who was not born in the UK is a lot lower. This is probably due to the fact that one needs quite a lot of money to live in those areas. So, in rural areas of Dorset, you have a very wealthy traditional English population.

I think that this separation makes Dorset particularly interesting, because you can get the best of both worlds. So such rural areas around Dorset allow non-UK-born individuals to fall in love with this part of England. Therefore, the environment gives you the option to embed yourself in the culture but still have a massive cultural impact if you stay in, for instance, the Poole or Bournemouth area.

I am not sure that rural Dorset takes a lot from overseas talent; the pace at which rural Dorset absorbs different cultures is very slow and I think this is part of what is great about it. When it comes to Bournemouth and Poole, talent from overseas is one of the main attractions; it is the reason why these places are so diverse. It is diverse, not just in terms of international backgrounds, it also brings the flavour of living in London without having to live in London. So Dorset does feel a lot more diverse and a lot more international and that attracts a certain type of individual attracted by this type of community.

Q: By 2030, only half of Dorset's population is forecast to be of working age. Can residents in Dorset who were born overseas play a positive role in reversing this trend?

I think due to the nature in Dorset that may not be a problem due to the natural beauty of the county. There is that temptation of people to retire in Dorset and that is not a new trend. In terms of the active population, the problem is that if you have a high concentration of wealthy people retiring in Dorset, then that will drive up house prices. This will make it harder for middle-class, working families to relocate here. And that trend has the potential to curve the economic development in Dorset if we don't have solutions for the housing problem.

And this problem is not due to immigration but simply because there is high demand for high-quality housing and accommodation from retiring people. Both

(Continued)

(Continued)

UK and non-UK-born talent will experience exactly the same challenges, which is how on earth we can afford to live here.

So, if we build more affordable housing, we can bring in more global talent. So I think that the real problem we have is one of housing. I think, as long as the UK economy remains open, overseas talent will have a role in that context of reversing the trend, where we see a high concentration of non-working people in Dorset.

REFLECTIVE EXERCISE

The most important contribution of global talent to cities, regions and countries – Essay or Discussion

Chapter 10 has discussed the role of global talent in shaping cities, regions and economies through their economic, socio-cultural and demographic contribution. You also had the opportunity to find out more about Nuno Almeida, founder and CEO of NourishCare, and his contribution to his region in the UK, Dorset.

Reflective exercise: Having read this chapter and the interview with Nuno Almeida, write a 500-word essay or discuss with other students from your course the most important contributions of global talent to cities, regions and countries. Consider your response through the perspective of the country, region or city that you live in.	
Question	**Response**
Develop your response around the following broad areas of contribution of global talent to cities, regions and countries: • economic contribution • socio-cultural contribution • demographic contribution.	

Further reading and resources

Deloitte (2016). *Global cities, global talent: London's rising soft power.* Available at: www2. deloitte.com/content/dam/Deloitte/uk/Documents/Growth/deloitte-uk-global-cities-global-talent-2016.pdf [Accessed 9 August 2018].

JLL (2018). *World cities: Mapping the pathways to success.* Available at: www.jll.com/cities-research/Documents/benchmarking-future-world-of-cities/Cities-Research-Mapping-Pathways-to-Success-2018.pdf [Accessed 9 August 2018].

REFERENCES

China Daily (2016). *Shenzhen needs to build more affordable housing to retain talent.* Available at: www.chinadaily.com.cn/china/2016-01/29/content_23312896.htm [Accessed 27 February 2018].

Committee on the Future Economy (2017). *Report of the Committee on the Future Economy: Pioneers of the next generation.* Available at: www.gov.sg/~/media/cfe/downloads/mtis_full%20report.pdf [Accessed 27 February 2018].

East Asia Forum (2017). *Immigration: The solution to Japan's population problem.* Available at: www.eastasiaforum.org/2017/10/26/immigration-the-solution-to-japans-population-problem [Accessed 28 February 2018].

Ferrer, J. R. (2017). *Barcelona's Smart City vision: An opportunity for transformation.* Available at: http://journals.openedition.org/factsreports/4367#tocto1n3 [Accessed 27 February 2018].

Financial Times (2012). *Cities must be cool, creative and in control.* Available at: www.ft.com/content/c09235b6-72ac-11e1-ae73-00144feab49a [Accessed 10 March 2018].

Financial Times (2018). *A cautionary tale from an ageing Japan for China.* Available at: www.ft.com/content/7fe77124-05dc-11e8-9650-9c0ad2d7c5b5 [Accessed 28 February 2018].

Global Talent Competitiveness Index (GTCI) (2018). *Global Talent Competitiveness Index 2018: Diversity for competitiveness.* Available at: https://gtcistudy.com [Accessed 24 February 2018].

Government of Canada (2017). *Speaking notes for Ahmed Hussen, Minister of Immigration, Refugees and Citizenship at a news conference on Canada's immigration plan for 2018.*

Available at: www.canada.ca/en/immigration-refugees-citizenship/news/2017/11/speaking_notes_forahmedhussenministerofimmigrationrefugeesandcit.html [Accessed 28 February 2018].

Harris, B. (2017). *The astonishing rise of Shenzhen, China's gadget capital*. Available at: www.weforum.org/agenda/2017/11/inside-shenzhen-china-s-gadget-capital [Accessed 27 February 2018].

Hays (2017). *Not all immigration is bad*. Available at: www.hays.co.uk/blog/not-all-immigration-is-bad/index.htm [Accessed 28 February 2018].

IBM (2018). *Welcome to the IBM Smarter Cities challenge*. Available at: www.smartercities challenge.org [Accessed 27 February 2018].

JLL (2018). *World cities: Mapping the pathways to success*. Available at: www.jll.com/cities-research/Documents/benchmarking-future-world-of-cities/Cities-Research-Mapping-Pathways-to-Success-2018.pdf [Accessed 28 March 2018].

Lee, A. (2017). *China's Bay Area is the next big thing, but where is it?* Available at: www.scmp.com/business/global-economy/article/2099244/chinas-bay-area-next-big-thing-where-it [Accessed 28 February 2018].

LinkedIn (2018). *LinkedIn workforce report: San Francisco Bay Area – February 2018*. Available at: www.linkedin.com/jobs/blog/linkedin-workforce-report-february-2018-san-francisco-ca [Accessed 28 February 2018].

McDermid, R. (2017). *Bay Area economy growing three times faster than national average*. Available at: www.bizjournals.com/sanfrancisco/news/2017/09/26/bay-area-economic-growth.html [Accessed 28 February 2018].

Malaysia Digital Economy Corporation (2017). *Attracting investors, globalising local tech champions*. Available at: https://mdec.my/msc-malaysia [Accessed 3 March 2018].

Migration Policy Institute (2017). *As its population ages, Japan quietly turns to immigration*. Available at: www.migrationpolicy.org/article/its-population-ages-japan-quietly-turns-immigration [Accessed 28 February 2018].

Municipal Corporation of Greater Mumbai (2017). *Report on draft development plan 2034*. Available at: www.mcgm.gov.in/irj/go/km/docs/documents/Draft%20Development%20Plan/5.%20Draft%20DP%20Report/DRAFT%20DP%20REPORT%20-%202034%20Final.pdf [Accessed 27 February 2018].

New York Times, The (2017). *Why Silicon Valley wouldn't work without immigrants*. Available at: www.nytimes.com/2017/02/08/technology/personaltech/why-silicon-valley-wouldnt-work-without-immigrants.html [Accessed 28 February 2018].

New Zealand Treasury (2003). *Population ageing in New Zealand: Implications for living standards and the optimal rate of saving*. Available at: www.treasury.govt.nz/publications/research-policy/wp/2003/03-10 [Accessed 28 February 2018].

Phadke, M. (2018). *Modi says Mumbai's new infrastructure will be up by 2022, but the past isn't encouraging*. Available at: https://theprint.in/2018/02/19/despite-politicians-gung-ho-bhoomi-poojans-mumbais-infrastructure-projects-languish [Accessed 27 February 2018].

Royal Society, The (2014). *Our futures Te Pae Tāwhiti: The 2013 census and New Zealand's changing population*. Available at: https://royalsociety.org.nz/what-we-do/our-expert-advice/all-expert-advice-papers/our-futures-te-pae-tawhiti/summary-and-report [Accessed 28 February 2018].

Shenzhen Investment Ltd (2018). *Project in Shenzhen*. Available at: www.shenzheninvestment.com/html/projects.php [Accessed 27 February 2018].

Simonson, S. (2016). *Global immigration to the Bay Area at 5-year high*. Available at: www.siliconvalleyoneworld.com/2016/03/24/global-immigration-to-the-bay-area-at-five-year-high [Accessed 28 February 2018].

Tech Nation (2017). *Tech nation report 2017: Bournemouth and Poole*. Available at: https://technation.techcityuk.com/cluster/bournemouth-and-poole [Accessed 28 February 2018].

11

THE GLOBAL TALENT MISMATCH AND THE ROLE OF EDUCATION

Chapter contents

The global talent mismatch: The evidence

- The scale of the global talent mismatch
- Key challenges and opportunities related to the global talent mismatch
- Skilled mobility and migration as an opportunity
- Education as an avenue to solve the mismatch

The education continuum

- The UN Sustainable Development Goals and education
- The role of HE in skills development and in solving the talent mismatch
- Evidence from international policy
- Establishing mechanisms to ensure the quality and relevance of education and training

Education–industry interaction

- University–industry collaboration as a means to solving the talent mismatch
- International policy and practice in university–industry collaboration

Workforce development through the interplay between education, industry and government

- The role of government in addressing the global talent mismatch

- Solving the talent mismatch through large-scale multilateral partnerships
- Ideas and implications for organisations and policymakers

Case study 11.1: Hays Global Skills Index and the global talent mismatch

Hays GSI – compare the performance of a developed versus a developing economy

Learning objectives

After reading this chapter, you will be able to:

- understand the concept of the global talent mismatch and its implications
- critically reflect on the role of education in resolving the global talent mismatch
- gain an understanding of the role of university–industry collaboration and large-scale multilateral partnerships in this mismatch.

THE GLOBAL TALENT MISMATCH: THE EVIDENCE
The scale of the global talent mismatch

In the previous chapter of this text, we discussed the role that talent plays in shaping cities, regions and countries through their economic, socio-cultural and demographic contribution and impact. The dividends from global talent such as skills, expertise and global competence are, however, not evenly distributed across all the cities, regions and countries that need them. Nor are they distributed sufficiently across all sectors of the economy that benefit from the diverse knowledge, experience and expertise of global talent.

Within the context of this uneven distribution of talent, often the available human capital does not match the requirements of the economy. This shortage of skills in the global workforce creates a global talent mismatch. The global talent mismatch, according to Hays, is defined as the gap between the skills that businesses are looking for and the skills available in the labour market.

This chapter provides a critical reflection on the scale and scope of the global talent mismatch and the role of education in reducing this mismatch. We adopt an international perspective in our discussions that will enable students and policymakers to gain a global insight into the talent mismatch and its implications. We also provide a critical insight into how governments and other policymakers have been responding to the global talent mismatch through policy interventions in the domains of global talent mobility, higher education, university–industry collaboration and large-scale tripartite partnerships.

The scale and scope of the global talent mismatch is not restricted to a particular country, region, city, industry, sector of the economy or organisation. The global talent mismatch is a global challenge, which has profound implications for development and competitiveness and, as such, it takes centre stage in economic policy and planning for cities, regions and countries. Extensive global research by professional services firm PricewaterhouseCoopers (PwC), in collaboration with LinkedIn, reveals that poor talent adaptability or, in other words, the inability of talent to re-skill, up-skill and change roles and industries, costs the global economy billions in lost productivity. This poor talent adaptability or alignment includes organisation-level challenges and economic implications, such as the need to mobilise additional training and recruitment resources. The talent mismatch, according to PwC and LinkedIn, could cost the global economy a total of $150 billion in lost productivity (PwC, 2014).

The economic implications of poor talent alignment are also reinforced by the challenge employers, recruiters and organisations face in identifying and recruiting the required talent. Employers are facing the most acute talent shortage since the 2008 global economic downturn, according to the 2017 Talent Shortage Survey, compiled by ManpowerGroup – a global recruiting consultancy firm. The Survey, which reflects the voices of over 42,000 employers surveyed, concludes that 40% of them experience difficulties filling roles (Figure 11.1) – the highest level since 2007 (ManpowerGroup, 2017). This provides further evidence of the extent of this talent mismatch on a global scale.

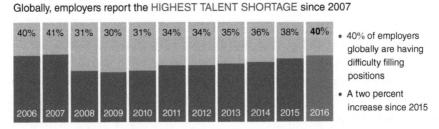

Globally, employers report the HIGHEST TALENT SHORTAGE since 2007

Figure 11.1   ManpowerGroup Talent Shortage Survey results

(Source: ManpowerGroup, 2017)

Amid the acute talent and skills shortages experienced by organisations and recruiters the world over, there is evidence that points to large-scale unemployment, regardless of this shortfall of talent and skills. The World Employment and Social Outlook: Trends 2018 study by the International Labour Organization (ILO) estimated that as many as 192 million people across the world were unemployed in 2018 (ILO, 2018). This creates a paradox whereby over 5% of the global workforce is estimated to be unemployed, even though many countries and sectors of the economy are experiencing global talent shortages. This is due to poor alignment of talent with requirements in the world of work across sectors of the economy and across political and economic geographies.

This global snapshot of current developments in the supply and demand for global talent points to the scale of the impact that talent mismatch and poor talent alignment have on economies, people and organisations. With this comes the need for policymakers and governments to be able to measure the progress of policy initiatives aimed at the alignment of talent with skills and requirements in the world of work.

How do we measure the global talent mismatch? The Global Skills Index (GSI), compiled by global recruiting firm Hays, is a reliable global comparative indicator of the challenges employers face in recruiting the right kind of talent. Through its comparative country-level insights, the GSI also provides an independent assessment of government-led initiatives aimed at reducing the global talent mismatch. We will discuss the Index in more detail later in this chapter.

Key challenges and opportunities related to the global talent mismatch

This gap between the skills that industry is looking for and the skills available in the labour market leads to some key challenges and opportunities for recruiters and policymakers. These include reduced individual and organisational output, lower operational capacity and economic productivity, and increased costs in training and sourcing talent, among other challenges.

Governments and policymakers have frequently cited reduced economic and workforce productivity as the single most important challenge resulting from the talent mismatch due to its wide-reaching economic implications. Hays highlights that the increased talent mismatch contributes to a rising productivity challenge on a global level. Low productivity negatively affects economic development and competitiveness. We now go on to explore one country's insight, where we critically reflect on the state of the talent mismatch and its impact on the economy in the UK through the perspective of Hays and its Global Skills Index.

COUNTRY INSIGHT

Talent mismatch and the UK's productivity problem

The UK has experienced a notable talent mismatch over the past decade. This particularly acute talent mismatch has been estimated to cost the UK economy, industry and recruiters over £1 billion in lost productivity. As a result, key sectors of the economy in the UK, such as financial and professional services, the automotive sector and technology have become less competitive and productive. A good indicator of the UK's performance in aligning talent with the right employment opportunities is the Index developed by Hays.

How does the UK's performance stack up against the other 32 countries included in the Hays 2017 Global Skills Index? Despite the fact that the UK has improved its overall GSI score, a breakdown of Index indicators for the country provides a somewhat worrying insight. This is particularly evident in the case of 'talent mismatch' – one of the seven key indicators used by Hays. GSI's talent mismatch indicator suggests that the UK is experiencing a high level of poor talent alignment when compared with the remaining 32 global economies included in the study, with a score of 8.4 out of 10 (Hays, 2017). Amid its low unemployment levels and forward-thinking employment policy, the UK is experiencing talent and skills shortages in more specialist areas: 'Businesses are finding it easier to recruit employees with the right skills, with unemployment, including long-term unemployment, falling. However, in niche high-skill areas skill shortages still persist.'

Skills shortages in more specialist or niche areas are not a surprise as the country's economy is increasingly diverse and, as a result, some sectors of the economy often face challenges in recruiting the right kind of talent.

This high talent mismatch score (Figure 11.2) may pose long-term, wide-reaching implications for the UK's workforce and economy. The score also provides evidence that the country may be experiencing greater pressure to align the skills and competences of its workforce in order to meet specific industry demands.

Acute talent mismatch essentially means high unemployment, alongside an upward trend in unfilled job vacancies. Talent mismatch has a direct impact on labour productivity and, in the long run, on economic productivity and, ultimately, the competitiveness of UK Plc. Talent mismatch, as Alistair Cox, CEO at Hays, points out, occurs when highly skilled jobs are being created and then go unfilled due to difficulties in finding the right kind of talent.

Cox often highlights in his blogs the wider, long-term implications of a skills mismatch, such as lowered economic growth and national competitiveness: 'We see a pervasive shortage of skills in the UK. Skills shortages have now started to impact economic growth.' The need to address high levels of talent mismatch through policy interventions is imperative for the UK economy and its status on the global index relative to competitor economies.

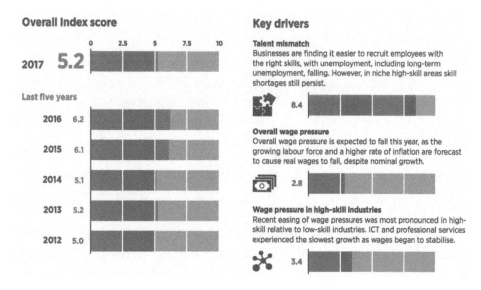

Overall Index score

Key drivers

Talent mismatch
Businesses are finding it easier to recruit employees with the right skills, with unemployment, including long-term unemployment, falling. However, in niche high-skill areas skill shortages still persist.

8.4

Overall wage pressure
Overall wage pressure is expected to fall this year, as the growing labour force and a higher rate of inflation are forecast to cause real wages to fall, despite nominal growth.

2.8

Wage pressure in high-skill industries
Recent easing of wage pressures was most pronounced in high-skill relative to low-skill industries. ICT and professional services experienced the slowest growth as wages began to stabilise.

3.4

Figure 11.2   The UK's Hays GSI score

(Source: Hays, 2017)

However, it is not just the UK that has been impacted by poor global talent alignment. Japan's talent mismatch levels, for example, are among the worst in the world. Japan's unemployment rate is low, at 3.1% in 2016, and its labour market participation is 76%, which is relatively high. Japan's talent mismatch has, nevertheless, been ranked as one of the most acute in the Asia Pacific region and, indeed, in the world, according to Hays' GSI. In the 2017 edition of the Index, Japan had a score of 9.9 out of 10 for its acute talent mismatch, indicating the country's inability to align its talent pool with the skills, attributes and requirements that are in demand in the world of work.

ManpowerGroup also provides insights into the state of the global talent mismatch through its investigation into countries where employers are having the most difficulty filling roles (Figure 11.3). This serves as another indicator of the global talent mismatch, which, as shown in Figure 11.3, is a truly global challenge that affects both developing and advanced, high-income economies.

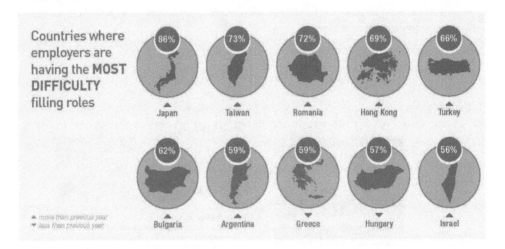

Figure 11.3   Countries with the most acute skills shortages (Source: ManpowerGroup, 2017)

In addition to challenges, there are opportunities related to this mismatch – opportunities for countries to train, skill and re-skill the workforce to better align talent with current requirements in the world of work. There are also opportunities provided by increased levels of talent mobility and skilled migration on a global level. Consideration must also be given, following on from Chapter 4, to the alignment of talent and technology in the workplace, leading to improved productivity of the economy.

In all cases, talent adaptability, as highlighted by PwC, is key to the provision of a response to the global talent mismatch – that is, the ability of talent to seek out and find opportunities across multiple employers, locations and industries (PwC, 2014). The notion of talent adaptability takes us back to our discussion in Chapter 1, where we introduced the concept of learnability, which is the ability to learn, up-skill and adapt in order to remain employable and gainfully employed. The question, however, remains as to how governments and policymakers should address the need for their workforce to learn, up-skill and adapt, particularly when large-scale policy initiatives require substantial investment and other resources. The increased mobility of talent is an avenue to overcome the global talent mismatch experienced by many, particularly middle- to high-income countries.

Skilled mobility and migration as an opportunity to solve the mismatch

The scale and pace of global talent mobility are fierce and two global forces have played a key role in fuelling this process – globalisation and technology. Globalisation and advanced transportation have enabled talent to move across borders more easily, while rapid technology adoption in the workplace means that we can now work from almost anywhere in the world as long as we have access to the internet. These forces have resulted in the rapid growth of global talent mobility and skilled migration. A study by global consultancy firm, Strategy Analytics, highlights that the global mobile workforce is set to increase from 1.45 billion in 2016, to 1.87 billion in 2022, accounting for 42.5% of the global workforce (Strategy Analytics, 2016). This large-scale pool of global talent that is increasingly mobile is an opportunity for some countries to shape a response to the talent mismatch they face, providing that they have adequate policies in place.

Global talent mobility, including skilled migration, is seen as an opportunity to address the high levels of talent mismatch globally, according to a study by INSEAD, one of the leading European business schools. The study found a significant correlation between movement of talent and economic prosperity. Bruno Lanvin, Executive Director for Global Indices at INSEAD, notes that the global mobility of talent is vital to fill the skills gap. The high proportion of innovative, entrepreneurial people who were born or studied abroad, provide opportunities for enhanced competitiveness and economic wellbeing that should be addressed by governments and policymakers alike (INSEAD, 2016):

> As globalisation deepens, talent mobility becomes an important element of dynamism, innovativeness and competitiveness. This is a matter that national governments, and also regional and municipal leadership, need to address in practical ways, focusing on both the immediate concerns of their constituencies as well as what should be the longer-term interests of their citizens – building the basis for sustainable growth, peaceful cross-border relations, and opportunities for younger generations.

This large-scale 'fluid' human capital that crosses borders provides avenues for nations to improve their economic productivity and competitiveness on the global stage.

Yet, a range of barriers exist, primarily from a legal and policy perspective, as different governments adopt contrasting approaches to global talent mobility influenced by economic, political, socio-cultural and demographic trends and developments in their countries. We discussed a number of national, regional and city-level approaches to policy making for talent attraction, development and retention in Chapter 10 of this text. Creating an enabling policy environment is key to tapping into the opportunities provided by a rapidly expanding and highly mobile pool of global talent. Governments and policymakers have a key responsibility to create an enabling environment to attract, develop and retain global talent.

Not all countries, however, may benefit from the opportunities provided by global talent mobility. Evidence suggests that middle- to high-income countries have been the winners in this increased mobility of talent on a global level. This is due to developing economies not always having the resources, nor the capacity and capability, to create an enabling environment that attracts talent and contributes to narrowing the talent mismatch.

However, even some high-income countries like the UK and Japan, which have created an enabling environment, face challenges in aligning talent with requirements in the world of work. The UK and Japan may not be as open to the global talent pool and the talent opportunities created by global mobility as other states are, for example Singapore and Canada. This lack of openness is seen as another reason why countries like Japan and the UK experience an acute talent mismatch, despite being high-income advanced economies.

Education as an opportunity to solve the mismatch

Alongside skilled migration, education and the provision of tailored education and training provision is another avenue to the resolution of the talent mismatch. This is achieved through a concerted, government-led effort to increase the capacity, productivity and skills base of home-grown talent through education and training. The provision of large-scale education, training and employment opportunities has been a priority for governments and policymakers due to the impact of these interventions on the economy, productivity and society that collectively bring about improvements in economic and societal wellbeing. We discuss the role of education, training and employment in the following section.

THE EDUCATION CONTINUUM
The UN Sustainable Development Goals and education

Access to quality education for all has been a priority for most, if not all, governments across the world, as is the provision of adequate training, skills development and employment opportunities for the many, not the few. The United Nations Millennium Development Goals (MDGs), adopted in 2000 with a deadline of 2015 and superseded by the Sustainable Development Goals (SDGs), are probably the biggest and most significant manifestation of the importance of improving the state of education, skills and employment on a global level (see Figure 11.4).

Figure 11.4   UN Sustainable Development Goals (Source: UNDP, 2018a)

The fourth Goal, Quality Education, emphasises that inclusive and quality education is one of the most powerful tools for sustainable development, which promotes economic and societal wellbeing. In order for this to be achieved, this Goal places an emphasis on the importance of exposing and involving as many children and young people as possible at different education levels ranging from primary through to higher education (UNDP, 2018a):

> This goal ensures that all girls and boys complete free primary and secondary schooling by 2030. It also aims to provide equal access to affordable vocational training, to eliminate gender and wealth disparities, and achieve universal access to a quality higher education.

In addition to quality education, the provision of full, meaningful and productive employment, and respectable work, for all women and men by 2030 has also been reflected in the SDGs. The eighth goal, Decent Work and Economic Growth, aims to respond to slow global growth, widening inequalities and a lack of jobs to keep up with a growing labour force following the 2008 global economic downturn. This Goal advocates that the development of entrepreneurship and job creation opportunities is central to sustained economic growth, higher levels of productivity and technological innovation (UNDP, 2018b).

These two SDGs provide strong evidence of the role of creating large-scale, sustainable education and employment opportunities as a means of nurturing knowledge economies and communities. They also highlight some fundamental challenges related to the current progress of the provision of education and employment opportunities for the many, not the few, and the fact that policymakers have perhaps been unable to provide a meaningful response to these challenges. This has been the case in many low- to medium-income countries.

A concerted effort led by governments, policymakers and other stakeholders with an interest in education and skills can contribute to improving the state of the global education and workforce, including tackling productivity and the global talent mismatch. One example of this concerted effort has been the historic UNESCO World Education Forum 2015 held in Incheon, Republic of Korea, where ministers alongside heads of states and agencies have committed to the provision of equitable and inclusive quality education and lifelong learning for all by 2030 (UNESCO, 2015).

The role of higher education in skills development and in resolving the talent mismatch

The education continuum includes primary, secondary, post-secondary and higher or tertiary-level education. We acknowledge that levels on the continuum may differ from country to country but these four are the most universal and widely accepted ones.

These levels of education, form an education continuum, indicating the importance of having as many people as possible involved in as many levels of this continuum as possible. The SDGs highlight not only a need for the provision of quality education opportunities, but also a need to ensure that all children complete primary and secondary education by 2030 as a minimum, while working towards achieving universal access to a quality higher education. Hence, there is a sustained commitment to the exposure and engagement of most, if not all, youth to all four levels of education.

While all education levels are important, tertiary-level education, or simply higher education, is where talent has the opportunity to develop specialist skills and knowledge, alongside higher productivity and capacity, with a view to achieving competitive advantage in the global job market. It is at this level where individuals, whether youth or seniors, have the opportunity to develop as future-ready global talent, enabling them to become both confident job seekers and job creators; and equally to make a meaningful contribution to the economy, the environment and society through the capacity and productivity premium they acquire through higher education.

What follows is a discussion on the perspective of higher education in more detail and the important function of this level in the alignment of talent with requirements in the world of work, where the latter contribute to increased workforce productivity and a narrowing of the talent mismatch gap.

Let us consider the UK as an example.

Our earlier discussion of the 2017 GSI by Hays, together with a country insight, suggested that the UK has improved its overall skills position but further work needs to be undertaken to address the prevalent talent mismatch, particularly across more specialist niche areas and sectors of the economy. The UK Commission for Employment and Skills (UKCES) estimates that, by 2024, 46% of all UK employment will exist within highly skilled occupations, which may further amplify the widening talent mismatch problem and its subsequent influence on economic productivity (UKCES, 2016). Higher education serves as an important function in improving the state of the graduate talent pool and youth who are yet to enter the world of work.

The Industrial Strategy sets out a pathway to build a future-fit Britain through investment in the education and skills, industries and infrastructure of the future are highlighted as a key priority (Department for Business, Energy and Industrial Strategy, 2017). The Strategy aims to enable talent to develop the skills needed for jobs of the future amid acute skills gaps and shortages across the UK. The Strategy also places skills development and employability high on the agenda through its emphasis on the role of the UK higher education sector in developing relevant skills and attributes to improve the productivity of the workforce and the economy.

Graduates play an important role in economic productivity, both at a regional and national level. At least one third of the UK's productivity growth in the decade to 2005 can be attributed to the substantial accumulation of graduate skills in the labour force. The House of Commons Business, Innovation and Skills and Education Committees also examined the strong links between higher education, coupled with the accumulation of graduate skills, and economic performance and productivity. Econometric analysis for 15 countries that include the UK suggests that a 1% increase in the graduate share of the workforce is linked with 0.2–0.5% growth in long-term productivity levels (Hristov and Minocha, 2017a).

Evidence from international Contexts

Higher education plays a pivotal role in narrowing the talent mismatch and improving economic productivity, not only in the UK but also further afield. Germany and Sweden experience high rates of productivity and low talent mismatch levels, partly through the provision of good higher education and skills development opportunities.

The largest democracy in the world provides another country-level policy perspective that has recognised the interplay between higher education and narrowing the talent mismatch, which leads to an increase in economic productivity. India is on the verge of recognising and utilising higher education as a tool to solving its acute talent mismatch and productivity challenge amid a strong workforce of over 700 million and a growing youth population. With its 33 million students across tens of thousands of colleges and universities, India has the second largest HE system in the world, second only to China. The skills development agenda is well placed to play a positive role in improving the workforce productivity and capacity building of India through addressing the prevalent talent mismatch. Indian HE institutions can support the process of developing skills, attributes and competencies that are relevant to the industry, not just in India but internationally.

India's working-age population will grow to over a billion by 2050, according to recent United Nations Development Programme projections (UNDP, 2016). This puts more emphasis on scaling up 'India's efforts, including channelling HE as a means to develop work-ready graduates, to increase its workforce and respond to its productivity and talent mismatch challenge. Challenges, nevertheless, remain ahead due to the lack of scalable skills development opportunities and targeted employability interventions across the majority of HE institutions in India (Minocha et al., 2018).

Building on the challenges for the Indian HE sector in the provision of education and skills development opportunities, independent reports and global employer surveys highlight the skills shortage and talent mismatch in India as an important country-level challenge – Manpower's 2017 Talent Shortage Survey is one example (ManpowerGroup, 2017). These perceived and real skills shortages and India's talent mismatch affect workforce productivity and capacity and have a negative effect on the economy. Poor talent alignment costs the Indian economy and businesses as much as $8.61 billion in lost productivity, according to global consultants PwC (PwC, 2014). The lack of a skilled workforce, which is a key driver for productivity at local, state and national levels, also affects the competitiveness of the Indian workforce and economy on a global stage. Amid this challenging context, higher education is set to play a key role and is, indeed, a priority for the Indian government through its recently established Ministry of Skills Development and Entrepreneurship.

Like India, developing global talent and a skilled workforce that can meet the requirements of the labour market and reduce the talent mismatch has also been at the forefront of government initiatives in China. As China evolves from an investment-led economy to a consumption-oriented one, from being the workshop of the world to being a services powerhouse, the country will need a skilled workforce, according to a McKinsey study. China too faces challenges that are similar to those in India despite considerable improvements in the quality of its higher education system.

Amid the steady increase in the number of enrolments in universities and colleges in China over the past decade, demand for skilled labour is likely to outstrip supply by 24 million people in 2020, according to a McKinsey study (McKinsey, 2013). McKinsey also estimates that if China does not bridge this skills gap, it could lose opportunities worth more than US$250 billion, which represents about 2.3% of the country's current gross domestic product.

Equally, data from the Chinese Ministry of Human Resources and Social Security reveals that skilled workers account for only about 19% of the entire workforce in the country, with highly skilled workers constituting only 5% (JP Morgan, 2016). The Chinese government has outlined ambitious plans and policy interventions to provide industry-relevant skills development opportunities, and universities are thought to serve an important function in this process.

China's President Xi Jinping stressed the role of higher education in fostering talent. This commitment is also reflected in China's 13th Five-Year Plan, which highlights the importance of higher education in skills development, such as through university–industry cooperation, as well as innovation in teaching and learning and a focus on vocational education and training (Hristov and Minocha, 2017b).

Canada also leads the way in creating links between higher education and skills development, with a view to addressing the talent mismatch in the country. In 2016 the Canadian Minister of Finance established the Advisory Council on Economic Growth to develop advice on concrete policy actions to help create the conditions for strong and sustained long-term economic growth.

Learning Nation: Equipping Canada's Workforce with Skills for the Future, released by the Council in December 2017, concluded that Canada's skills development infrastructure is not equipped to meet the challenges that lie ahead, particularly as nearly a quarter of all current work activities in Canada are estimated to be displaced by automation by 2030 (Government of Canada, 2017).

Canada's performance in both higher education and skills development has been strong, as per Canada 2020 – a leading think tank working towards redefining the role of federal government in the country (Canada 2020, 2014). However, as the Advisory Council on Economic Growth notes, Canada lacks the education and training infrastructure to support working adults, leading to a lost economic opportunity and widening skills gap among this growing demographic. The Council sees higher education as being central to addressing the education and training needs of working adults (Government of Canada, 2017): 'Higher education institutions play a critical role in producing curious lifelong learners, who renew their knowledge on a regular basis as new developments in their fields emerge.'

In addition to the provision of education opportunities, a recommendation of the Advisory Council on Economic Growth is the need to support innovative approaches to skills development. This includes encouraging, identifying and co-financing innovative pilot programmes that address known skills gaps among workers of all ages, together with post-secondary students and youth.

Canada 2020 also concludes that challenges related to excellence and equity in the country's skills and higher education performance would need to be addressed as a means of reducing skills gaps and improving the economic prosperity and societal wellbeing of all Canadians.

These policy insights from the UK, India, China and Canada provide evidence of the vision of these countries' governments to improve the state of their talent pools through higher education. The impact, success and outreach of these government interventions are, nevertheless, yet to be assessed, particularly in the case of the world's two most populous countries – China and India – which raise important considerations related to the quality and relevance of their higher education systems.

Establishing mechanisms to ensure the quality and relevance of education and training

The quality and relevance of education and skills provision was reinforced by the shared commitment of governments and policymakers during the UNESCO World Education Forum 2015 in Incheon, Republic of Korea, who collectively committed to the Incheon Declaration: Education 2030 (UNESCO, 2015). While education systems in high-income, advanced economies have a reputation for meeting quality standards, this is not always the case with emerging economies, especially those in Africa and Asia, that have a large tertiary-level population. For example China has a 174 million-strong population aged 15–24, while the tertiary-level population in India is even higher, at 243 million. India's capacity to educate the next generation of global talent and equip them with industry-relevant knowledge and skills has been a challenge, with over 780 universities and over 37,000 colleges being unable to accommodate the large youth population. Alongside challenges related to capacity, universities and colleges in India face quality issues, especially vis à vis the relevance of the curriculum. This widens the talent mismatch gap in the country as its higher education system produces a large pool of job seekers that are not necessarily workforce-ready, nor equipped with industry-relevant skills and knowledge.

The challenges related to the alignment of graduate talent with requirements in the world of work are multifaceted and are by no means unique to China and India alone. With many other countries still facing challenges related to the quality, capacity and relevance of higher education and training provision, it is important to establish policy mechanisms and initiatives that ensure these challenges of higher education systems are addressed, particularly in emerging, low- to medium-income economies.

EDUCATION–INDUSTRY INTERACTION
University–industry collaboration as a means to solving the talent mismatch

The policy insights, including international examples and case studies, discussed in this chapter signal a gap between education and employment in terms of a skills mismatch. Governments alongside universities have adopted a range of policy-informed interventions and approaches to address the skills mismatch. The purpose of these interventions and approaches by governments is to ensure that university leavers are equipped with skills and knowledge that are both industry-relevant and sought after by employers, regardless of their field of study. Among these approaches, university–industry partnerships hold a prominent place as a widely accepted and often highly effective approach to developing workforce-ready and globally competent graduate talent.

University–industry collaboration is seen as a means to solving the global talent mismatch. Michael D. King, Vice President and General Manager of IBM's Global Education Industry, noted that an integrated partnerships approach is necessary as 'the speed of technological innovation and industry demands is moving faster than higher education's ability to adapt' (*Harvard Business Review*, 2015). King also notes that the emergence of new university–industry collaboration models is already starting to reshape education, but more evidence is needed beyond the arguably few pockets of excellence demonstrated across the higher education sector.

There have been a number of examples internationally but the industry voice, coupled with high graduate unemployment levels on a global scale, suggests that mainstream and mass approaches to university–industry collaboration might be due for a rethink. Partnerships with universities and other types of organisations to promote good practice and skills development are certainly avenues that need to be exploited further. Partnerships could take the form of systematic and synergistic approaches to employer engagement, industry-led curriculum innovation and the co-creation of industry-relevant teaching and learning.

International policy and practice in university–industry collaboration

How do higher education providers work with industry and how do they facilitate it? We use this section to provide an insight into the UK, Brazil and Germany and some of the large-scale, government-led programmes that these countries have adopted to enable closer university–industry interaction.

The UK government has reinforced the importance of apprenticeships through the apprenticeship levy to foster greater links and partnerships between training providers, including higher education institutions and employers to address the current skills gap of the economy. Let's take the case of degree apprenticeships in particular. Since their launch in 2015, over 30 universities in the UK are offering degree apprenticeships and progressing this priority with some pace. While in its early days in the assessment and impact of the policy, it is clear that policy interventions influence institutional behaviour and potentially accelerate progress against the talent mismatch in the economy.

Further afield, Brazil has taken a different approach to strengthening the links between universities and industry.

Marta Lucia Azevedo Ferreira, a Professor at the Federal University of Rio de Janeiro, provides an analysis of mechanisms developed and implemented by Brazilian policy-makers with a view to fostering university–industry interactions. Some of these policy responses, created in the late 1990s, include Sectorial Funds of Science and Technology – the 'Technological Innovation Law' – aimed at the development of technology networks and international research projects, entrepreneurial activities and science and technology parks and incubators alongside other initiatives (Azevedo Ferreira and Rezende Ramos, 2015). Following this and other policy initiatives and institutional innovations, the subject of university–industry interactions has been receiving more attention and, as such, it has gained further traction in Brazilian higher education. Despite recent university–industry collaborations in sectors including health, mining, agriculture, oil and gas, Sérgio Queiroz, a professor at the University of Campinas, concluded that there is still a challenge to broaden the types of university–industry interaction and scale up the impact and reach that these partnerships deliver across the country (Queiroz, 2013). Amid the political shake-up and major socio-economic challenges that Brazil faces, a World Bank study notes that the country has taken steps to improve the relevance of its higher education and introduce greater flexibility in the way degrees are delivered, often in partnership with industry (World Bank, 2002). Universities and colleges, nevertheless, should pursue a more meaningful and impactful relationship with employers that would enable them to participate in the design of curriculum and pedagogic interventions, with a view to further improving the relevance of Brazilian degrees. The development of relevant government policy and a body of good practice is of key importance in enabling tailored university–industry collaboration, which, for example, focuses on the development of graduate talent for priority sectors of the economy in Brazil that often face skills shortages.

Germany offers another forward-thinking, policy-driven approach to collaboration between higher education institutions and industry representatives, especially in the area of the inclusion and integration of refugee and asylum seekers in the workforce. An estimated total of 1.2 million refugees and asylum seekers arrived in Germany between 2015 and 2016, fleeing the Syrian war. Refugees in Germany provide another untapped resource of global talent and, indeed, an opportunity to narrow the talent mismatch in the country. Despite the strong vocational orientation of universities and colleges in Germany, there is still a notable mismatch between graduate talent entering the workforce and employer requirements. How does the German government approach this opportunity through policy and partnerships? There have been some successful government-led partnerships for education and training, coupled with policy initiatives aimed at the workforce integration of refugees in Germany, which we discuss further in the policy insight.

POLICY INSIGHT

Government–led partnerships for education and training, and the workforce integration of refugees in Germany

With the arrival of over one million refugees and asylum seekers in the past three years alone, Germany is hoping to narrow its talent mismatch gap and improve the profile of its ageing population through the integration of these communities into the country's

(Continued)

(Continued)

workforce, economy and society. Many of the refugees are educated to a higher education level and this provides an opportunity for this predominantly youthful workforce to support the productivity of the German economy and enrich German society socio-culturally. Germany experiences a high talent mismatch across some sectors of national importance, including healthcare and midwifery, administration, science and engineering. This shortage of talent limits the country's ability to improve its productivity and economic competitiveness.

The German government has been working closely in partnership with both higher education providers and employment transition and integration agencies to provide education, training and employment opportunities for refugees in the country.

In terms of education, the Federal Ministry of Education and Research has made a channelled investment of €100 million for higher education programmes for refugees between 2016 and 2019 (Inside Higher Ed., 2017). Supported by this funding, the German Academic Exchange Service has developed a set of targeted interventions to enable more refugees to participate in higher education and improve their knowledge and skills base. Nearly 200 higher education institutions, close to 50% of all universities in Germany, have joined the two most popular education and integration programmes for refugees.

In addition to education and skills development interventions by policymakers, a policy note by the OECD states that the regional government in Germany has implemented a range of integration measures and pilot projects to support the labour market transition of asylum seekers and refugees in the country. The Integration Act introduced a new programme, 'Integration Measures for Refugees', which seeks to create 100,000 employment opportunities targeted at refugees and asylum seekers (OECD, 2017). Many of these employment opportunities aimed at refugees are expected to feature sectors of the economy that experience talent and skills shortages.

In the context of our discussion of macro, government-led interventions to enable more impactful university–industry interaction and perspective of the UK, Brazil and Germany, we acknowledge that individual countries' approaches are all very different and usually tailored to the specific socio-economic and workforce characteristics of these economics. Hence, the objective of our discussion is not to provide a single policy response to the opportunities enabled by university–industry partnerships. The above discussion of good practice from various countries at different stages of development of their graduate talent pool provides practice examples, which may be of relevance to policymakers tasked with furnishing a response to the talent mismatch through university–industry collaboration.

WORKFORCE DEVELOPMENT THROUGH THE INTERPLAY BETWEEN EDUCATION, INDUSTRY AND GOVERNMENT

The role of government in addressing the global talent mismatch

Governments in both developing and developed economies have a primary role in shaping a response to the global talent mismatch. Earlier in this chapter, we provided international insight and evidence that some high-income economies with advanced higher education systems and university–industry collaboration frameworks, such as Japan and the UK, are not immune to global talent mismatches. Workforce development, with a focus on the alignment of talent with requirements in the world of work, is, therefore, of key importance, and policy initiatives led by governments are central to narrowing the talent mismatch.

Harold Sirkin, a senior partner at the Boston Consulting Group, notes that while governments take a lead role in addressing the talent mismatch, there is a need for policymakers to adopt a proactive approach to engagement with industry representatives, universities and other key stakeholders that can support workforce development and a reduction in the levels of talent mismatch (Sirkin, 2016). This challenge for policymakers to establish productive, large-scale collaborations is faced by both developing and developed economies.

Solving the talent mismatch through large-scale multilateral partnerships

Large-scale, innovative tripartite partnerships involving a 'Triple Helix' of university–industry–government provide another platform to nurture innovation in addressing the global talent mismatch through workforce development, and to assist with improving the relevance of education and skills development initiatives. This good practice in large-scale partnerships, however, is not widely adopted. Triple Helix partnerships can however provide an integrative approach to addressing what is now becoming a global challenge – the global talent mismatch – while fostering economic and social development through innovation and research.

Unlike university–industry partnerships, in Triple Helix collaboration the government assumes an active role in these partnerships, which goes beyond the provision of policy. According to the Triple Helix Research Group at Stanford University in the

USA, university–industry–government relationships take centre stage in the knowledge economy era. This tripartite relationship has a transformational impact and reaches beyond universities to capture areas of economic development and progress in society at large (Stanford University, 2018):

> The Triple Helix thesis is that the potential for innovation and economic development in a Knowledge Society lies in a more prominent role for the university and in the hybridisation of elements from university, industry and government to generate new institutional and social formats for the production, transfer and application of knowledge.

The 'entrepreneurial university' is also a central concept in the Triple Helix model whereby enterprise-driven higher education, enabled by tripartite collaborations, has a high capacity to provide students with training and skills development opportunities and to nurture entrepreneurial talent (Stanford University, 2018). India, the largest democracy in the world and a country that has demonstrated a keen commitment to inculcating an entrepreneurial mindset in its rapidly growing generation of job seekers, has taken a comprehensive, government-led approach to capitalising on the benefits of the Triple Helix.

High-level skills development and solving the talent mismatch are areas of key priority for the Indian government, which has introduced a number of initiatives under Skill India, including the National Policy for Skill Development and Entrepreneurship. The establishment of key government bodies, including the Ministry of Skill Development and Entrepreneurship (MSDE) and the National Skills Development Corporation (NSDC), underlines the importance of aligning Indian talent with requirements in the world of work for the economy, the environment and society at large.

Key stakeholder groups in India, such as employers, higher education institutions and non-governmental organisations (NGOs), are important delivery partners for the Indian government's Skill India initiative and play an important role in improving the state of the country's large-scale workforce and talent pipeline. For example, the NSDC partners with a wide range of higher education providers, central ministries and industry representatives in the implementation of skills development interventions and capacity building in vocational education and training. This initiative includes the inception of 38 Industry-led Sector Skill Councils, which conduct research on standards and requirements in the world of work, alongside providing sector-specific training in partnership with government and universities (MSDE, 2018).

Still in its infancy, Skill India and the range of policy initiatives provide the basis for a transformation in the way the Indian workforce is being developed that is underpinned by university–industry–government partnerships. The case of India provides evidence on how emerging, low- to medium-income countries shape their response to the talent mismatch through policy interventions aimed at large-scale tripartite partnerships between universities, industry and government.

Australia provides a developed economy insight into how Triple Helix partnerships have contributed to the foundation of the country's first innovation district in Adelaide that connects industries and graduate talent. Led by the South Australian government, Tonsley Innovation District has been founded around a partnership between government, university and industry.

At the core of Tonsley's model has been the development of a large-scale, mixed-use urban project that brings together regional government, higher education and training institutions and industrial partners that represent four highly specialised sectors of the economy in Australia – Health, Medical Devices and Assistive Technologies; Cleantech and Renewable Energy; Software and Simulation; and Mining and Energy Services (Tonsley, 2018). The South Australian government has enabled Flinders University and TAFE SA, a vocational skills training institution, to establish campuses on site and collaborate with both new and established high-profile businesses, including Siemens, ZEN Energy Systems and Micro-X.

Looking ahead, the intention for this initiative, kick-started by the government is to become firmly established as an economic growth engine for South Australia by attracting a critical mass of industry, research, education and commercial activity in Tonsley Innovation District in Adelaide (*University–Industry Innovation Magazine*, 2017).

Tonsley Innovation District provides an example from a high-income economy of how Triple Helix is being adopted to enable a range of knowledge, research, skills and entrepreneurship development partnerships across highly specialised and high-growth sectors – sectors within the capacity and interest of South Australia and where talent serves an important function to enable future growth, innovation and development.

Ideas and implications for organisations and policymakers

This section offers some indicative ideas for universities, government and employers. These aim to support each stakeholder groups in shaping their response to the challenges related to talent mismatch:

• There is a need for universities to intensify their employer engagement agenda with a view to providing students with opportunities to develop industry-informed skills, gain industry exposure and access placements – all leading to future employment opportunities. University–industry collaboration requires reform at a systemic level, particularly in developing economies where the employability of graduates is well below the OECD average (e.g. up to 50% in Africa), and deeper university–industry interaction is a key response. Establishing an enabling environment for industry and employers to engage with higher education institutions and provide industry-informed input into curriculum and pedagogies is central to the transitioning of graduates into the workforce.

- Employers should seek out incentivisation from governments to engage with higher education institutions in training and skills development initiatives through the relevant government-led frameworks in place. They should seek to play an active role in curriculum and graduate development training to ensure that this talent are work-ready to meet the demands of industry.

- Policymakers and governments are important coordinating bodies that should create an enabling environment for multilateral partnerships that include higher education institutions, employers and government bodies. A collaborative environment that is coordinated by policymakers and local governments is key to meeting challenges related to the quality and relevance of education and skills development opportunities. Governments, particularly those in developing countries, also need to incentivise university–industry partnerships with a focus on the design, development and delivery of courses and modules on entrepreneurship, job creation and innovation.

CASE STUDY 11.1

Hays Global Skills Index and the global talent mismatch

In this chapter, we have provided insights into the importance of skills and skilled talent for the productivity and competitiveness of individuals and organisations which collectively shape the economies of cities, regions and countries. The contribution of skills as a competitive advantage was covered in Chapter 9, which discussed the Global Talent Competitiveness Index and measuring competitiveness through talent and skills.

The ability to measure the skills mismatch of individual countries is, nevertheless, just as important. Measuring skills mismatches provides an independent analysis of the effectiveness of policy interventions aimed at the better alignment of talent with skills requirements in the world of work.

The Hays Global Skills Index, as highlighted by Hays, one of the world's largest recruiting firms, is a complex, statistically based analysis, which is carried out in collaboration with Oxford Economics and is designed to assess the dynamics of skilled labour markets across 33 countries. Seven indicators make up the Hays GSI, which also considers the

Talent Mismatch or the gap between the skills that businesses are looking for and the skills available in the labour market (Hays, 2017).

Oxford Economics (2016), supported by Hays, highlighted the economic and productivity implications of skills shortages and talent mismatches for economies and businesses:

> Skills shortages and skills mismatches are worrying issues for businesses. When employers find it difficult to recruit the people with the skills they need, there are real costs. These may be lost business, reduced productivity or a need to undertake additional training to up-skill people. There are also implications for the workload and welfare of existing staff with increasing pressure to meet growing demand.

The impact and implications of poor talent alignment reinforce the importance of the Index and the underlining assessment of talent mismatches, which serve as an opportunity to inform government policy and industry practice.

Structure of the Global Skills Index

The Index consists of seven indicators. The indicators are given equal weight when the overall Index score is calculated for each country. Each indicator measures how much pressure different factors are exerting on the local labour market:

- **Education flexibility:** In today's global and technology-driven economies, raising educational standards is crucial to bridging skills gaps. This indicator provides a comprehensive view of the state of education. The lower the score, the better the chance that the education system is flexible enough to meet labour market needs. The higher the score, the less likely it is that an education system is equipped to build a solid talent pipeline.
- **Labour market participation:** Bringing more people into the workforce is a powerful way to improve economic and labour market performance. Countries that can raise the employee participation rate may gain an edge over countries with less scope to do so. The lower the score, the larger the potential pool of workers. The higher the score, the lower the number of workers there are available to join the workforce.
- **Labour market flexibility:** Governments play an important part in determining how well labour markets function. For instance, they can cut red tape, avoid laws that discourage hiring and adapt policies that welcome talented people from abroad. The lower the score, the better aligned governmental policies are with labour market dynamics. A higher score means that there are more barriers restricting the local labour market.

(Continued)

(Continued)

- **Talent mismatch:** This indicator measures the gap between the skills that businesses are looking for and the skills available in the labour market. A higher score indicates that businesses are facing a serious problem in matching available talent with unfilled jobs. A lower score suggests that employers are having an easier time finding workers with the skills they need.
- **Overall wage pressure:** Skills shortages are likely to be an important issue when wages are growing faster than the overall cost of living. A higher score indicates the presence of overall wage pressures that are higher than the historic norm for that country. A lower score tells us that wages are not rising quickly and that those pressures are not as apparent.
- **Wage pressure in high-skill industries:** Some industries require higher-skilled staff than others. As it takes time to undertake the training necessary to work in those industries, it potentially makes them more vulnerable to skills shortages as the number of people qualified to start work cannot be changed quickly. A higher score indicates that wages in high-skill industries are growing faster than in low-skill industries relative to the past, which is indicative of the emergence of sector-specific skills shortages (such as in engineering or technology). A lower score tells us that wages for those in high-skill industries are rising more slowly or in line with wages in low-skill industries.
- **Wage pressure in high-skill occupations:** Some occupations require a higher than average amount of training, education and experience. These are called high-skill occupations. Rising wage pressure in this category signals that these occupations are experiencing a shortage of workers with the necessary skills. The higher the score, the greater the presence of skills shortages affecting high-skill occupations. A lower score tells us that wages for those in high-skill occupations are rising more slowly than those in low-skill occupations.

Higher scores mean that a country is experiencing more pressure than has historically been the case. Conversely, lower scores across each of the above indicators on the Index provide evidence that a country feels less pressure than before.

Global comparative perspective on the talent mismatch

The Hays Global Skills Index touches upon the wider socio-political and economic landscape by highlighting the recent instability and uncertainty that can be noted in most parts of the world. It suggests that the skills gap will quickly turn into a 'skills chasm' if it isn't addressed by governments and business leaders. There is also, clearly, a role for the HE sector in tackling this critical issue. According to the 2017 Index report, the macro picture is mixed, whereby some economies have strengthened and others have weakened their position on the Index.

From a UK perspective, the Index demonstrates a high level of pressure predominantly in talent mismatch, which is projected to impact the output and productivity of industries. The UK demonstrates a Talent Mismatch score of 8.4 out of the 10 possible. The higher the Index score, the more 'pressure' the country is experiencing in aligning its talent with the skills requirements in the labour market. While the UK is in a good position overall, more needs to be done to close the skills gap, particularly in some niche sectors of the economy – a challenge that we discussed in the country insight earlier in this chapter.

Japan is equally experiencing a high level of mismatch between the skills available on the job market and those required by industry and business. The country has a Talent Mismatch score of 9.9 out of the 10 possible, which has been ranked as one of the most acute in the Asia Pacific region. Japan is now positioned close to the USA, Ireland, Portugal and Spain for the severity of its talent gap – countries which all demonstrate a score being close to the maximum one of 10 for Talent Mismatch (Figure 11.5).

Paradoxically, emerging economies such as China and India, on the other hand, have lower Talent Mismatch scores – 3.8 and 5.0 out of 10 respectively. These emerging superpowers, however, face other challenges in their labour markets, which in the longer term could influence their standing and performance on the Talent Mismatch indicator of the Index.

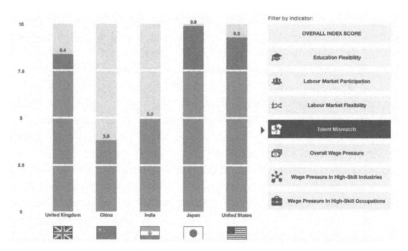

Figure 11.5 Talent mismatch in comparative perspective

(Source: Hays, 2017)

(Continued)

(Continued)

China has a Talent Mismatch score of 3.8 out of 10, which is relatively low when compared to the UK's score of 8.4. China, nevertheless, has a high Labour Market Flexibility score in the 2017 Hays Global Skills Index – 8.1 out of 10. The lower the score, the better aligned governmental policies are with labour market dynamics. A high score means there are more barriers restricting the labour market, which may influence the country's performance on the Talent Mismatch indicator going forward. The New Skills at Work report by JP Morgan Chase already suggests that the supply–demand gap for highly skilled labour in China is widening and the country is projected to face an acute skills shortfall.

India, similar to China, has a high Labour Market Flexibility score on Hays' GSI – 8.7 out of 10. The lower the score, the better aligned government policies are with labour market dynamics. A high score means there are more barriers restricting the labour market and such barriers might impact the level of talent mismatch at a time when the country stated that it will need 109 million additional skilled individuals across 22 key sectors of the economy by 2022.

Future-proof countries: recommendations

Hays provides three key recommendations for policymakers and practitioners. These are very much aligned with the imperative to respond to the mismatch of available skills in economies that experience high talent mismatch across the world:

1. **Address skilled migration to tackle the ever-growing skills gap**. This recommendation suggests that governments need to identify skilled roles that local workers cannot fill and then develop strategies which serve to attract and retain the relevant talent globally. Government and policymakers are also urged to distinguish between skilled migration and mass migration and to identify approaches to attract the best and most relevant talent to address this problem.
2. **Implement smarter training programmes to ensure businesses are future-proof**. The importance of employee training that features employability skills, including technology, digital literacy and, more importantly, softer employability skills, such as problem solving, communication and negotiation – all being in demand across specific sectors of the economy – is highlighted by this recommendation. This training should be implemented across the board and hence cover new graduates, middle managers and older workers.
3. **Tackle low productivity through better technology and employee engagement**. The recommendation here is directed at policymakers and businesses to focus on more meaningful employee engagement as low productivity continues to be a pertinent challenge to economic growth in many countries. Hays contends that a wider integration of technology in the workplace may facilitate this and offer sustainable avenues for workforce engagement.

Further case study resources

Hays (2017). *Hays Global Skills Index 2017*. Available at: www.hays-index.com/the-index/introduction [Accessed 5 April 2018].

Oxford Economics (2016). *Hays Global Skills Index 2016*. Available at: www.oxfordeconomics.com/recent-releases/the-hays-global-skills-index-2016 [Accessed 5 April 2018].

REFLECTIVE EXERCISE

Hays GSI – compare the performance of a developed versus a developing economy

Chapter 11 has discussed the global talent mismatch and its implications for individuals, organisations, sectors of the economy, cities, regions and countries. This chapter also explored the role of governments, businesses and HE in solving the global talent mismatch. You had the opportunity to find out more about Hays' Global Skills Index as an approach to measuring the talent mismatch across both developed and developing economies, alongside other determinants of labour market flexibility.

Question	Response
Reflective exercise: Having read the Hays Global Skills Index case study in Chapter 11, use the Hays GSI at the following page: www.hays-index.com/comparison-tool to compare the performance of a developed versus a developing economy of your choice, based on the Talent Mismatch indicator of the Index.	
Write a 500-word essay or discuss with other students from your course the findings from your cross-country analysis in light of further country-level data available at the following page: www.hays-index.com/countries and in a way that you can: • highlight three key challenges related to talent mismatch for your selected countries; and • propose three key ideas to address high levels of talent mismatch for your selected countries.	

Further reading and resources

Sustainable Development Goals Fund (2018). *Goal 4: Quality education.* Available at: www. sdgfund.org/goal-4-quality-education [Accessed 9 August 2018].

UNESCO (2018). *Connecting the UN Sustainable Development Goals: Education plays a key role.* Available at: www.unesco.org/new/en/media-services/single-view/news/connecting_the_un_sustainable_development_goals_education [Accessed 9 August 2018].

REFERENCES

Azevedo Ferreira, M. L. and Rezende Ramos, R. (2015). Making university–industry technological partnerships work: A case study in the Brazilian oil innovation system. *Journal of Technology Management & Innovation*, 10(1), 173–87.

Canada 2020 (2014). *Skills and higher education in Canada: Towards excellence and equity.* Available at: http://canada2020.ca/wp-content/uploads/2014/05/2014_Canada2020_Paper-Series_Education_FINAL.pdf [Accessed 5 April 2018].

Department for Business, Energy and Industrial Strategy (2017). *The UK's industrial strategy.* Available at: www.gov.uk/government/topical-events/the-uks-industrial-strategy [Accessed 2 March 2018].

Government of Canada (2017). *Learning nation: Equipping Canada's workforce with skills for the future.* Available at: www.budget.gc.ca/aceg-ccce/pdf/learning-nation-eng.pdf [Accessed 5 April 2018].

Harvard Business Review (2015). *Why higher ed and business need to work together.* Available at: https://hbr.org/2015/07/why-higher-ed-and-business-need-to-work-together [Accessed 2 March 2018].

Hays (2017). *Global Skills Index: Executive summary.* Available at: www.hays-index.com/the-index/introduction/#introduction [Accessed 3 March 2018].

Hristov, D. and Minocha, S. (2017a). *The role of graduate employability in economic productivity in the UK.* Available at: https://charteredabs.org/role-graduate-employability-economic-productivity-uk [Accessed 2 March 2018].

Hristov, D. and Minocha, S. (2017b). *Are universities helping China compete on skills?* Available at: www.universityworldnews.com/article.php?story=20170801064540606 [Accessed 2 March 2018].

INSEAD (2016). *The Global Talent Competitiveness Index 2015–16: Talent attraction and international mobility.* Available at: www.insead.edu/sites/default/files/assets/dept/glo balindices/docs/GTCI-2015-2016-report.pdf [Accessed 1 March 2018].

Inside Higher Ed. (2017). *Providing access to higher education for refugees in Germany.* Available at: www.insidehighered.com/blogs/world-view/providing-access-higher-education-refugees-germany [Accessed 2 March 2018].

International Labour Organisation (ILO) (2018). *World employment and social outlook: Trends 2018.* Available at: www.ilo.org/global/research/global-reports/weso/2018/WCMS_615594/lang—en/index.htm [Accessed 1 March 2018].

JP Morgan (2016). *New skills at work: Skills shortages in the Chinese labour market.* Available at: www.jpmorganchase.com/corporate/Corporate-Responsibility/document/skillsgap-in-chineselabor-market-exec-summary.pdf [Accessed 2 March 2018].

McKinsey (2013). *The $250 billion Q: Can China close the skills gap?* Available at: www.mckinsey.com/industries/social-sector/our-insights/the-250-billion-question-can-china-close-the-skills-gap [Accessed 2 March 2018].

ManpowerGroup (2017). *2016–2017 talent shortage survey.* Available at: www.manpowergroup.com/talent-shortage-2016 [Accessed 1 March 2018].

Ministry of Skills Development and Entrepreneurship (MSDE) (2018) *National skill development corporation partnerships.* Available at: www.skilldevelopment.gov.in/nationalskilldevelopmentcorporation.html [Accessed 3 March 2018].

Minocha, S., Hristov, D. and Sreedharan, C. (2018). *Global talent in India: Challenges and opportunities for skills development in higher education.* Available at: https://issuu.com/globalbu/docs/global_talent_in_india_online_versi [Accessed 2 March 2018].

Organisation for Economic Cooperation and Development (OECD) (2017). *Finding their way: Labour market integration of refugees in Germany.* Available at: www.oecd.org/els/mig/Finding-their-Way-Germany.pdf?TSPD_101_R0=1ca458960d3cb84f7019cade214 53a63aYI00000000000000007a4150c2ffff00000000000000000000000000005a9964b b00261c0709 [Accessed 2 March 2018].

PricewaterhouseCoopers (PwC) (2014). *Talent mismatch costs global economy $150 billion.* Available at: https://press.pwc.com/News-releases/global-economy-misses-out-on-150 bn-due-to-talent-mismatch/s/c433d953-6669-41c1-9225-fd63ac9298d6 [Accessed 1 March 2018].

Queiroz, S. (2013). *Challenges and opportunities in university–industry collaborative research.* Available at: www.fapesp.br/week2013/london/pdfs/D3_queiroz.pdf [Accessed 2 March 2018].

Sirkin, H. (2016). *Hiring foreign talent won't close the skills gap.* Available at: www.forbes.com/sites/haroldsirkin/2016/06/24/hiring-foreign-talent-wont-close-the-skills-gap/#64e6c2d66bb0 [Accessed 3 March 2018].

Stanford University (2018). *The triple helix concept.* Available at: http://triplehelix.stan ford.edu/3helix_concept [Accessed 3 March 2018].

Strategy Analytics (2016). *Global mobile workforce forecast update 2016–2022.* Available at: www.strategyanalytics.com/access-services/enterprise/mobile-workforce/market-data/report-detail/global-mobile-workforce-forecast-update-2016-2022#. WpgvDa2caqC [Accessed 1 March 2018].

Tonsley (2018). *Tonsley: About.* Available at: https://tonsley.com.au/about [Accessed 9 March 2018].

UK Commission for Employment and Skills (UKCES) (2016). *UK labour market projections: 2014 to 2024.* Available at: www.gov.uk/government/publications/uk-labour-market-projections-2014-to-2024 [Accessed 2 March 2018].

United Nations Development Programme (UNDP) (2016). *UNDP: Fastest population shift in history means make or break for Asia-Pacific.* Available at: www.in.undp.org/content/ india/en/home/presscenter/pressreleases/2016/04/26/undp--fastest-population-shift-in-history-means-make-or-break-fo.html [Accessed 23 June 2017].

United Nations Development Programme (UNDP) (2018a). *Quality education.* Available at: www.undp.org/content/undp/en/home/sustainable-development-goals/goal-4-quality-education.html [Accessed 2 March 2018].

United Nations Development Programme (UNDP) (2018b). *Decent work and economic growth.* Available at: www.undp.org/content/undp/en/home/sustainable-develop ment-goals/goal-8-decent-work-and-economic-growth.html (Accessed 2 March 2018).

United Nations Educational, Scientific and Cultural Organisation (UNESCO) (2015). *Incheon declaration: Education 2030.* Available at: http://unesdoc.unesco.org/ images/0023/002338/233813M.pdf [Accessed 8 March 2018].

University–Industry Innovation Magazine (2017). *Collaborate or crumble: How Australia's tri ple helix is being challenged to drive an innovation nation.* Available at: www.uiin.org/ index/downloadissue/issue/UIIM_2017_Issue1/type/Print [Accessed 3 July 2018].

World Bank (2002). *Higher education in Brazil: Challenges and options – A World Bank country study.* Washington, DC: World Bank.

INDEX